THE SONGS

1. Still Monday   4:03

2. Can't Keep Us Down   3:53

3. Free   5:46

4. I'm Stupid & So Are You   4:10

5. Let Me In   3:23

6. Looking Up At Her Thighs   4:22

7. Talkin' Nina Pennington Blues   3:17

8. Talkin' Nina Pennington Blues (accoustic mix)   1:53

9. Zero King   5:22

10. Take It Away   3:20

11. If I Had A Dick   3:48

12. While I'm Dead...Feed The Dog Underture   2:50

13. White Heat   10:10

14. Author's Guarantee

All songs ASCAP (see pages 234-236 for publishing information.)

D1528768

While I'm dead... Feed the dog

Ric Browde

First published in the United States of America in 1997 by
COMENT PUBLISHING, a division of COMENT MEDIA GROUP, INC.
3932 Wilshire Boulevard Suite 212
Los Angeles, CA 90010

E-Mail.   xsesscdzne@aol.com
Ordering information.   www.allmediadist.com

Library of Congress Cataloging in Publication Data
Browde, Ric
Ric Browde, composer, author, producer.
1. Browde, Ric
2. Fiction, United States

ISBN 1-57787-099-9 single copy
ISBN 1-57787-097-2 pack of Seven

It all starts off with my mother's first suicide attempt. I'm upstairs practicing guitar when the phone rings. I figure she's going to pick it up, but it just keeps on ringing so finally I answer it.

"Is your mother home?" I recognize the voice as that of my fat cousin with the face lift. "Hold on a second and I'll get her."

I go downstairs and there she is lying real still surrounded by a veritable who's who of saints on hundreds of prayer candles. Through the blazing inferno I see these sixteen envelopes all addressed to people whose fault it is, two pill bottles, and the requisite empty bottle of vodka. I shake her but she won't move...so I guess she's kicked the bucket and I better get rid of my piglet cousin and use the phone for some 911 action.

"She's too dead to come to the phone right now, so hang up and let me make some calls." Fatso starts babbling so I tell her, "Hang up right fucking now Julie, this is an emergency and I need the phone." She continues on. "Now." *Click.*

So I do the 911 thing and being that we live in a small suburb of St. Louis where the only doughnut shop is two blocks down, four cops and an ambulance are over in two minutes.

By the time they arrive I've figured out that Seconal is what's put her in God's little waiting room. So, the ambulance guys go into their official suicide drill... you know – do some earnest CPR, see that doesn't work, shout a few obscenities and throw the body onto the stretcher and get her to the stomach pump pronto.

As the paramedics are taking her out one of the cops starts doing an interrogation number on yours truly.

"What's her name?"

"Lucretia Garbo Thibault."

"Date of birth?"

"July 9th, 1928."

"Religion?"

"Let's see – she was Catholic this week, but last week it was Unitarian and two months ago I think she was a Buddhist or was it Hindu, I know it wasn't Jehovah's Witness because I haven't seen the *Watchtower* in about a year. Anyway who cares?"

"These are questions I have to ask," he says officiously, "now what's her education?"

It's just then while the ambulance drivers are navigating their way through the side door that I see the note, taped in big letters on the garage:

while I'm dead...Feed the dog

Now I don't know about you but when I read a suicide note that says "While I'm dead feed the dog" I laugh. I don't care if it's written by my mother or goddamn Mother Theresa it deserves a good chortle. Unfortunately the cops and ambulance drivers don't see the note yet and are starting to give me the 'I bet she did it because of you – you uncaring son of a bitch long hair drug consuming commie' look. Meanwhile Duke is barking out back, probably because he's read the letter and damn well wants to make sure that I fully understand it. He'll have to wait. Finally one of the cops notices the note and he breaks out laughing and can't control himself either, causing the ambulance guys to see it and lose it too; so we end up having a whole procession of hysterical emergency workers carrying my mother off to the emergency room.

My sister shows up just in time for me to ask her to go with Mom to the hospital. I hate waiting in those type of places and besides this way I can make some calls. As he loads my mother into the back I hear the ambulance driver saying she's probably dead but he's going to hurry to the hospital anyway and give it the old college try.

So while the obnoxious cop resumes his questioning I feed the dog who seems okay with the program now that he sees he still has clout around the place.

"I didn't hear your answer. What did you say is her education?"

"Does this determine whether she gets sent to smart doctors? I mean don't you have anything better to do?"

"Look we need this information for statistical purposes," the burly doughnut king of Clayton, Missouri retorts, eyeing his nightstick longingly.

"Fuck yourself, my mother may be dead and you want to know how far in college she got? Is this what they teach you in your sensitivity training courses?"

"Listen we have a potential homicide investigation here and you may be a suspect."

"Homicide my ass, how do you explain the suicide notes?"

Finally the cop's boss shows up and realizes it's in bad taste to badger suicide victims' next of kin and that I might be interested in discussing other things than her educational development. "Look son you must be stressed out – we'll just leave this questionnaire here. Fill it out at your convenience and mail it to us, okay?"

"No problem. I have some calls to make before I go to the hospital, so thanks for coming and have a nice day," I say, reaching for the sixteen unread suicide notes.

"You can't have these."

"Why not?"

"They're evidence."

"This one's addressed to me and I want to read it."

"Only if you let us look at it first." The doughnut cop grabs it from my hand. He starts reading, I can tell because his lips are moving a mile a minute until he gets to a big word. "What does opprobrious mean?"

"Abusive or malevolent," I answer, thankful that I read my mother's *Readers Digest* 'Improve Your Word Power' column.

"Well you're opprobrious," he says as he reads on, "and you've been fucking her best friend."

I suddenly feel the dread that has so far eluded me through this situation. How did she find out? Marge Bender better not be letting on. She's my best friend's mother and I only did it after she blackmailed me. Was it the same detective that she hired to catch my dad? Mom's a psycho-bitch alcoholic whom no one will take seriously if she lives, but if she knows, who else? Billy Bender will be pissed that I was nailing his mother, not to mention how his father – her husband the ex-college football player turned neo-Nazi sporting goods salesman who does a very good business in shotguns might feel. What happens if Nina Pennington the subject of many a late night wet dream, finds out; will I be dead in the water with her, especially since we were just getting somewhere in our relationship? I mean I had my hand inside her bra for five minutes last night while my tongue was halfway down her throat. There could be big trouble in River City.

"Enough about me...I want to know what this one says," I say, picking up the one addressed to 'My Son-of-A-Bitch Husband.'

"Leave it alone," Dunkin' Donut cop decrees, snatching the epistle from me, not noticing that I have with my other hand slipped the one addressed to Marge Bender under my shirt.

"What's it say?"

"This is official police business and it isn't addressed to you anyway. We'll hold on to these until after our inquiry is complete."

So it takes the cops a few more minutes to gather all the evidence of wrongdoing before they clear out. I try to convince them that the candles are important to the investigation and need to go to headquarters, but they aren't that dumb. Too bad. I hate those candles.

I finally have the place to myself. Time to open Lucretia Thibault's message from slightly before the grave. The phone rings as I open the envelope.

"Hello." Oh no, it's Fatso. If I tell her the truth she'll be on the way over to show how much she cares. I start perusing the ramblings from my recently departed (but how far?) mom.

"What did you mean by she's too dead to come to the phone? What's going on? Why did you tell me to hang up?"

"Uh, mom tried to commit suicide they just took her to the hospital... Yeah, it's drugs, 50 Seconal, she might be dead... I think they might need blood donors down there, I can't go because I think I'm coming down with bronchitis but maybe you can give. Kristen's there with her; and I'm making calls and answering the police's questions." She wants to press charges against Marge for corrupting me? I read on, "I think you better hurry down to the hospital Fa...um, I mean Julie. Quick!"

That should keep Fatso out of my hair for a few hours or so. Maybe if Mom hangs on, Julie will work a few pounds off pacing earnestly back and forth in the waiting room. Hang in there Mom, for the good of humanity. Don't die for at least twenty million calories or so.

It was Marge, the bitch got drunk and told her. She left out how it happened. I had no choice. It's kind of embarrassing, but here's the way it went down.

You know I have the job at the radio station filing the records after the jocks get through with them. A few weeks ago this promotion woman, which is a record company term for 'prostitute', comes in to blow everybody in exchange for them playing the new album by David Bowie, who I can't stand. Now believe it or not, at this point I'm the most naive kid in the world.

I'm sixteen years old and I have never had sex with anyone including myself. Nobody explained the old birds and bees to me, Dad was off in California shacked up with his mistress, Mom was too boozed up to care, and I was too busy playing guitar.

Everyone at the station knows I'm a twentieth century Vestal Virgin, and decide it is their job to initiate me. There's a woman sitting in the news booth, which is a small glass cubicle in between the control room and record library. Jimmy Leach, the deejay, tells me she wants to meet me. Her name is Dominique and she's wearing a leopard print bikini which barely exists, and a pair of knee length

FEED THE DOG

matching leopard high heel boots. She has platinum blond hair and is alternately sucking on a Tootsie Pop and a bottle of cognac which is a violation of FCC regulations, although I'm not going to be the one to mention it to the feds.

"Hi, uh, Dominique, Jimmy said you want to see me."

"Yeah, drop them," she says, nodding towards my pants.

"Excuse me?" I notice Jimmy Leach and a couple of the other guys watching me through the glass.

"Take off your pants silly."

"Uh, I, um," I stammer while seeing Jimmy nodding his head at me to do what the lady asks. I don't want to be a nerd so I guess I'll go along with the joke.

"Your underpants too," she says giggling into her cognac bottle.

"Uh, I can't."

"Why not?"

"Because you'll see my..."

"Prick? I've seen lots of pricks today. Are you shy? Maybe this will put you at ease." She removes the bikini, leaving me totally speechless. Jimmy nods again but I'm frozen in place with my pants down around my ankles. I see the station manager and two other guys watching me while they run one of the tape recorders. This must be my lucky day, I've won the Publisher's Clearing House sweepstakes booby prize and get to be the biggest moron in the world. Dominique rips my underpants off. "Come here."

Jimmy is besides himself as is everyone else in the rapidly swelling control room. Fortunately that isn't the only thing rapidly swelling. She puts my cock in her mouth and I utter the single most inane sentence of my life.

"Don't you know I piss with that?" Jimmy tells me later that he wet his pants he was laughing so hard. Dominique is on the floor in more ways than one too, but it isn't her pants that get wet.

As I pull myself back together I make a mental note to go buy all of David Bowie's albums since he's my favorite rock and roll star of all time. Meanwhile Jimmy's playing back the tape of my close encounter of the finest kind. While my face turns redder than Nikita Khrushchev on May Day everyone slaps my back in congratulations. Dominique comes up, kisses me on the lips, and hands me two backstage passes to tonight's Bowie show.

I saunter on home and call Billy Bender to ask him if he wants to see Bowie. "Bowie sucks," says Billy. I correct Billy about who does the sucking in the Bowie camp, and all of the sudden Billy wants to come to the show.

We go down to Kiel Auditorium and get herded backstage into the V.I.P. lounge which is actually the men's room with a couple of garbage cans full of beer. We share the hospitality room with two writers with bad breath from the *Evening Tribune*, a satin jacketed hoodlum type from Bowie's record company, Jimmy Leach who is going to introduce Bowie, and about a dozen leather and lace clad groupies eager to service the star of the evening.

I look for Dominique who eventually saunters in like she owns the place. She's radiant in her outfit of gold lamé hot pants, gloves, and halter top. She sees me and waves. Any doubts Billy has about me telling the truth disappear as she comes over and plants a lingering kiss on my lips while exercising my zipper with her gloved hand. But then she stops and says she has an important business conference with some deejay from Cedar Rapids. They vanish into the farthest stall and I can see through the bottom opening that she's indeed on her knees taking care of business.

Billy whispers to me that he's in love with Dominique – and I'm the proudest guy there as I'm sure with his big mouth everyone back at school will soon be regaled with the exploits of Ric Thibault, backstage stud.

A few minutes later Dominique returns and while fixing her lipstick tells this girl with incredible tits how we met this morning. Unfortunately Billy hears the whole story and he's giving me the 'you were a god, but now you're kind of a geek' look. But luck returns when Dominique suggests that Big Boobs take me to the back room and complete my education. She seems willing and Billy is flashing me the 'you were a geek, but now you're the luckiest guy in the world and can I come along?' stare. I ignore Billy and trot along with Marie, whose friends call her Boom Boom.

We go into this little room where I complete my sex education class with honors. I try to get some post graduate study in but Boom Boom doesn't want to miss Bowie and so I go back and search for Billy. I can't find him so I watch Jimmy Leach get booed while trying to introduce Bowie. Bowie is amazing – but being his number one fan I'm prejudiced. After it's over I walk backstage trying to hook back up with Billy since he is the one with the car. He's nowhere to be found, but a friend of Boom Boom's tells me Dominique had him thrown out for getting drunk and puking all over her.

It's midnight and I'm stuck at Kiel Auditorium with no ride. I don't have enough money for a cab and it's a ten mile walk home to Clayton. To further complicate things I was supposed to be back one hour ago. Mom will be up drunk waiting for me and I need a better excuse than "I was getting laid by some big titted bimbo named Boom Boom at the Bowie gig after getting my first blowjob earlier this afternoon."

The truth just is never good enough. I need a good lie. I run through all the old reliables, but I don't have a car to blame for mechanical trouble, my dog could not have eaten my homework, and I haven't been held hostage by bank robbers. Think man think. There has to be a good alibi out there somewhere with my name written all over it. I've already walked four miles and I'm still looking for that one big whopper to make things right when Providence smiles upon me.

Passed out face down on the sidewalk is a genuine miracle from above. Not only have I been blessed with a generic smelly wino, but the Almighty has been putting in overtime, 'cause this one's bleeding. Good Samaritan that I am I call the cops who upon my insistence that the man claimed to have been beaten by a gang of thugs before he passed out from his concussion, reluctantly ("Not this old wino again") take my savior to County General. I insist on going with them to make sure the guy is okay. This enables me to make the safe call home.

"Hello?"

"Hi, it's me."

"Do you know what time it is young man?"

"No, I called you just to find out what time it is."

"It's two in the goddamn morning and you're grounded until the 21st century smarty pants."

"Before you start grounding me don't you want to hear what happened?"

"It better be good."

"I'm at County General..."

"Are your legs broken?"

"No, they're fine."

"Then I suppose you're hooked up to a life support system and called me for Father O'Brien's phone number so he can come and give you the last rites?"

"No, I'm fi.."

"Well then, you better have come up with a real good story, or..."

I interrupt her and test my alibi, "You see, I found a guy who got beaten up pretty badly by some muggers...He was unconscious on the sidewalk when I found him, so I had to bring him here and wait for the police to take a report. You can call County General's emergency room and ask for me if you don't believe me."

"Original," she pauses while I hear her take a drink of something, "Assuming I believe you, you did the right thing."

My fib works! I try and press my luck a little,"Um, Mom can you come get me? The busses aren't running anymore."

"I'm too tired," she hiccups, "take a cab."

"I don't have any money."

"I'll pay for it when you get here."

"Okay, thanks Mom. See you soon." I hang up relieved. After all if that is the biggest lie I ever tell I'll probably be in good with St. Peter when it's my time – plus Lucretia is springing for the taxi.

It's the morning after the concert and I'm over at Billy's house. He's pretty mad about me going off with Boom Boom and leaving him alone. He says he was just having a few beers minding his own business when a security guy tells him he has the wrong pass to be in the hospitality room. Billy argues and gets in a shoving match with the bouncer. Dominique walks in and Billy does a Technicolor yawn all over her from drinking and being punched in the stomach. She's pissed and he's 86ed from the place. So he goes home and when his mom asks what happened he tells her the whole story including my coming out ball, so to speak.

I apologize to Billy and tell him what he missed making sure to give him the blow by blow action with Boom Boom. I embellish it a little telling him how I hung out with Bowie and Dominique who were trying to get me to go on the road with them. The only reason I didn't go is because I was looking for Billy who, it turned out had stranded me. I'm playing that tune out when Mrs. Bender marches into the room and she's not a happy camper.

"Billy told me what happened to you yesterday." I shoot Billy the 'How could you have told her the whole story you bastard' glare. "Billy go upstairs to your room while I talk to Ric." Billy leaves with a 'sorry you're in trouble but it's your fault' expression on his face.

Marge Bender is one of those women who could audition for a role as a TV mom. She can bake cookies with June Cleaver, clean a house like Donna Reed on black beauties, and dispense morality like June Allyson when she still had a bladder. But she would never get the part because unlike TV moms she chain smokes, drinks Seagrams straight up and swears like a wounded sailor. She's also my mom's best friend.

"So Billy tells me you got both a blowjob and laid yesterday." So much for Mrs. Subtle.

FEED THE DOG

"Congratulations." I'm sort of unsure where this conversation is going so I decide to take the 5th and remain silent. "Of course Lucretia isn't going to be happy about you messing around with sluts is she?"

I silently give myself the Miranda warning "*You have the right to remain silent, you have the right to an attorney. If you cannot afford one...*"

"What are we going to do about this, Ric?"

"Deny everything?"

"No, no I didn't mean to come off angry with you. I'm your mother's best friend and..." she's starting to smile and get TV mom sincere, "I'm your friend too."

Oh no, it's the schizophrenic version of good cop/bad cop, and she wouldn't give me a dime to call my lawyer if I had one. Remain calm...admit nothing...shit I can't stand up to much more of this prosecution or is it persecution?

"Tell me what happened."

"I thought Billy already told you."

"You tell me."

"It's too embarrassing."

"Then show me."

"I can't."

"Why not?"

"Because we, um, kind of didn't have all our clothes on all the time."

"Like this?" Forget what I said about TV moms, because unless you've got some special channel which I don't know about, you never get to see Mary Tyler Moore's breasts. I mean you can tell she has good ones but you never see more than the bulges under those tight sweaters. Marge Bender takes off her shirt and I get an unobstructed view of my best friend's mother's tits. I'm ready to plea bargain.

"Sort of."

"Were her breasts bigger?"

"I don't remember."

"What did you do to them?"

"With Dominique I just looked."

"And Boom Boom?"

Goddamn big mouthed Billy, isn't he an accessory after the fact? Get him in here I'll turn state's evidence.

"Ric, just answer the question, or better yet, show me."

"Show you?"

"Yes, just like you did to Boom Boom."

"I can't."

Billy's mother grabs my hand and presses them to her rather large boobs. "Yes you can, I won't tell your mother, I want you to... you know it feels good when a boy does that to a girl," she starts breathing heavy and moaning, "You know I love it, don't stop," and she starts to grind her chest all over my face. So one thing leads to another, and I show her everything I learned. Suffice it to say that evidently my education is not quite as complete as I think because Mrs. Bender is insisting on showing me other things that two people can do together. I think I'll save the details for the TV pilot show I'm going to write for that secret channel the Benders must get. I think it will get better ratings than *Make Room For Daddy*.

Kevin Bender used to be my favorite neighbor. He had season tickets to the Blues, and he took Billy and me to the playoffs the year that asshole, Bobby Orr, scored the goal in overtime to win the Stanley Cup. He, however, could not be a TV dad.

Ward Cleaver always had good advice like 'turn the other cheek' when Beaver got into a fight. When Billy and I got in a scrap with our class bully, Kevin Futterman, Mr. Bender gave us a tear gas pistol and showed us how to use it. "Disable the other guy and then kick him in the nuts," was his fatherly advice. When we were driving back from the movies one night he hit this parked car because he was trying to look at two hookers walking down the street. Mr. Bender sped off and Billy and I got ice cream cones every day for the next month.

And now I'm fucking his wife.

And his wife doesn't believe in one morning stands.

I know there is a term for a woman who isn't happy unless she's getting laid all the time. I ask Billy what it is. "Nymphomaniac," he says, "Why?" Now I can't tell Billy that I'm banging his nymphomaniac mother every day in his garage, in my garage, in the bathroom, in the backyard, etc., so I tell him Boom Boom called and is always wanting to get it on. Billy's impressed. His mother is a nympho, and I'm fucked.

♪

Nothing ever happens in the small suburb of St. Louis, Clayton, Missouri – unless you count the time there was a near riot at the A&P during the two day Wonder Bread strike of 1965. There was also the time that Frankie Dzierwa shot himself in the head after leaving the ten pin standing in the final frame – blowing a 300 score and a one thousand dollar prize at the Tropicana bowling alley. But all in all it is a place where boredom is measured by the clock – you know, it's two o'clock and I'm pretty bored, it's five o'clock I'm really bored, it's eight o'clock God I'm fucking bored, it's twelve o'clock I'm so bored I think I'll go to bed.

Therefore, Marge Bender and I playing 'Hide the salami' would probably keep the town occupied for the next two millennia.

I'm keeping my mouth shut, Billy's already told everybody about Dominique and Boom Boom, so my stud reputation does not need any bolstering. Also, I'm trying to make a move on Nina Pennington, who, to quote Nabokov is, "*the light of my life, the fire of my loins*", which I've underlined and highlighted in *Lolita*. I'm supposed to write a paper on the book tonight for English class – but I haven't read much past the first page due to Marge interrupting me every free moment I have. Duke may have to eat another paper if she doesn't leave me alone.

Nina Pennington is the most beautiful girl in the world if you don't count Raquel Welch or Brigitte Bardot, and Jane Fonda in *Barbarella*. She's got straight blond hair, big boobs, and an ass you can base a religion on. I forget what color her eyes are. Anyway she's really smart and wants to go to an Ivy League college or join the Peace Corps. Like me she's a big Bowie fan, and thanks to my p.r. man, Billy, she thinks I know David personally.

In the newly revised paperback edition of *How To Pick Up Girls* it says anything is fair in trying to score with a chick. So I lie. Worshiping Nina Pennington's ass goes against the 'Thou shalt not worship false idols' commandment, so I would be doing everybody a favor in nipping this potential infidel upheaval in the bud by removing her from the competition. God will understand. I'll explain it to Father O'Brien next time I happen to remember to go to Confession. He'll understand too.

"Nina, David called last night and I've got tickets to see Bowie Friday night in Chicago. Since it's Good Friday we get the day off from school, so do you want to go with me?" It's safe as milk. I know the chance of Nina convincing her parents to let her go on a date two hundred fifty miles away on Good Friday with anyone, much less me, is roughly the same as the chances of hell freezing over.

She'll decline and maybe we'll go on a date somewhere where I can practice all the moves on her I learned from reading *How To Pick Up Girls*.

Before I can finish patting myself on the back I learn of stunning developments concerning a sudden cold front blowing down Satan's empire. "My parents are away in Europe so they'll never know. I'd love to."

I'm a dead man. Today's Monday, and Bowie is in Chicago in four days. All I have to do is get enough money for tickets, if there are any to be had, borrow a car, and figure a way to break the old midnight curfew by ten or twelve hours. Even if that works, I'm going to have to figure a plausible explanation for why I don't have backstage passes to my friend David's show. I'm desperate but I can't let Nina feel it. "Great. I'll pick you up around noon. It'll be far out."

I panic. My next class is Latin. It's bad enough that I live in the most boring city in the most boring state in the United States, but I take classes in dead boring languages spoken by no one other than celibate priests, reading boring poems by one named poets in pentameters which no one other than flatulent bastards, like Mr. Apgar, who teaches the class, understand. Skipping class is punishable by suspension. However, Apgar is so into Ovid that there is a chance he won't miss me. I gamble.

I go down to the radio station and find Jimmy Leach who knows everybody at Bowie's record company. I tell Jimmy my emergency and he calls someone and arranges to get me not only tickets, but backstage passes. I promise never to boo a disk jockey again when he introduces a band.

Now I need to get a car. I obviously can't ask my mother for her keys so I can go to Chicago. I'm too young and too broke to rent one. None of my friends are about to lend me theirs, so there is only one option – Marge Bender.

I go over to Marge's. She kisses me and starts making out before I get a chance to ask. Consequently we roll around the living room for a few minutes before I can pop the question.

"Marge, I need a favor."

"Anything sweetie, just keep doing what you're doing."

"I need to borrow your car Friday, I promise to bring it home clean with a full tank of gas Saturday."

"Sure baby, what's going on?"

"Um, I have to..." Well here comes another doozie. I can't tell her that I'm borrowing her car to go screw Nina Pennington, and I can't tell her I'm going to Chicago because she'll tell my mom.

I've got to make this one really good,"...follow my father and catch him with his mistress for mom's lawyer. Only I don't want her to know because she's liable to do something violent and get in trouble...you know how she is."

"Sure honey, that's sweet."

So I finish my business with Marge and tear back to school.

I luck out, Mr. Apgar never noticed I wasn't there. In fact Mr. Apgar didn't notice anything, because he had a heart attack and died while reading Ovid.

Billy Bender is filling me in on the details, "Man, you should have seen him, Apgar's just about to give a surprise quiz when he grabs his chest, mumbles something in Latin, belches and dies. Where were you?"

After some of the lies I've told one more is not really going to hurt. I can't tell Billy, "I was fucking your mother on your dining room table." I'm lying to protect his feelings. God will understand this one too. I might want to go to Easter Mass Sunday. A few Hail Marys, a couple Our Fathers, a little penance, everything's fine. It's great to be Catholic!

"I had to run down to the radio station, there was an emergency."

"What happened?"

Jesus what is it everyone's Perry Mason around here trying to break me on the stand? Don't I get one lie free? "The F.C.C. found out that I was with Dominique and they wanted to question me."

"What did you tell them?"

"I denied everything."

"Who ratted on you?"

"I don't know maybe that guy backstage from the *Evening Tribune*. I think he might have overheard Dominique talking to Boom Boom."

"Yeah, he was a creep." Billy believes me. I might have a gift for this lying stuff. Maybe I should become a salesman or a politician instead of a musician.

It's still Monday. I've got Nina, the tickets, the backstage passes, Marge's car, and now there is only one more hurdle, Lucretia Garbo Thibault, a/k/a Mom.

Unless they make *What Ever Happened to Baby Jane* into a sitcom, Lucretia doesn't have a shot at TV momdom. She hasn't been sober since she caught my dad with his secretary eight years ago in 1965. Each day she wakes up, downs the half a bottle of vodka on her night stand and then gets out of bed prepared to avenge herself upon those closest to her. Unlike her namesake Garbo speaks and speaks loudly and menacingly. After a hard day of spitting venom she downs a couple of martinis, makes sure that her two kids and one inmate are in their bedrooms, and then takes some pills so she can relax.

I'm low man on the totem pole around our house. First, despite his philandering, is Dad. Even though they seem to have lawyers and detectives permanently on retainer for their impending divorce they never quite make it to court. There's always some temporary reconciliation followed by three weeks of holding hands and cooing at each other. Then Johann announces he has to leave town on business, leading to loud shouting matches mainly in German which, other than 'Schweinhund', I don't understand. Then they break up and I have to help my dad load up a U-Haul and move to a singles complex in Creve Couer. While my older brother Stephan and I carry everything in we get to hear Dad on the phone with his mistress telling her to catch the next flight to St. Louis, "because this time it's for good." This will last for three to four months whereupon Dad will get tired of his 'blow in her ear and she'll thank you for the refill' bimbo and make up with Lucretia. Then Stephan and I will have to go load up the U-Haul and bring everything back, while Dad is on the phone with his lawyer canceling the divorce.

Second from the top on the totem pole comes Duke. He's always happy and glad to see everyone. The dog can do no wrong, even when he chews up the genuine reproduction Louis XIV settee.

Batting third is Kristen. Kristen is eighteen, two years older than me, and has never been caught doing anything wrong in her life. She gets straight A's in school and speaks four languages fluently. She looks like butter wouldn't melt in her mouth, but she also strips under the name 'Bambi Bosoms' on Friday nights in Gaslight Square. I found that out when I caught her stashing two hundred bucks in a hiding place behind the garage. She swore me to secrecy and for ten percent of what she grosses my lips are sealed.

Next is Stephan. I hate Stephan. We have not gotten along since the day JFK got killed. I was home sick that afternoon watching TV when they interrupted *My Little Margie* to announce the shooting. Stephan came home from school for lunch and I bet him five dollars that he didn't know who the President of the United States was. He took the wager and said Kennedy. I told him he was

FEED THE DOG

wrong it was Johnson. He got pissed off and refused to pay. I appealed to Lucretia and she got angry at me for having the bad taste to make such a bet. No one respects my entrepreneurial spirit.

Every structure needs a good foundation, and I serve that function for the Thibaults. If someone goes hungry in Bangladesh it's my fault. If the Bay of Pigs fails, blame Ric – and if a lamp should accidentally shatter while Stephan and I are upstairs playing hockey you know who will take the penalty. Our private in house public address announcer goes, "we have a two year penalty for roughing to #3 Ric Thibault." I argue with the ref, Lucretia, and end up getting whistled off for another ten years for misconduct.

Classes are called off so the whole school can attend Mr. Apgar's funeral. We go out to St. Mary's and listen to the revisionists already at work telling us how much we're all going to miss his wisdom and counsel. I'm sitting in the fourth pew directly behind the open casket. Apgar looks a little waxy, but he always looked that way come to think about it. I kind of halfway expect him to jump up out of the coffin and scream "Okay Mr. Thibault conjugate the Latin verb for fucking skipping my class and causing me a heart attack," but thankfully he is not in the mood for it. Billy whispers he heard that they have hidden cameras in the classrooms and that I'm in big trouble. I'm not buying this one however. I know if there had been any hidden cameras catching Apgar's last gasp it would have been the biggest story ever in Clayton and would therefore have been shown in slow motion freeze frame replay on the six o'clock news, with live team coverage at ten. I'm about to tell Billy to fuck off when I notice Nina, looking really stacked in a tight black sweater, crying in the next pew. She looks like she needs comfort and I vow to provide solemn solace just as soon as Father O'Brien stops telling us how we would all be taking a little part of Apgar with us throughout our lives. I wonder which section of Apgar I get, probably his dandruff.

After the funeral I catch up with Nina. She's not in the best of moods. What with her parents being in Europe she spent the night alone replaying the death of our beloved Latin teacher a thousand times in her mind. "I was in the front row and he collapsed right at my feet," she sobs, "wasn't it the worst thing you ever saw?"

Nina hadn't noticed I had been playing hooky. "Oh yes it was a terrible tragedy that will haunt me every night for as long as I live," I say not altogether untruthfully, thinking of what I went through to get the tickets and car – and what I still need to do vis à vis Lucretia. "I forgot you were alone, why didn't you call me? I would have come right over," I add in my most sincere sympathetic voice.

I hold her hand as we walk up the aisle. Out of the blue someone elbows me and I spin around to see an angry Marge Bender giving me the 'lose the crying slut, buster' look and my mother who is crying, probably because there's no liquor at the service. This day is not off to a good start.

The only safe thing to do is hang out with Billy until Marge cools out. Marge can't say anything in front of Billy about my love of life. Of course I can't tell Billy too much about Nina because he's already proven he has a big mouth which is what got me into this mess with his mother. So I'm sort of treading water until the next undertow strikes, in the form of Marge Bender.

"Ric dear, I've been thinking about what you said to me yesterday about needing the car Friday. I don't think you should be alone that late outside your father's." Please Lord, I pray, show some mercy and don't let her volunteer to escort me. "so, I want you to take Billy with you." My prayer has been answered – and I'm still fucked.

"I can't ask Billy to get involved."

"I can, and I want him there. I don't want to worry about you falling asleep, and that's final."

Billy, sensing an adventure at hand, is thrilled to be going on my spying mission.

I need another Bowie ticket.

It's Wednesday and Jimmy Leach is furious. The new ratings book has come out and he has fallen into last place in morning drive time. Evidently even Brother Theodore and the Send Your Money To God, (care of Brother Theodore, P.O. Box 666, San 'We have no extradition treaty with the U.S.' Jose, Costa Rica) Radio Show is doing better than Jimmy. Jimmy is in no mood to help me score another ticket. He tells me to attempt something which is biologically impossible. I now remember why people boo deejays at rock concerts, and vow to throw a firecracker at him at the next show.

I call Chicago on the radio station's phone. There are no tickets left. According to the ticket outlet, scalpers, if you can find one, are getting fifty dollars a seat. I've only got seventeen dollars and one possibility. I have to borrow Marge's car, pick up and seduce Nina, kidnap Billy, go to Chicago, find Dominique, who might not recognize me with my pants on, get her to give me a ticket for Billy, and then explain why I'm not home to my mother – all this while writing a paper on the degeneration of western culture as represented by Humbert Humbert in *Lolita*, which on account of

FEED THE DOG

Apgar's croaking is now due on Monday.

Well God, do you love me and, if you do, would you mind proving it? I promise never to swear again if You help me. I'll be like everyone else and listen to Brother Theodore rather than Jimmy Leach. How about it?

So it's Thursday. I've decided to put my fate in the hands of God and wing it. Marge wants me to come to her house for a 'box lunch'. Since I need the car, I figure I can't refuse. We fuck for forty-five minutes and then she gives me a sandwich to eat on the way back to school. I ask her if she has any vitamins. She does. I chug a handful of vitamin E. I think I'm going to need them.

Nina is still being sensitive. I tell her it's okay if she'd rather have a prayer vigil for dear Mr. Apgar than go see Bowie. But she says he would have wanted us to have fun, so Chicago is still on. She asks if we can have dinner with David.

"I'm not sure because he might be busy, but I promise to ask if and when I talk to him tonight." It's not quite a lie since I didn't say that I was definitely going to talk to him.

After school Billy has to go help his dad at the store, so I go back to Marge's and make out with her until eight which coincidentally is when Kevin and Billy close up shop. As I get dressed Marge finally pops the question.

"Ric, love, who was that girl you were with at the funeral?" *Ladies and Gentlemen, Marge Bender presents 'The Spanish Fucking Inquisition'* (God hasn't proven anything yet and He can't hear me swear in my mind so I'm still okay), *make way for the Grand Inquisitor.*

"Nina? Oh she's the girl that Apgar fell on when he died. She took it real bad and I was trying to comfort her." *How much does she know?*

"She's very pretty." *Do I look guilty?*

"Yeah, come to think of it she is attractive." *Spoken like a gentleman!*

"I'd say sexy." *Is that an iron maiden behind the dresser?*

"Yeah, she is a bit." *The defense rests.*

"Have you been putting the moves on her?" *The bad cop has returned for an encore.*

"Hardly," the first syllable being truthful – therefore it is at most a half lie.

"I'd hate to find you with some young piece of fluff, it would break my heart." *We the jury find the defendant guilty. Quick, file an appeal for executive clemency.*

I lick between her legs. "Don't worry Marge I'm not going anywhere." *Full pardon!* "Marge, can I ask you for one more favor?"

"Sure love."

"Can you tell my mom I'm spending tomorrow night with Billy here...we might be up real late past curfew and I don't want to get in trouble for helping her."

"Sure dear. In fact why don't you spend the night, maybe I can come in and visit you after Kevin falls asleep."

Knowing that we won't get in until six in the morning at the earliest I'm willing to take the risk. "That'd be fun." She kisses me, and I escape just as I hear her husband's car in the driveway.

It's Good Friday and Lucretia is actually smiling. She tells me that she's been listening to this new radio program hosted by Brother Theodore. She sent him one hundred dollars and just received in the mail a green glow in the dark plastic Jesus which will ward off the Devil. I ponder the irony that I have to leave immediately.

I go over to Marge's. Billy's there so I don't have to make out with her. Giving me the keys to her brand new red Oldsmobile 98 with leather seats AM-FM radio and an eight track player she warns us to be careful. We go out to the garage where Kevin Bender is cleaning a shotgun. "I'm going hunting tomorrow morning," he says with a 'guess what type of hunting I'm doing with this you cuckolding motherfucker' look. Suddenly my boots are wet and I have to go home to change my pants.

I run into my house and find my mother giggling, wildly dancing with her new plastic Jesus. She stops abruptly when she sees me. "Back so soon?" the joy is totally gone from her voice. I tell her I forgot something and run upstairs and change. Running back out, I notice she's happy again.

We're two miles from Nina's and it's time to kidnap Billy. I'm driving and Billy's showing me the Nikon camera with the telephoto lens which we're supposed to use to take pictures of Johann.

"Billy, Dominique called a few minutes ago."

"I hate that bitch ever since she got me thrown out of backstage." This lie needs a little more embellishment.

"I explained to her what really happened was you got sick from food poisoning. Now she feels so bad that she had you kicked out she wants to make it up to you personally."

FEED THE DOG

"What do you mean?"

"Well, she asked if we would come visit her tonight so she can show you how sorry she is."

"Really?"

"Uh huh, there's only one small hitch. She's at the Bowie show in Chicago. She promised us backstage passes again and all we have to do is get there. I figured it all out and all we have to do is drive there and tell your mom we were staking out my dad in Creve Couer. It'll work."

"No it won't. Mom will know we drove the car five hundred miles – she keeps an odometer log."

Thankfully I've watched every episode of *Mission Impossible* so I know how to disconnect the odometer. "See, Billy, no problem." Billy's nervous but quiet. "Oh yeah, and one other thing I promised Nina Pennington she could come too as my date. So while you're scoring with Dominique I'll have something to do." Thankfully the prospect of getting his pipes cleaned by Dominique is enough to make Billy agreeable.

So we pick up Nina. She is even more beautiful than I remember her from this morning's jerk off session. She's a walking wet dream wearing a black vee neck sweater that promises unimaginable treasures, black satin hot pants, and five inch stiletto heel pumps. Her legs lead up to heaven and my mind is right down in hell. She doesn't even seem to mind Billy's being along for the ride.

"So Ric, are we going to get to meet David?"

I've already told Billy I talked to Dominique this morning, so I can't just turn around and tell Nina that I haven't. Try to squirm out of this one silver tongue. "It's all taken care of," I pat Nina on her thigh which is of course in close proximity to the much revered Sacred Ass of Pennington. Billy turns on the radio and Chuck Berry's playing *Sweet Little 16*.

So I'm heading over the Mississippi when I see the sign, 'State Line, Welcome To Illinois'. A little voice inside starts shouting "Hey asshole, what do you get when you add Chuck Berry, State Line, *Sweet Little 16*, Nina Pennington, and a semi-stolen car? That's right stupid – Mann Act." Suddenly I don't feel so good. I shove in the 8-track that's in the player and Johnny Cash's *Folsom Prison Blues* comes blaring out. Feeling absolutely wonderful I quickly eject the tape and switch the radio back on. That's when I also notice we only have one eighth of a tank of gas left. So I pull into the Fina station where gas is only fifty-eight cents a gallon. While Nina is in the bathroom I pay the cashier and ask Billy how much money he has.

"Eight bucks, why?"

"Well your eight bucks and my remaining five aren't going to get us back from Chicago."

"Does Nina have any money?"

Now I still have some values left and I'm not about to go Dutch with a Goddess. "I can't ask her," Nina returns with a couple of sodas for Billy and me. "Where did you get these?"

"From the vending machines out back, why?"

"I just wondered thanks." A light bulb goes on in my head. "Nina could you wait in the car while Billy and I go to the bathroom?"

"I don't have to go," Billy complains.

"Billy, it's a long way to Chicago and I don't want to have to stop too often, come on." I give him the 'come with me or you may be walking home from Edwardsfuckingville Illinois' look.

So we go around back to where the bathrooms and vending machines are. It is a documented fact that the Mafia owns every vending machine ever made. The Mafia are killers and thieves. Therefore, stealing from the Cosa Nostra boys is a way of fighting crime and not a sin. "Help me turn this cigarette machine upside down."

"Why, what the fuck are you doing?" Billy helps me and all the money falls to the top of the machine.

"What the fu... we are doing," I correct him without cussing while turning the machine back right side up, "is getting money." And money it is as we liberate the sixty-seven dollars twenty-five cents in quarters and two packs of death sticks that fall out the machine from the evil clutches of the Mob.

We run back to the car and are off. Nina doesn't realize anything even though our pockets are clanging like an epileptic slot machine. I'm thinking what a great day this is. The Feds want me for the Mann Act, and the underworld is probably at this very moment mobilizing hit teams for the great cigarette machine heist. Meanwhile Kevin Bender has a shotgun and is going hunting for me tomorrow morning.

I look in the rear view mirror. Isn't that J. Edgar Hoover in the '69 Cadilac tailgating me? There's only one way to find out if we're being followed – I slam on the brakes. He tries to swerve to avoid me and smashes into a guard rail. I resume speed. Mr. Hoover is going to have car problems for the next few days.

"Ric, why did you hit the brakes so suddenly?" Nina asks.

"I didn't want to hit that squirrel crossing the road," not remembering until it is too late that squirrels do not inhabit the cornfields of Illinois.

"That's noble of you," Cool. First, she thinks I'm noble. Second, she's not majoring in zoology so she doesn't know much about the native habitats of squirrels. Lastly, she didn't notice the accident behind. Things aren't too bad here after all.

"Man aren't you going to stop for the accident you caused?" Saint Billy the all-of-a-sudden-righteous-with-a-short-life-span asks from the floor in back where he's checking to see if he lost any teeth when he flew into the front seat after I hit the brakes.

"I didn't cause an accident Billy, the guy was tailgating me, it's his fault that he didn't maintain a proper distance. Right Nina?"

"Was there an accident?" she asks turning around.

By this time we've gone around a bend and she can't see anything so I tell her Billy was just joking, while giving Billy the 'you better say you're joking if you don't want to be sucking the rest of your meals through a straw' look in the rear view mirror.

Billy mumbles, "Just kidding," while shooting me the 'I better get a blowjob out of this if you want to live' stare.

Nina Pennington radiates sex. She sits voluptuously, she breathes seductively and talks in the most sensuous husky voice, and she doesn't even know it. It's extremely hard to keep my eyes on the road and off of her. So I pull over and make Billy drive so I can sit by her undistracted in the front seat.

Billy is so eager to get his reward in Chicago that he starts speeding. I'm just about to try and kiss Nina on the neck when I see a police car pull out behind us. "Billy it's the cops!" Evidently Billy's even more scared of our recent criminal past than I am, and he freaks out.

"They're not going to take me," he says having seen too many *Cannonball Run* movies and not enough *Adam 12* episodes. We're in the left hand lane of a three lane in each direction highway. Billy speeds up as do the cops.

Nina doesn't say anything but she's a little bit tense, which isn't the worst thing in the world because she clutches me tightly. Very tightly. Extremely tightly – and in places which can be very interesting when held tightly. I'm feeling no pain at all...I could even learn to enjoy being chased by cops.

So we're heading down Highway 57 about one hundred miles per hour when Billy sees his opening. There is a truck in the middle lane. Billy zooms past the truck and then abruptly pulls into the extreme right hand lane and slams on the brakes. The cops whiz past the truck while we pull off into a ditch. Nina can't look and buries her head in my chest holding onto me even tighter. Billy kills the engine and whoops, "We made it!" just as I make it.

While we wait and make sure the cops are gone I can feel my picture being tacked up on every post office bulletin board in the country:

WANTED DEAD OR ALIVE!

Richard Alouitious Thibault for kidnapping, Mann Act violation, leaving the scene of an accident, unlawful flight to evade arrest, car theft, robbery, and illegal betting with brother. Also suspect in mysterious death of Latin teacher. Thibault is known to be in the company of **William Bender** a/k/a/ **Billy "I'll do anything for a blowjob" Bender** and her holiness, **Nina Pennington** (See accompanying *Vogue* photo layout) Shoot first, ask questions later.

Nina is mad at Billy. "You could have gotten us all killed, I want Ric to drive." Her wish is my command, so I get out of the car only to sink six inches into a mud puddle. By the time I get to the other side of the Oldsmobile my boots are ruined and my feet are soaking.

I start the car, shove it into gear, the wheels spin but we don't move. I shift into reverse...again nothing. We're stuck.

Billy suggests we use an emergency call box to summon a tow truck. I reluctantly come to the conclusion that Billy is not going to be a rocket scientist if he lives long enough to grow up.

"Billy, who answers the emergency phone?" I ask.

"I dunno, an operator?"

"Yes, and now for the bonus question – who does the operator work for?"

"The government?"

"Billy it's like using the Batphone. You're calling the police when you use it, and by the time you hang up we'll have the entire Illinois Highway Patrol, the Army, National Guard, and the Navy because there is a puddle of water involved trying to hire us to make license plates for the next twenty years. So get out here and push."

Nina slides behind the wheel and we get in front and shove. The tires spin. Mud flies and the car doesn't budge. We go around to the back and try pushing forward. The tires spin, mud flies, and eventually the car lurches out of the ditch and back onto the shoulder.

Billy and I are filthy. Nina laughs. "The good news is the cops are looking for two white guys, so they'll never find you. The bad news is there is absolutely no way I'm going to go to Bowie with

FEED THE DOG

you looking and smelling like that."

The Lord is on my side after all! We decide we have to find a shower and a laundromat. This will take at least two hours. We'll be so late to the concert that I will be able to blame Billy for making us miss being able to pick up our tickets at the will call window, thereby saving me the embarrassment of looking for Dominique.

A few miles down the road we find a twenty–nine dollar a night motel which, according to its marquee, also features special short stay rates. Nina goes in and asks about the hourly cost. She returns saying we can get a room for three hours for only ten bucks. I cough up the last of my paper money and she goes back in and registers. Nina brings back the key to room 107. Upon entering the sparsely furnished room I strip down to my underwear marveling at my good fortune. Who would ever have thought I'd be half-naked in a motel room with Nina Pennington? I give Nina a handful of the Mafia's quarters to do our laundry while we clean up.

We take our showers and watch television while waiting for Nina to return with our clothes. The only program on is a rerun of *The Fugitive*. My dad is always telling me to learn from the best so I pay close attention to Richard Kimble who is experienced at evading both cops and bad guys. Kimble is cornered in a warehouse when the show is interrupted by a news bulletin about a snow storm moving in on Pekin, Illinois. Evidently Pekin is much like Clayton because this news is of such magnitude that three earnest newscasters and two remote cameras are required to tell us that six to ten inches of snow are being forecast.

"Jerry how's it doing on highway 57?" the anchor asks some poor slob reporter who is shivering in the middle of a field.

"Well, Frank it's snowing pretty hard."

"Can you describe the snow Jerry?"

"It's cold, wet, and white," Jerry says with great profundity.

"Elaine Sutherland is standing by outside Jeremy's truck stop. Elaine what does it look like where you are?" Frank queries a shivering woman.

"It's cold, wet, and windy," Elaine adds, bringing a woman's perspective to this momentous story.

I switch channels but they have all interrupted their programming to discuss this fast breaking story. I look out the window and see that snow is indeed falling. My faith in the hard hitting integrity of the American press is unshaken. In case God is still listening I tack on a silent addendum to my prayer of earlier this week. Please God let it snow, let the highway be closed, and let me be stranded throughout eternity in a motel room with Nina Pennington.

I'm sitting in the motel room watching the snow coverage thinking up the best way to get rid of Billy so I can be alone with Nina when she gets back. I can't ask him to go sleep in the car, and it will look really suspicious if we try to pay for a another motel room with quarters. I'm still racking my brains when Nina finally returns with our clothes. She's crying.

"What's wrong?"

"I was coming back from the laundry when I skidded on some ice and crashed into a stop sign," she sobs.

"Are you okay?" I ask trying to appear caring although I'm more concerned about how fucked up Marge's car is.

"Yes, but the car is messed up."

"Mom's going to kill us," Billy says.

So we get dressed and go outside to examine the formerly brand new Oldsmobile. The fender is falling off and the front end is pretty dented. "Mom's going to kill us," Billy cries, repeating the bloody obvious. "What are we going to do?"

"If you hadn't tried to outrun the cops this wouldn't have happened," I try to blame Billy.

"It's not my fault your girlfriend doesn't know how to drive."

"I'm sorry." Nina cries harder but doesn't protest being called my girlfriend!

"Let's go back inside," I say not feeling quite so bad about the day's developments. I put my arm around Nina and tell her everything will be fine as we walk to the room. She's still sobbing and looks like she needs a hug. I'm more than happy to provide such services. Meanwhile Billy's on the verge of tears too – but I decide he doesn't require a squeeze.

I try to think of what Father O'Brien would say in such a situation. Girls always respond to that warm Irish Catholic charm. "I'm sure the car is insured so we're not looking at the end of the world. The most important thing is that you're all right. Did anyone see the accident?"

"No, I don't think so."

"Good, all we need now is a little white lie and we'll be fine. Let me think a second." I contemplate calling the cops to report the Oldsmobile as stolen, thereby getting us off the hook for the chase, but that would not account for how we are still in possession of the car. I need a better lie.

My deliberations are disturbed by some loud moaning from the room next to us. It sounds like some lucky bastard is having serious sex. I'm pondering the accident and hoping Nina will want to

FEED THE DOG

keep up with our motel neighbors when through the wall I hear a female voice plead, "Fuck me harder Johann," followed by grunting sounds. Billy and I look at each other and Nina stops sobbing. We grab a couple of glasses and put them up against the wall to hear better. Evidently some guy named Johann has just gotten his rocks off. We hear moaning and the squeaking of bedsprings, and then the same female voice asks, "Are you ready for your turn Kevin?"

I have an idea we know who is in the next room. From my experience there are not too many men named Johann in the United States, and probably only a handful of them would be in a motel room within driving distance from Clayton with a guy named Kevin. I run out to the car and get the camera and the telephoto lens. I ask Billy if he knows how to use it. He says he does. The sounds from next door – a bed moving back and forth, punctuated with occasional grunts, groans, and heavy breathing – are getting louder. I tell Billy to get into the Oldsmobile and aim the camera at the door of room 108. "Don't let anyone see you, but when the door opens take as many pictures as you can."

Billy goes outside and I instruct Nina, "Ring room 108. When they answer say you're the desk clerk and you want to tip them off that the vice cops are on their way." She nods and makes the call.

I hear the phone ringing in the adjacent room. The bed stops shaking and the grunts subside as Nina announces the impending raid. Johann shouts, "It's the police, get dressed and let's get out of here." The woman whines, "I'm not going anywhere mister until you fork over the hundred smackers." There's a lot of frantic rustling as I move over to our window and peek out through the curtains. Bingo! out come Johann Thibault, Kevin Bender, and a platinum blond woman, none of whom look happy. I spot several bursts of light from Billy's camera. The idiot is using the flash attachment! Our fathers can't help but see Billy too. While another car tears out of the parking lot they nab the fool.

"It wasn't my idea, it was Ric's, and I didn't crash the car it was Nina, I didn't even want to be here, it's not my fault," Billy rats us out without hesitation. I have no choice but to move quickly, opening the door and walking out. This is one time when the old saying 'the best defense is a good offense' seems beyond dispute.

"Hi Dad! Hello Mr. Bender, how's the hunting?" I think we're having what's called a pregnant pause because Dad and Mr. Bender look like guppies with their mouths opening and closing with no words coming out. I decide to break the silence. "Oh, I'm so sorry ma'am, please pardon my family's lack of manners, allow me to introduce myself I'm Ric Thibault and this is my girlfriend Nina Pennington – and I see you've already met Billy Bender. What's your name?"

"Trixie Montana, say Mr. Smith and Mr. Jones how about that extra tip we were talking about?" Billy's dad, Mr. Smith, reaches into his wallet and takes out some money. The woman grabs it and splits.

"Well, fancy running into you here Mr. Smith and Mr. Jones, we have so much to talk about, but let's not stand out here freezing to death. There's a diner over there why don't we grab a bite to eat and have a father/son gab fest." I figure we should be in a place with plenty of witnesses in case our discussion turns out to be less than friendly.

We trudge over to the diner and Nina whispers she's not too happy about being dragged into this family discussion, but I assure her we're holding most of the cards. Billy is quiet and all zombie like, he must be exhausted from the one billionth of a second of torture he endured before cracking.

According to its sign, A.J.'s Fine Eats is world famous. I must be ignorant because I never heard of the place before. I'm not the only ignorant one though because the two state troopers drinking coffee at the counter seem unaware of the certain promotions which await them if they would only pay attention to the five dangerous criminals entering the restaurant. Besides Billy's and my own recently documented crime spree you have our two adulterous whoremongering fathers, and making her debut into criminal life, hit and run driver Nina Pennington. But the cops just sit there chatting up the waitress while we walk right past them. Suckers! They'd probably miss Ma Barker's gang too.

The waitress brings us menus and no one is talking. I figure it's up to me to break the ice. "Trixie seemed like a nice lady, too bad she had to run off before we got a chance to talk and get to know one another." Johann glares at me. "I don't know if I ever properly introduced you to Nina, a classmate of ours from Clayton High. Nina Pennington, this is my father Johann Thibault, and Billy's dad, Kevin Bender."

They murmur how do you dos. Kevin asks Nina "Is your dad Zachary Pennington, the banker?" Nina nods. Kevin winces. I sense we might be in an even better negotiating position than I thought.

"Look I believe in laying all my cards on the table. You've got some problems and we have a few too. Maybe if we put our heads together on this one we can help each other out. As I see it, and correct me if I'm wrong, you would like us to forget you were ever here. We'd also like to forget we were ever here. The only thing which is preventing us from falling into a state of total amnesia is this little car problem we have. Now if our car problem just went away we could forget everything, and it won't even cost you one single ice cream cone extra. What do you say?"

"Deal," Mr. Smith and Jones respond in unison.

"Let's eat," I say, joining Nina and Billy in a collective sigh of relief. During dinner we negotiate

FEED THE DOG

the terms and conditions of our pact. There will be no reprisals and my dad will take the blame for the damage. In exchange for Johann having backed into Marge's parked car in a Creve Couer parking lot, we turn over the film.

Johann wants to know what we are doing out here. I've told enough lies for a while so I tell him the truth, we were going to see Bowie in Chicago. "You're grounded."

"I think that constitutes a reprisal."

"No it doesn't, it has nothing to do with Kevin's and my, um, activities."

"I want an appeal."

"Your mother is the Supreme Court on these matters."

"We're out of her jurisdiction, I'll ask the state troopers over there," I bluff.

"How about if you're only grounded one non-weekend night?"

I take the plea bargain. Dad asks for the check telling the waitress we're in a hurry due to us having a long drive home ahead of us. She says we're not going anywhere because the troopers have just closed the highway due to the snow.

We go back to the motel for the night. Nina, Billy and I head back to our room. "Where do you think you're going?" Johann demands.

"To our room."

"Since when do you share a bedroom with a girl?"

I could tell the truth and tell about the numerous times I have shared a bed with Marge Bender, but discretion is the better part of valor so I lie, "Never."

"Okay young lady we're going to get you your own room, Billy you sleep with your dad, and Ric you come with me."

The trip back is excruciatingly boring. Johann and Kevin have Nina drive with Billy and his father in Marge's car. I'm Johann's sole passenger. Nina probably hates me after missing Bowie and, over my objections, winding up riding with Billy and Kevin. I think this too falls under the reprisal category. Johann warns me to be quiet or else. I sit in angry silence worried that Nina will never talk to me again. Johann drops me off and I slink back into the house.

Lucretia is passed out snoring on the couch next to an empty tequila bottle. Stephan and Kristen aren't home so I should have a few hours of peace.

Leave it to Billy to blow it. It takes him exactly eight seconds to tell Marge that Nina was with us last night. I find out when Billy calls me two minutes after I walked in the door. "I don't know what you did to my mom, but she hates your guts. She says she's going to cut your balls off next time she sees you."

"What did you tell her?" I ask wondering about the sex lives of eunuchs.

"That you have a really beautiful girlfriend and are getting a reputation for going out with the most exotic women in town. I told her that I'm jealous of you, stud." I make a mental note to check how much it will cost to have Billy's tongue removed.

At least Marge can't go and tell Kevin that I've jilted her for Nina. I don't think he'll be the most sympathetic audience, although I'm sure that emptying a couple of clips of ammunition in my general direction would not be the most odious task in the world for him.

Well there is nothing I can do now other than avoid being around Marge and sharp objects. She has nothing to be mad about. I never told her I loved her or anything. Our relationship is purely sexual. She's almost twenty years older than me...when I'm 30 she'll be 50, and when I'm 45 she'll be in some geriatric center eating Jell-O. She has to know this will never work in the long term. Men can mess around with younger women – like Humbert Humbert in *Lolita* – it's gross but okay; but what guy wants to go out with an old hag? I contemplate this while bullshiting my way through my paper on Nabokov and the degeneration of western society.

Lucretia is on the warpath and that path leads straight to me. It's about five o'clock and my mother is screaming something in German into the phone. I guess she's yelling at Johann about something or other. He probably doesn't need the phone to hear her – he only lives eight miles away. Since Kristen's out I have no one to translate what's going on, but I figure hiding in my room until Lucretia calms down might be a good idea.

No such luck. My door flies open and the Madwoman of Chaillot, Clayton division, has landed. "I know where you, Billy, Kevin and your son of a bitch father were last night. It's bad enough that your father is hiring tramps, but you and Billy, at the same seedy motel in Pekin, Illinois? How could you?"

"How could I what?"

"Don't even try to deny it. I've got pictures. I had a detective follow your father last night. Not only does he find your son-of-a-bitch father and Kevin Bender with some floozy, but in the next room you and Billy have your own tramp. What is it with the men in this family – you're such rotten fucks that you have to bring along the neighbors to pinch hit for you?" She slams the door before I can either recover from the shock or attempt an explanation.

I'm still trying to figure everything out when I hear Lucretia on the phone with Marge. "I'll be right over," she says, and hangs up.

Hurricane Lucretia is roaring and the emergency early warning system has failed. I can't alert Billy, and even if I could he'd probably only make things worse. Johann is supposed to be catching a plane to France – and I can't exactly be honest with Kevin.

I try to call Nina. There's no answer.

I pick up my guitar. If I were black I could be playing authentic blues but I have to settle for the ersatz, white boy blues. I compose the first half of *Talkin' Nina Pennington Blues* instantly:

> *I'm a liar with a beautiful girlfriend*
> *Nina be her name*
> *I'd die here for my beautiful girlfriend*
> *Like a worn out flame*
> *I'm a sucker with a gorgeous girlfriend*
> *Nina be her name*
> *Wanna fuck her, my gorgeous girlfriend*
> *'Til I cause her pain*
> *Gonna stick my tongue down my splendid girlfriend*
> *Nina moan my name*
> *Then I'll put my dick down my splendid girlfriend*
> *Oops! I think I just came*

The phone rings. It's Stephan. He's going to see *Love Story* with his girlfriend tonight at the Shady Oak Theater and wants me to tell Lucretia that he won't be home for dinner. I assure him I'm writing the message down, even though I'm not, and promise I'll give it to Mom as soon as I see her.

Since Stephan is going to be gone for a few hours it's the perfect time to break into his room and check out all his hiding places. I know he keeps his dirty magazines behind his bookcase, and his marijuana in a plastic bag behind a dresser drawer. I check to see if he has anything new. I search all of his traditional caches, looking under the bed, in his closet, and in the vent. All I find is a package of rubbers and his dog-eared illustrated copy of the Marquis de Sade's *Philosophy in the Bedroom*.

I crawl out onto the roof and check inside the TV antenna where I find his latest treasure, psychedelic mushrooms. I borrow just a few, so he probably won't notice.

If ever there was a time to be high on mushrooms, this is it. I swallow half of what I took from the antenna. I wait ten minutes and nothing has happened so I eat the rest – just in time for Lucretia to return from the Benders.

Normally my mother is five foot two and weighs maybe one hundred pounds with Clairol reddish-brown hair and no sense of humor. But on mushrooms she's got arms forty feet long and is the world's greatest stand-up comedienne. She's telling me some joke about a detective who follows her husband, her neighbor, and a hooker to a motel room in Pekin Illinois and finds her son and her neighbor's son with another girl who is mistaken for a hooker. Her forty foot arms are flapping wildly around the room making the story hilarious. I'm rolling on the floor in hysterics. Maybe Lucretia should have her own TV show, it would get higher ratings than snow coverage.

She's now telling me that she's sorry for the misunderstanding, but pissed off at my dad. I ask her to keep telling jokes but she says Marge wants to see me. Her arms are shrinking and turning orange while the walls explode open revealing a hidden passageway leading directly to the Benders'. I plead, "I don't want to join the Vienna Boy's Choir," but Lucretia shoves me through the opening and I'm in Marge's operating room, the kitchen.

Evidently while we were on our Illinois excursion Marge had a boob job. Her tits are now 110 FF's and are poking me in the eye from across the room. I'm getting a hard on, although it also sort of itches. Marge is telling me that I let her down by going out with Nina. Her tits are still growing as they push their way through her tight sweater. Her nipples peel back revealing twin silos preparing to launch small nuclear missiles in my direction. Marge babbles on totally unaware of the havoc her breasts are causing. I think I've hit the mother lode of Nabokovan degeneration – maybe I should rewrite my paper.

"Why are you staring at my breasts?"

Shit! she noticed, "'cause they're so huge."

"They are huge, but you might never get to see them again unless you're a good boy." The silos retract, and she bends over the table revealing that she's not wearing panties. "Do you want to fuck me?"

Even if I wasn't on a such a gonzo mushroom rush I wouldn't know how to answer the question. "No" would be an insult, and a "yes" would just pull me further into this mess. I play it safe, "I want what you want."

FEED THE DOG

"I want to fuck, but I don't want to catch you with anymore slut girlfriends."

She unzips my pants and despite her constant questions of "What's so funny?" we do the deed.

The mushrooms have subsided, I'm back home and my dick still itches. I take a shower and make a startling discovery in my pubic hair. I have crabs. If I have crabs Marge for sure has them, and so does her husband. I wonder how long Kevin will torture me before using his shotgun.

I've got to get rid of them without anyone knowing about it. I can't call our family doctor – he might tell Lucretia. So I go down to the free clinic.

The appointment nurse is a nasty troll-like creature. "What's your reason for coming?"

A fair and reasonable question, but how do I answer it? "I've got a problem with my, uh..." I keep stammering hoping that will fully explain my plight.

"Your what?"

"You know, my um."

"Oh your penis! Why didn't you say so," she says loudly so everyone in the waiting room can hear. "What type of problem?"

"Um."

"Syphilis?"

"No, I don't think so."

"Herpes?"

"No."

"NSU?"

I don't know what NSU is so I blurt out "Crabs."

The troll tells me to have a seat while she gets something for my condition. I sit down on the couch next to a ninety year old woman with a walker and a Hispanic lady with two young kids. The mother grabs her kids and flees to the other side of the waiting room. The old woman pulls herself up with great difficulty and starts across the room. She hasn't made it to safety yet when the nurse returns with a bottle of Kwell shampoo for me. "Take a shower with this, lathering up your whole body especially your hair. Leave it on for twenty minutes and rinse. Also wash all your clothes and sheets in hot water."

I go home and start by washing the sheets and all my clothes. Lucretia gets excited, "Since you already know how to do laundry, from now on do your own." She waltzes away.

I take a shower and hope the stuff works. I get out and wait the twenty minutes. The lather smells awful – if I were a crab I'd want to definitely vacate the premises. Kristen yells I have a phone call. "Tell whoever it is I'll call them back in twenty minutes."

"Are you sure? It's Nina Pennington."

"Okay, I'll be there in a second." Suds and all I walk over and take the phone from Kristen. My sister starts sniffing and then smiles and goes into my room. I can't stop her and talk to Nina at the same time.

Nina doesn't hate me! "I'm so sorry I crashed the car and made you miss Bowie. I want to make it up to you so what are you doing tonight?" I assure her that it wasn't her fault, but that I would love to see her. I hang up feeling great.

"Got the crabs, Ric?" Kristen asks, having reappeared with the Kwell bottle. "I'll make you a deal. I don't say anything and you stop commissioning my dancing." I agree to her terms.

Billy wants me to go to the movies. "Come on, *Love Story* is showing at the Shady Oak. I've already soaked the corn flakes just like you showed me." Billy was with me when I used the corn flake trick during *Romeo and Juliet*. We sat in the balcony and during the mushiest love scene, when there wasn't a dry eye in the theater, I made ralphing noises for a couple of seconds and then dropped the bag of soggy flakes on the audience below. People screamed and panic ensued. The lights came up, the movie stopped, and we were long gone before anyone knew what happened. Knowing that Stephan is going to be there on a date makes it tempting, but I use my Nabokov paper as an excuse. I can't let 'Big Mouth' know anything about my seeing Nina. Billy says he's going anyway. I hope he nails Stephan.

I check my dick for any surviving crabs. I don't find any. In honor of Nina I throw on some deodorant, I'm now ready for the big rendezvous. I don't want Lucretia to notice me leaving so I go out my window and slide down a tree. A two mile walk to Nina's won't seem that long knowing she wants to make up for yesterday. You can atone for everything baby, just spread your legs.

I'm crossing the corner of Hanley and Forsythe Roads when Kevin Bender pulls up in his car. He rolls down his window, "Can I give you a lift Ric? It's a bit chilly to be out walking."

"I'm just heading down to the stationery store, but thanks," I lie, noticing Mr. Bender scratching

FEED THE DOG

his crotch while he's talking.

"Okay, well don't freeze to death," he says driving off. He probably doesn't want me to die of the cold because it's not painful enough.

Five minutes later Nina's door opens and she surprises me with a big kiss right on the lips. I wonder if I can slip her the tongue...it's worth a try, I swallow my gum and stick it out. She's opening her lips! God does her tongue feel good. Life doesn't get better than this, I think, noticing I have another hard on. I'm just reaching for her tits when she breaks off the kiss and invites me in before we die of frostbite.

"I've got this evening all planned out, it'll be so romantic," she says, giving me another kiss, "we're going to go see *Love Story* and then go dancing at the Depot."

When you have had Nina Pennington's tongue down your throat you do not argue. If left to my own devices I could think of very few things I would less rather do than go to *Love Story* especially considering that Stephan will be there and Billy is going to launch his corn flake vomit attack. I'm under her spell.

Nina takes her father's Buick and we drive to the theater. The place is packed but we manage to get two tickets. I don't see either Billy or Stephan, but just in case I choose seats far under the balcony overhang, safely out of range of any stray cereal.

In reality the movie is terrible, but it's not so bad when you're holding hands with Nina. We exchange a few quick kisses about halfway through the movie. I try to kiss her while accidentally on purpose brushing my arm against her breasts. She moves away. Embarrassed by the rejection I shift to the other side of my seat. A couple of minutes later I feel Nina's tongue in my ear. She whispers, "Come here silly," and places my hand underneath her sweater. I'll never understand girls but I take what I'm offered. So we're fooling around, until Ali McGraw finds out she's dying. Nina decides it would be in bad taste to do anything more than hold hands during such a heartrending scene. The movie is in full tearjerker overload when I hear Billy begin. He takes his time doing the vomiting noises. Everyone starts fidgeting in their chairs, a few start giggling, and then Billy lets loose. A whole box of Kellogg's pride tumbles from the balcony. A couple of girls scream, people are scurrying for cover, the lights come up and the movie stops.

I'm laughing, and Nina drops my hand. "That's gross, I can't believe you find it funny." I try to control myself but then I see Stephan standing up covered with soggy corn flakes. Way to go Billy! Stephan is looking up at the balcony and is pissed. I sink into my seat. He must see Billy because like a bat out of hell he starts running up the aisle right past me.

We wait for the movie to resume, but evidently Ali McGraw got a reprieve from the governor, because the theater manager announces they aren't going to finish the screening until they can clean up the mess. We are told to go out to the lobby for a refund. When we get there we see the ushers have grabbed someone. Stephan is trying to reach over the ushers to punch him. I figure the best course of action is to get out of here before anyone sees us, but Nina realizes who the suspect is. "Look, they've got Billy Bender," she exclaims. "I'm sure he didn't do it, we've got to help him."

An usher tells us Billy is being held for the cops. Stephan sees me and accuses me of being an accomplice. A security guard seizes me just as two policemen in full riot gear come through the door.

"These two dumped vomit from the balcony on our patrons," the theater manager complains.

"I'm innocent, let me go," I shout, but no one other than Nina is defending me.

"Shut up," the lead cop orders, jabbing my chest with his nightstick. "Do you have any witnesses?"

"I saw the whole thing officer," says an Italian looking guy in a seersucker jacket, "and this one," pointing at Billy, "dumped the bag. I didn't see anyone else."

Nina also provides an alibi, and after a few minutes I'm released. The manager is apologetic. I threaten to sue the theater for unlawful detention. He offers me two free passes for the next five years if I'll forget anything happened. I feel a case of selective amnesia coming on; I don't remember where I am but I do recall Stephan trying to get me into trouble.

Meanwhile the cops are hauling Billy downtown. The theater is pressing charges for disturbing the peace, inciting a riot, littering, and unauthorized dumping of hazardous waste materials. I yell to Billy to keep his mouth shut. Not too likely, but it's the best advice I have other than to keep his back to the wall at all times.

Nina wants to help Billy, but the cops will only release him to his parents. She asks me for a dime to call them, but the last thing Marge will want to hear is Nina's voice telling her we witnessed Billy being thrown in jail while out on a date. "I know Marge better," I say, "I'll call."

I dial the number of the phone I'm calling from. I let Nina hear that it's busy. "We'll have to call back later." She tells me to get the operator and ask her to do an emergency interrupt. I'm stuck, so I say I'll try the call once more. This time I dial the right number.

"Hello," Marge answers.

"Hi, it's me."

Marge is whispering so I know Kevin is close by "I'm so glad you called, there's something I've got to talk to you about..."

"Marge can it wait? We've got a problem."

"What sort of problem do we have?"

"Billy's in jail."

"For what?" she gasps.

I tell her the story of Billy, *Love Story* and the corn flakes.

"Why didn't you stop him?"

"I wasn't with him, I didn't know what happened until afterwards."

"Oh. If you weren't out with Billy who were you with?"

I'm damn well not about to say "Nina," so I answer, "Some friends."

"Which friends?"

I try to change the subject, "They've taken him down to the police station, hurry."

"Which friends, Ric?"

"Some friends of mine from school."

"Nina Pennington?"

"She may be here too, but there are a whole lot of us." I try to sound convincing.

Marge isn't buying it. "Listen, I don't want Kevin to know anything about this, I'll meet you downtown and you better be alone." She slams down the phone.

"What did she say?" asks Nina.

"She's going to meet me at the police station."

"Good, let's go."

"Uh, Nina, I don't know how to say this but I'm just going to tell you the truth. My mom doesn't know I'm out with you, and if Marge tells Lucretia my ass will be grass." Nina's not happy but she believes my story. She drives me to the police station and gives me a good tonsil swabbing kiss.

"Call me as soon as you get home, no matter how late it is, okay?"

"I promise."

The apprehension of the Shady Oak vomiter is the biggest collar the Clayton police have made since Joseph Cleveland Grant and his prized heifer Maude were arrested for bestiality two years ago. Being that it is a sure ticket to the six o'clock news every cop wants in on the Billy Bender bust. Therefore I arrive to a mob scene at the police station. Due to my previous few days' activities I don't want to be anywhere near places with wanted posters so I elect to wait for Marge outside.

Five minutes later she pulls up – and she's got a pissed off look. "Where's Billy?"

"In the station," I start to walk back in.

She yanks me back, "Before we go in there I want to talk to you about something. It's embarrassing and I want you to think really hard before you answer it."

Just like in *12 O'clock High* I can see the bombers circling overhead. "We have target sighted, open bomb bays, bombs away." Twenty megatons of bombs are headed my way. Remain calm, I say to myself. Remain calm? You've got twenty megatons of bombs about to come crashing down on your head and you say remain calm? What type of idiot are you? Panic you fool, run around like a chicken with your head cut off – do something reasonable!

Marge is on her final approach, "Did you give me the crabs?"

It's times like this when I fall back upon the wise fatherly advice hammered into me since birth, 'when all else fails play stupid, you'll always be amazed how believable it will be to most people.' I respond, "Crabs? We live in Clayton there's no ocean anywhere near here where am I going to get crabs? and even if I did get some I think I'd remember having given them to you."

Marge gives me one of those soul penetrating stares. Little does she know that I've got my lead shields up and we all know even Superman can't see through lead. "Ric, crabs are repugnant little insects that nest in your pubic hair."

"Oh. I don't think I have any crabs but do you want to check?"

"We can't here," Marge says her voice making that fine line transition from hostile to horny.

It takes five hours for Billy to get his mug shots, fingerprints and posed pictures with the arresting officers completed. The arraignment takes one minute, but I feel good because I get to be on TV. Channel 3 is covering the Shady Oak riot live. They interview me as Billy's next door neighbor and eyewitness to the crime.

"Was Billy Bender always a vicious criminal?"

"No."

"Is he a member of a gang that terrorizes your community?"

"I don't know if he's a member of a gang or anything, but he does have friends in Chicago."

The reporter finishes with me and does a wrap-up from headquarters for the cameras. "The police are investigating whether Billy Bender, the young hoodlum arrested at the Shady Oak crime scene, has underworld ties to Windy City mobsters."

While Marge is occupied filling out some bail forms I find a phone and call Nina. She's been watching everything on TV. "You look so cute on TV," she purrs, "that I just want to kiss you all over!"

My pants are getting tight again. "You want to use the free tickets tomorrow and see the end of the movie?"

"My parents are getting back tomorrow night, I don't think I can go out, but what are you doing during the day?"

"Whatever you want." I see Billy and Marge emerging from the crowd of reporters. "Look Nina, I gotta go, call me when you wake up." I hang up.

Marge is angry. "Who were you on the phone with?"

"I was just calling some friends to let them know I was on TV," I lie.

I notice there is something about driving in cars with parents that inhibits conversation. Just like last night with Johann we drive back in quiet until Marge decides to stop and pick up the early edition of the morning newspaper. She has me check and see if there is anything in it about her criminal son.

I don't have to look too hard. I read her *The Evening Tribune's* special riot edition front page editorial railing against the liberal, soft on crime judge who sprang Billy on bail:

> For a mere fifty dollars the streets of Clayton have been transformed into Sodom and Gomorrah where dangerous criminals lurk in every doorway. Judge Irving Heinz's Easter gift to us is to set Billy the Kid Bender loose to perpetrate more heinous acts of depravity upon our society.

My paper on Nabokov seems to be getting more timely by the moment.

We find a couple of reporters staked out in front of the Benders' so we pull into my driveway instead. Lucretia is in the kitchen drinking straight shots of vodka. "You look like you could use a drink Marge," she slurs offering her the bottle.

"I don't want to drink the last of your booze..."

"There's plenty more," Lucretia points to the two fifths sitting on the counter. "Drink up."

So Marge pours the rest of the bottle into a glass and tosses the empty into the trash. She shuts the trash can and then quickly reopens it and pulls the Kwell bottle out.

All around the country morticians are rubbing their hands in glee, casket makers are being put on double shifts, and the editors of both *The National Enquirer* and *Guns And Ammo* are planning their next year's worth of issues just off the one look that Marge Bender has on her face. I now understand how the Catholic Church has operated for so long. Pope Paul probably was a kid in Italy and ran into a woman with the same facial expression and a butcher knife right before he took the vow of celibacy. He wasn't going to be able to fuck again anyway so he may as well swear to it. Suffice it to say Marge is not a happy camper. Thankfully she can't scream, "Your son gave me the crabs when he fucked me on the kitchen floor," to Lucretia. All she can manage is a weak mumble, "I need a double."

I decide this is the perfect time to go to my room. I'm too nervous to sleep so I pick up the guitar and work on *Talkin' Nina Pennington Blues*.

> *I'm a eunuch with no beautiful girlfriend*
> *Nina can't be my wife*
> *I'm a eunuch with no beautiful girlfriend*
> *'Cause Marge Bender's got a knife*

I can hear them talking well into the morning. From the sounds of it Marge is as drunk as my mother. Hangover remedies are going to be in big demand tomorrow. I finally drift off to sleep and that's when she tells Lucretia.

I finish reading the suicide note addressed to Marge. She is to inherit my mother's genuine Brother Theodore Enterprises plates of the saints, and is to stop having sex with me. Lucretia is quite clear on the subject.

Meanwhile Clayton, a town still struggling with the ordeal of last night's Shady Oak riot, is coming to life. The whole neighborhood is gathered outside trying to ascertain why the emergency vehicles have come. The smart money is on the theory that our well known local hooligan, Billy Bender, has broken into the house and reenacted the Manson killings.

From the assembled horde emerges a very hungover Marge Bender. She's pounding at the door just as the telephone rings. I open it while running to get the phone. "Could you excuse me for one moment?" I shout.

It's Nina. "Hi, are we still on for this afternoon?" the goddess asks as my heart pounds.

I whisper, "I can't talk now but I'd love to get together. My mother won't need her car today so you don't have to pick me up." Then in a full voice, "I'll call you back in a few minutes. 'Bye."

When I hang up Marge is standing almost on top of me while probably casing the joint for knives to use in her castration act. "What's going on here and who was that on the phone?"

"My mother tried to commit suicide, she may have succeeded, the ambulance just took her to the hospital." To avoid answering the second part of the question and prevent Marge from wreaking any acts of vengeance upon me I hand her the purloined note, and add, "She left you this letter explaining everything."

Marge is stunned and sinks into a chair to read Lucretia's anguished message. "I don't remember telling her about us, I must have been drunker than I thought, does anyone else know?"

"Unlike some people in this room I haven't told anyone. You know the police want this as evidence."

"Have they seen it?"

"No, I figured they don't need to know." I decide to press the circumstances to my advantage. "I feel awful that I've hurt my mother by having sex with you, so I promised God I wouldn't make love to you anymore if He spares my mother's life." Although it may do the trick, it sounds too melodramatic rolling off my tongue so I add, "the plates are over there."

"We should get to the hospital. Who's there with her?"

"Kristen and Julie. I'm going to stay here and man the phone. You're welcome to go, I think they took her to County General."

So Marge runs off to the emergency room, probably to insure that in case Lucretia pulls through she can deny everything. She forgets the plates.

I dial Johann at the Hotel Georges V in Paris. "Hello, je veux parler avec Monsieur Johann Thibault," I say in my best high school French.

The operator apparently doesn't like my accent, sneeringly responding, "I speak English sir, and Monsieur Thibault is not accepting calls, may I take a message?"

"Can you tell him his son is calling from St. Louis and that there is an emergency back home?"

"What type of emergency?"

"His wife has attempted suicide."

"Oh, hold the line sir, one moment please." The operator stays on the line while putting the call through. A French woman answers and she and the operator talk. All those years of French have not been in vain because I understand most of it. She's asking this woman to let my father come to the phone for an emergency. "No," she assures the person, it is not the police, it is a call from the United States."

The woman seems disappointed and asks us to wait a second. In the background I hear her telling my father to be a good boy and come pick up the phone.

"Hello," my father's voice is a little shaky and he sounds out of breath.

"Hi, dad, it's Ric. Sorry to bother you but Mom took 50 Seconal and is in the hospital. The ambulance driver said she's probably dead."

"What do you mean – probably dead?"

"Well, she wasn't yelling at anyone, and she didn't have a drink in her hand. Is that dead enough?"

"Where are you?"

"Home."

"Where did they take her?"

"County General."

"Who's with her?"

"A bunch of doctors and nurses."

"Very funny. Where's Stephan?"

"I don't know."

"Did she leave any notes?"

"Sixteen not counting the one on the garage door that says to feed Duke."

"What did they say?"

"I don't know, the police took them," I say protecting the confidentiality of Mom's correspondence with Marge.

"How did the police get them?"

"They were here."

"I see. Here's what I want you to do, let me know what happens with your mother and I'll make some calls and try to get those letters back. Your mother is a very sick woman. I hope we can keep our family's dirty laundry within the family." I hear more than one woman giggling in the background.

"Dad, who's with you?"

"I'm in a business meeting."

Now I may have been the most naive person in the world several weeks ago, but I've gotten a lot smarter in the last few days. I know it's eight o'clock at night on Easter Sunday Paris time and Johann is in a hotel room with at least two women. I don't think he's working in the conventional sense. "What type of business?"

"It's classified, you know I'm not allowed to discuss my business," he says abruptly, "call me later when you know something." *Click.*

I wish I was having the same sort of meeting with Nina. I'd have the front desk hold all my calls too, in fact I wouldn't even let them put emergencies through.

I think about Nina and realize she would be mad at me for coming over while my mother is in the hospital dying. Play up the sympathy angle stupid, chicks love to feel sorry for someone in a time of need. I call her.

I put on my somewhat-shaken-yet-firmly-in-control voice. "Hi, it's me, I can't come over, my mother tried to kill herself, they just took her to the hospital, they said she's (stutter a little, appear vulnerable for dramatic purpose, I tell myself) um, she's ah, she might die."

It works! Nina asks, "You shouldn't be alone, are you alone?"

"Yeah, I'm supposed to wait here and mind the phone while Kristen's at the hospital with her."

"I'm coming over, I'll be there in a minute, it'll be all right."

I hang up and run through the possibilities:

1. My mother is dead. Much sympathy from Nina. Don't have to fuck Marge again. A few days off from school. Johann moves back in.

2. My mother lives, but is a vegetable. Much sympathy from Nina for longer time. Don't have to fuck Marge again. A few days off from school. Johann moves back in.
3. My mother recovers. Less, but still substantial attention from Nina. Don't have to fuck Marge again. No days off from school, but get sympathy from teachers. Lucretia has to go to the loony bin for a while. Johann stays at his place.

I'm glad I don't have a say in the outcome, but if I had a vote I would take option three. Father O'Brien would agree with my decision. This being Sunday I should probably go see him – although under the circumstances, he'll understand if I don't make it.

A minute later the doorbell rings. It's a little quick for Nina to get here, I think to myself as I open it. Usually when I open the door for someone I can see the sky, trees, and some of the walkway behind them. This is not the case with this visitor, because all I can see is this huge man standing there blocking off the sun. Kevin Bender is scratching his crotch while waiting for me to invite him in.

"Hi, Mr. Bender," I say in a legitimately quivering voice.

"Marge told me everything that's happened and I wanted to come over." According to the dictionary the word 'everything' means 'all things pertinent'. Did Marge really tell him 'everything' and, if so, should I call Father O'Brien and see if the Vatican has some sort of bulk rate on the last rites? (Get your last rites here. Absolution, repentance, contrition, your one stop penance center – two for a sawbuck, yes siree, step right up...), "Ric aren't you going to let me in?"

"Oh, I'm sorry, all this stress, um, come in."

"Listen, I've always thought of you as family," (I pray he doesn't know how spot on he is) "and want you to know that I'm here for you." He's scratching himself again. "This must be pretty hard on you, you want to talk about it?"

"Not right now Mr. Bender, I think I'd rather immerse myself in phone calls to all our relatives and be alone to think. Thanks for dropping by, it means a lot to me."

"Don't hesitate to call."

"I won't. See you soon."

Yes, and thanks for appearing on the Cuckolded Fool With A Gun Show. As you know all departing contestants on the Cuckolded Fool With A Gun Show get a consolation prize of the home version of our game by Milton Bradley and a couple of targets as a souvenir of their appearance.

I push him out the door into the crowd which has swelled to several hundred people since the arrival of the emergency crews. Wanting to get rid of everybody so I can be alone with Nina, I conduct an impromptu news conference for the neighbors. "My mother has had a bad reaction to some prescription pills and has been taken to County General Hospital. At this time her condition is unknown. I called 911 and they sent policemen with the ambulance. Nothing else has happened, so will you please go home."

Brian Savage, the midget reporter from Channel 6, is still on the job from last night's Shady Oak riot story. He shouts a few questions. "What is the linkage between Billy Bender and the victim? Did he force her to take the pills? Is he in your house now and if so does he have any hostages?"

"Are you on drugs?" I ask hopefully. Maybe he will share whatever psychedelic he's taking. "Billy Bender is not here, and he has absolutely nothing to do with what happened this morning. Now please, this is a very trying time for the Thibault family. Could you please leave us alone?"

A reporter from *The Evening Tribune* asks if I could cry a little for the cameras. "It'll make a great shot for our extra edition."

I'm about to tell him to fuck off when Nina pushes her way through the multitude. "I came as fast as I could but I had to park a mile away because of all this traffic. I thought you said you were alone."

"Miss – could you give him a hug for our cameras?" shouts a lady from *The Globe Republican*. I decide to cooperate with the press, after all, aren't they the watchdog of the people?

"We didn't have our cameras ready," complains a reporter from Channel 7, "could you do it again for us?" Out of civic duty I kiss Nina.

"The show's over folks, sorry," I say walking arm in arm with Miss Pennington into the house. No sooner are we in the door than the phone rings. It's Kristen.

"She's going to live, but she stopped breathing for a while so there was no oxygen flowing to her brain. The doctors say she might have suffered brain damage but there is no way to know until she wakes up. They pumped her stomach but she's still going to be out of it for at least eight to ten hours. So Cousin Julie and I are coming home. Did you talk to Dad?"

I briefly sketch out our conversation and tell her I still haven't found Stephan. She says she'll be home in ten minutes. I hang up.

So it's either Option 2 or Option 3.

"That was Kristen. My mother's probably going to live, but the doctors won't know until later whether she'll make a full recovery or be a vegetable."

My relationship with Nina Pennington has ten minutes to flourish if I play my cards right. Nina puts her arm around me. What is the meaning of the gesture and if it's good how do I best exploit it? I debate whether to cry or not. Crying would show that I'm sensitive. Nina's sentimental, she's the one who dragged me to *Love Story*. However, she's not the Kahlil Gibran or *Jonathan Livingston Seagull* type. No, crying is too faggy.

Think. She's an existentialist. She's likes that dead guy Camus, who got the Nobel Prize for *L'étranger*. It begins, "Mama died today. Or was it yesterday? I don't remember." I only got through the first couple of pages, I wish I had read more – it must be chock full of existential insight. I rack my brain for knowledge of existentialist character traits. What could be more existential than a sigh? Can you sigh with a French accent?

I try an understated sigh, throwing in a barely audible 'merde' at the end for a French influence.

It works. She is hugging and caressing me. God she smells great and her tits feel really good rubbing up against my chest. I wish I had a beret. We'd probably be fucking by now if I had one.

I get cheated – my ten minutes are nowhere near up when Stephan comes barging in. "Why are all those fucking people outside? What the hell is going on?"

"Mom tried to kill herself."

"No she didn't."

"I'll bet you five dollars."

Stephan remembers our last bet and decides against it. "What happened? Is she dead?"

So I tell Stephan the relevant parts of the story finishing as Kristen and Julie return. They regale us with hospital stories, she has no pulse, she's dead, she has a pulse, no magazines in the waiting room, lots of doctors, EKGs, shots of this, shots of that...it goes on and on.

I'm getting bored with my family – and if they're boring me just think what they must be doing to Nina. Since it appears we're moving into Option 3, I figure it's time to get her out of here while I'm still ahead.

"Aren't your parents coming back from Europe today? You should probably be home before they get back." I escort Nina past the crowd to her car. She gives me a kiss full of promises.

Au revoir ma cherie.

There is no brain damage, Lucretia is going to be okay. Since it is illegal to attempt suicide in Missouri she has to either go to jail or the loony bin for a minimum of two weeks. It's a good thing she wasn't successful – the penalties are a lot stiffer for doing the job right.

My hatred for Stephan grows by the minute. I catch him ransacking Mom's purse right after I return from walking Nina to her car. He says he's only checking to find her hospital insurance card but I know he's full of shit. First of all, suicide is not covered by insurance. Second, there is now only seventeen dollars in her purse, and I know I left seventy-one bucks after I went through it during the Seconal search. I hope Lucretia doesn't remember she had ninety-two bucks before she tried to off herself.

The crowd outside eventually thins out, and is gradually replaced by a herd of relatives and friends of the family inside – each trying to out sincere the other in their condolences upon this trying occasion. Jumbo Julie is here shrinking the room with her three piglet children. Our deaf and partially senile seventy-seven year old great uncle Gene thinks that this is a surprise birthday party for Lucretia and wants to know when we're supposed to hide. Mr. Carlotta, the owner of the liquor store down the street, is looking most concerned of all. He's probably trying to figure out how he will be able to afford a vacation if Lucretia is out of commission too long. Father O'Brien is here being gentle and priestly and wondering why the hell he hasn't seen me at Confession for the past few months. There are a bunch of Kristen's friends, and some other people who probably think they are crashing a party, and finally there is the Bender clan. Kevin is laying the 'I consider you family' rap on Kristen, Marge is avoiding me like the plague, and Billy is hanging with me upstairs in my room. We're plotting our revenge on Stephan for being the asshole who got Billy in trouble last night.

Billy is telling me about the cops threatening him with an Army style boot camp for juvenile offenders. "That type of stuff scares me," I tell Billy, "I could never be in the armed forces. The moment someone ordered me to do something I'd tell them to fuck off and I'd be in the stockade."

Billy agrees, "Yeah, you have to live in a barracks with a bunch of guys, no girls, and dig holes wherever they want them. Only macho assholes like Stephan dig the army – though he might not like it so much after being fragged by his own platoon in Vietnam."

I get an idea. "Why don't we enlist Stephan in the Marines, they need a few good men don't they?"

"How are you going to do that?"

"Easy, we look alike. I'll steal his driver's license and go down to the enlistment center. I'll forge the papers, take the physical and then return home. A few days later no one will show up when he is supposed to report. He'll be AWOL, and they'll come looking for him, it'll be great."

"Yeah that would be cool."

"There's only one problem, you have to keep your mouth shut."

"You can trust me. When have I ever blabbed?"

I stare at Billy. He's actually serious.

Monday's morning assembly is eventful at Clayton High. Basil O'Reilly, our principal, is angry about having one of his pupils implicated in the Shady Oak Riot. A meeting of the faculty disciplinary committee is set for noon to consider suspension of any students found to have been involved. Billy's in trouble. I'm somewhat of an accessory before the fact so I'm sweating a little too.

He moves quickly to the second topic. "I have to tell you ladies and gentlemen that it is not easy to find an instructor to replace a great teacher like Mr. Apgar, especially on such short notice. It is extremely difficult to find someone who has command of such a rich language. We left no stone unturned in our pursuit of an individual possessing the qualities and traditions which we have come to expect here at Clayton High. It is therefore a great honor and privilege to introduce our new Latin teacher, Sister Margaret. Some of you or some of your parents may object to a nun teaching a public school class. If you do, you will be excused from the class with no penalties. For those of you who do pursue this fine course of study, a study that is viewed favorably when it comes to admission decisions at major universities throughout the country, Sister Margaret and I must ask for a little cooperation and understanding. Sister Margaret has been a Carmelite nun for the last seventeen years. A few of you may know that the Sisters of Carmelite have taken a vow of silence. Consequently we had to go to the Archbishop of St. Louis to get a special dispensation for her to speak. Thankfully His Excellency was gracious enough to give his blessing to our new Latin teacher. Sister Margaret will be free to converse only within the actual classroom. At all other times she will remain faithful to her order's vows. Ladies and Gentlemen I have spoken with this lovely woman, her voice is a little rusty but it will get stronger, trust me."

"One thing we teach at Clayton High is to be free of all prejudices with regard to race, color, creed, or handicap. It is with that in mind that I must beg you Latin students for one further indulgence. Sister Margaret has a mild case of narcolepsy. This is not something to either joke about or take advantage of. Please continue to be the gracious and caring students that I know you to be.

Our dear late Mr. Apgar would have wanted it that way. So without further ado, please give a warm Clayton High School welcome to Sister Margaret."

We all get up and give this old lady in a black habit a standing ovation, while everyone tries to find out what a narcoleptic is. Terry Borotsik thinks it's a heroin addicted epileptic, but Nina says it's a disease that has people falling asleep for a minute or two in the middle of the day. I sense that for the first time in my life, or anyone else's either, Latin is going to be where the action is.

O'Reilly is motioning for us to be quiet again. "One further announcement, Kristen and Ric Thibault's mother is in serious condition at County General. Our best wishes for a speedy recovery to Mrs. Thibault, and our sympathies to Kristen and Ric."

It is a little embarrassing being offered sympathy by the principal in front of the whole school, but on the positive side I don't think I will be implicated in the great Shady Oak Riot case.

Billy Bender, the high profile criminal, is to meet his fate at noon. All students facing disciplinary action are allowed an advocate of their choosing to represent them before the faculty court. I have a funny feeling that he's going to ask me to be his advocate, so I try to avoid him.

He's not in my first period English class. I hand in my Nabokov paper to Mrs. Lukowich and spend the rest of the hour looking at Nina who is wearing a tight red sweater, I can see her nipples through her bra. She's got big ones. They are far more interesting than J.D. Salinger's personal life which seems to be of great fascination to Mrs. Lukowich. Why should I give a rat's ass about some rich guy who wrote four books and now is a recluse in New Hampshire? Nina seems to care about Salinger. I guess I'll have to read *Franny & Zooey*. What a waste...the things I do for love.

Second period is Biology. Billy is not in my class, and Nina isn't either. Mr. Hucul is boring us with statistics on the heart rates of frogs. I spend this hour looking out the window and daydreaming about the only heart I care about – the one behind the semi-visible treasures packed into Nina's taut red sweater. J.D. Salinger would probably come out of seclusion for a chance at them – unless he's queer. I have a friend, Richie Pasquale, who knows if any famous person is a homo or not. I'll ask him about Salinger.

The bell rings and I'm leaving class when I see Billy in the hall. He's coming my way so I race out the other direction, down the stairs and into my French class. Madame Bourbonais is the strictest teacher in the whole school. She's from Guadeloupe and according to rumor is working for minimum wage because it's like being a millionaire back where she comes from. We're only allowed to speak French in her class – probably because she doesn't speak English. Billy knocks on the door and tries to talk to me in English. Madame Bourbonais starts screaming at us in French, so with a shrug of my shoulders and a big "excusez-moi" I get to ignore him.

French is pretty good. I proudly tell Madame Bourbonais how I put my acquired language skills to use rousting my father from his Paris 'business meeting' – omitting the part about the operator speaking English fluently of course. I'm thinking about Nina's breasts again when the school's public address system interrupts blaring, "Ric Thibault, please report to Principal O'Reilly's office immediately."

I walk slowly downstairs to O'Reilly's. I'm a little tense, I'm thinking he's going to tell me Lucretia croaked. I feel guilty about the twenty-one bucks in my back pocket. Wait a second – why didn't he ask for Kristen to come to his office too? It's too late to think it through because I open the door to find Billy waiting for me. O'Reilly tells me I have been asked to be Billy's defender. I have the right to turn down this assignment but I can't because Billy's my best friend.

"Can I have a moment with Billy alone?" I ask.

O'Reilly allows us to use his office, shutting the door behind him. This is the first time I've been in this office without the principal. Every previous visit was accompanied by the addition of another black mark to my permanent record. The feeling of power is awesome as I sit in O'Reilly's black leather chair. I go through the papers on his desk while talking to my client.

"Billy, they're not going to listen to a word we say – they've already made their decision. You're guilty as hell and they are going to suspend your butt out of here for a week until it all cools down." I open O'Reilly's desk drawers. I find the one with all the stuff that has been confiscated from kids. There are three squirt guns, some firecrackers, two packs of condoms, and a set of brass knuckles.

"I can't get suspended it will ruin my chances for college," Billy whines.

"Fuck that, I've been suspended four times already and you don't hear me sniveling about college," I lie. I'm scared shitless at the prospect of not getting into college and beginning a career working for Burger King while Nina is away at some snotty east coast university learning how to mix martinis, play croquet and date guys with English accents.

Billy begs me to come up with some sort of plan. He promises he'll do anything for me if I can get him out of this jam. I'm finishing my inventory of the confiscated goods when I feel something barely sticking out from behind the drawer. It's a thick envelope. I pull it out and open it.

Maybe Billy has a pipeline to God, or perhaps it's a miracle in honor of our narcoleptic nun –

FEED THE DOG

because I have just found our get out of jail free card! Basil O'Reilly has been taking pictures of the girls' locker room. There must be a two way mirror or something because he has all these shots of topless girls looking right into the camera while they are doing their hair and stuff. There are also photos of girls soaping up in the showers. I recognize several of them including the love of my life, Nina Pennington! I show Billy.

"God, look at Debbie Richardson, here she has tiny tits but when you see her in class she has melons." Billy and I have discovered a major fraud perpetrated by the padded bra.

"We should get Ralph Nader to investigate Playtex when he has some free time, but let's focus our attention on your situation. As your attorney I advise you to keep your mouth shut and let me do the talking. You are about to see the Clayton High judicial system at its best."

I open the door and tell Principal O'Reilly that I will serve as Billy's lawyer. He says fine and tells us to be in the faculty lounge in ten minutes.

"I'd like to bypass the disciplinary committee, Basil."

"Principal O'Reilly to you. Watch your ass Thibault – I can have you up there on charges – crazy mother or not," he snaps.

"I don't think so."

"What did you say?"

"Baz," I throw him a photo of a topless Gina Thomson "recognize this? Or," I toss him one of Mary MacEachern in the shower, "this?"

"You little shits, you went through my desk didn't you?" he sinks into his chair. "You can't prove anything...I can claim I confiscated these like all the other contraband."

"No, Bas, it doesn't work that way, 'cause I'm willing to bet the cameras are still there. Look at these pictures – it's a fucking disgrace."

O'Reilly is flustered and tries a different course. "What do you want from me?"

"First, we want Billy to get off. Second, we want all the suspensions removed from my record and third...have you got any more pictures of Nina Pennington?"

Before the pallid O'Reilly can answer Billy exclaims, "Here's one of Kristen!" I study the shot. Yes, my sister's integrity is unimpeachable. She is indeed 'Bambi Bosoms'.

"Okay, I'll give you everything you asked for, but how do I know you'll keep quiet about this, uh, monitoring system?" O'Reilly asks.

"A legitimate question," I respond while going through the pictures one more time, "you can either remove the cameras or pay us fifty dollars a week plus film processing charges to operate them for you."

As with Stephan my entrepreneurial spirit is not appreciated by my pal the principal. He decides to dismantle the cameras. Too bad, I only found one other picture of Nina and it is a little out of focus.

It's 2:25. Five more minutes to Latin class and everyone is already in the classroom. A red hot debate is raging on what Sister Margaret's first words are going to be and how rusty and squeaky her voice is. I've got two bets riding on how many times she clears her throat before speaking a full sentence. Both Billy and Roger Lefley say she'll do more than four 'ahems' before finishing the first phrase. I say less than four and they each give me two to one odds on a dollar.

The anticipation level is as high as waiting for David Bowie to hit the stage. I halfway expect Jimmy Leach to show up and introduce her. "Hi, ladies and gentlemen, this is Jimmy Leach from KDNA the rock of St. Louis, I know you all have been waiting a long time to see her – and let me tell you I've been hanging out backstage with her and she's a real motherfucker, put your hands together and give a warm St. Louis welcome to Sister Margaret." Too bad he doesn't make the intro, I still have the firecrackers that I swiped from O'Reilly's drawer.

Precisely as the clock strikes 2:30 Sister Margaret enters the class to a standing ovation. I think Billy and Roger are leading the ovation in an attempt to fluster her. They're cheating and I'm about to call the bets off when Sister Margaret holds her hands up to silence us. I have got to hand it to her, she has stage presence because everyone has shut up including me. I wonder if she has groupies; wouldn't it be cool if Boom Boom was giving blowjobs in the coat closet after class? She's getting ready to say something. Come on Sister spit it out.

In a strong Tallulah Bankhead-like voice she says without any prelude whatsoever, "Venividiesperevici." I won.

"Pay up suckers," I whisper to Roger and Billy.

Sister Margaret does not notice the money exchanging hands. The seventeen years of enforced silence have created a volcano, all the words have been pent up in her little body under tremendous pressure and now her mouth has blown open and words are pouring out like molten lava, "Ican'texpresshowhappyIamtobehereteachingatClaytonHighSchoolmynameisSisterMargaretandI willbeguidingyouthroughthebeautyoftheLatinlanguageanditspoetsVirgilOvid..." She still hasn't taken a breath. Maybe she takes the same diet pills that Lucretia uses.

I look around the room. It's not only me. No one can understand her. Everyone is either giggling or staring at her with their mouth open, even Nina.

I raise my hand. She doesn't notice.

"Sister Margaret?"

She keeps on going.

"Excuse me Sister Margaret." I yell a little louder.

She waves me off. "MyclasseswillbeconductedaslecturesandsincethereisnotenoughtimetogetthroughwhatIwantIwillnothavetimeforanyquestions..."

She's rattling on for another two minutes when, out of the blue, she conks out. Her head slumps down and she falls asleep in her chair.

"I'll bet you guys double or nothing she wakes up in less than two minutes without anyone doing anything to her," I proposition Roger and Billy. Billy takes the bet, Roger declines. However, he agrees to go double or nothing that she acts like nothing happened when she comes to.

Billy looks at his watch. "One minute." he announces, "one minute fifteen seconds...one minute thirty seconds...one minute forty..."

"ConquestofGaulwasnotdueonlytoCaesar'ssuperioirnumbersbutwasatriumphoftheforcesof civilizationoverthebarbariansipsofacto..."

I won! I'm eight bucks up on Latin class. Not too shabby.

About twenty minutes later Sister Margaret is walking in front of Nina when she falls down on top of Nina and snoozes off again. I bet Billy and Roger even money she'll be back in a minute. Roger declines, but Billy accepts the wager and gets his watch out. "Thirty seconds...forty-five seconds...one minute. I win!" I pay Billy. Oh well, I'm still seven dollars up, I hide my disappointment by helping Nina get out from under the slumbering Sister. With Billy's assistance we put her back in her chair.

"Okay, two dollars she's up and going in two minutes," I propose. No one takes the bet, which is pretty lucky because she still hasn't woken up two minutes later.

Five minutes later she still hasn't awakened. So we're all sitting there talking waiting for her to resume when Nina points out that Sister Margaret is looking a little pale.

"Have you ever seen nuns hanging out in bikinis trying to get tans? Of course she's pale," says Billy.

"I know that," Nina says, "but she looks different – kind of blue."

I look and Nina is right. She has that same look Lucretia had yesterday. I go up and tap her arm tentatively. I cautiously shake her shoulders. "Sister Margaret?" No response. "Sister Margaret wake up," I yell into her ear. I shake her again a little harder. Finally I take her arm and search for a pulse.

She's dead.

The same cops and ambulance drivers who picked up Lucretia arrive to haul the late Sister Margaret away. The fat cop is looking at me like I must have killed her.

"Hey, Mr. Opprobrious, you got anything to do with this dead nun?" he asks me.

"I didn't do anything, she just keeled over on Nina Pennington and died."

"Did she leave any notes?"

"This isn't a suicide; the woman fell over and kicked the bucket. I don't think she planned it."

Billy comes to my defense, "Ric didn't have anything to do with it, he lost a dollar on her croaking."

"What do you mean?" the other cop asks.

"We were betting on when she'd come to and Ric said in less than a minute. I won a dollar."

"You guys bet on when she was going to die? I ought to arrest you for that right fucking now."

"No, we didn't bet she was going to die. She's a narcoleptic and we were betting when she'd wake back up."

"So you're telling me she was a heroin using epileptic nun?"

Basil O'Reilly is explaining narcolepsy to the police when Father O'Brien arrives to administer the last rites. He mumbles through his task in Latin. I want to tell him to stop speaking Latin, O'Reilly will probably try to hire him to teach and he'll be dead within a week. I like Father O'Brien.

Meanwhile Nina is not taking it well. This is the second Latin teacher to drop dead on her in the last week. I try to comfort her. "Everyone always says you're drop dead gorgeous, but this is ridiculous." She cracks a smile and hugs me closely. I can feel O'Reilly's picture of her in the locker room getting wrinkled. C'est la vie!

I walk Nina home, but I don't get a good-bye kiss on account of her mother being in the front

FEED THE DOG

yard adjusting her lawn jockey. I have to settle for a handshake. I wonder if parents have some sort of secret union where they conspire to sap all the fun out of life. This train of thought occupies me the entire way home.

I call County General. Lucretia is physically okay but she's not allowed to have visitors for two days while she's under round-the-clock psychiatric observation. I pity the poor bastards who have to put up with her. They are going to earn their pay today.

I go into Lucretia's room and look through her purse. I'm really pissed off at Stephan. The seventeen dollars are missing from her wallet and so are her car keys. I wanted to borrow her Pontiac to get to work, now I'm going to have to ride my bicycle. I take her credit card and decide to scare Stephan. I call the cops and report the car as stolen.

I ride down to the radio station to find a happy Jimmy Leach. "Ric, how would you like to make some extra money?"

Due to the fact that I'm talking to a disc jockey, which is the lowest form of life on the food chain, I ask, "Is it legal?"

"Sure, it's pretty legal, you won't get into any trouble or anything."

"How much money do I get?"

"Twenty-five bucks and fifty record albums for five minutes work."

"Who chooses the albums?" I ask, not wanting to get stuck with Melanie records.

"You do."

"What do I have to do?"

"Go to the doctor."

"What's the catch?"

"You're going to tell him you're having trouble sleeping what with your mom's suicide attempt, and then he's going to write out some prescriptions which you're going to hand to me."

"Why don't you go?"

"I already went this week, he can't write too many prescriptions to the same person."

"What prescriptions is he going to give me?"

"Fifty Valium and forty Quaaludes."

"What are Quaaludes?"

"'Fuck Me' biscuits. They're the closest thing to Spanish Fly there is, one of them and even your Catholic girlfriend becomes a nympho."

I think about O'Reilly's pictures of Nina in my pocket, "I'll do it for twenty-five bucks, fifty record albums and five Quaaludes."

Five minutes later we're sitting in Dr. Morton Tudor's office. Tudor's waiting room is packed. Jimmy recognizes two guys from Suckerpunch, the band that are supposed to open for Jefferson Airplane tomorrow night at Kiel. Also in the room are two Cardinals football players, three girls who look to be either models or high class hookers or both, a couple of nervous kids from Ladue (the rich suburb) and a disk jockey from the other rock and roll station. I've never seen a doctor's waiting room with the magazine selection this one has, *Hustler, Penthouse* and *Rolling Stone* replace the usual fare of *Highlights For Children*, two month old copies of *Life* and *Better Homes and Gardens*. Jimmy slips me fifty dollars to pay the doctor.

I thumb through *Hustler,* I think one of those model looking girls is the woman in one of the pictorials. I show Jimmy. He agrees. I'm debating whether to ask for her autograph when I see an advertisement in the back:

> *We'll blow up any snapshot into a full four foot by six foot poster and rush it back to you within five days for only twenty dollars. Credit Card orders accepted.*

I think about Nina's picture and rip the ad out.

Patients come in and out really quickly, and five minutes later the receptionist who must have a monopoly on the blue eye shadow market calls my name. Walking back I see Jimmy heading toward the *Hustler* girl. I'm escorted to a back room where this old guy with a stethoscope asks my age, and weight.

"What are you here for?"

"I can't sleep, my mother tried to commit..." He hands me two prescriptions before I can finish my tale of woe.

"You can come back in a month for another examination. Please pay my receptionist."

Jimmy is mad; he tells me when I walk out that the model is a lesbian. All he did was go up to her and tell her who he was and that he admired her work. She slapped him and told him to fuck off. My view of girls who model for porno magazines has changed – they have good taste after all.

We drive to the drugstore. Jimmy doesn't want to come in because the pharmacists know him. He gives me money for the prescription and waits in the car.

I give the script to the Pakistani druggist behind the counter. "Another prescription from Dr. Tudor? Let me guess, fifty Quaaludes and fifty valium?" He laughs. I don't correct him that it's for only forty Quaaludes. I take the extra ten out before I hand Jimmy my haul. Jimmy hands me the twenty-five bucks and five Quaaludes. He tells me he's going to get me the record albums by rigging a promotion running on his show tomorrow. He's going to fix the contest by having me be the sixth caller to say "I love the Jimmy Leach show on KDNA the rock of St. Louis."

I hope God doesn't strike me down for lying.

♪

Stephan is angry when I get home. The cops pulled him over for stealing Lucretia's car, "What gives you the right to report the car as stolen?"

"Well the keys were in Mom's purse, and when I got home her wallet was empty and the car was gone. It was a logical conclusion, I figured someone had broken in and ransacked the place and, after finding her keys, stole her car."

"I only borrowed the money from her, I'm going to pay her back."

"Did you ask her if it was okay to take her car?"

"Yeah, I did this morning," he lies.

"That's weird because she hasn't been allowed any calls or visitors all day."

Watching Stephan squirm is a great spectator event. It could rapidly replace baseball as the national sport if given proper exposure. I can hear Harry Caray doing the play by play, "Here's the wind up and the pitch, and there he goes, it might be, it could be, it is an outrageous lie." I think I might have a career as a network television programmer ahead of me.

Stephan is getting ready to punch me out when Kristen comes in excited. "I got a scholarship to Stanford!" Unlike Stephan, who is going to St. Louis University and still lives at home, my sister is no fool. She got accepted to a prestigious university two thousand miles away from our family.

"We should have a celebration party," I suggest thinking about the opportunity to test the fifteen 'Fuck Me' biscuits in my pocket.

"I'll tell Mom," states Stephan, continuing his long-standing tradition of annoying me.

I suggest a compromise that will insure Stephan's silence. If he buys the beer for the party the contents of Lucretia's wallet will have been utilized for household expenses while she was in the nuthouse.

It's not a lie because the party is for all those members of the household who choose to show up Friday night. I'd be able to sleep with it, if it weren't for the pictures of Nina naked keeping me awake all night.

After a moment of silence in memory of our latest late Latin teacher, Basil O'Reilly is addressing Tuesday's special assembly, "For those of you who are interested there will be a memorial Mass for the late Sister Margaret tonight at 6 P.M. at Our Lady of the Sacred Assumption."

O'Reilly continues, "Tragedy often brings out the best in people. We are deeply indebted to our friends at Washington University for lending us their Senior Professor of Ancient Languages, Dr. Markus Kuntz. Dr. Kuntz is considered the leading scholar of third century B.C. Roman poetry, and has won numerous awards for his seven books on the subject. We look forward to having Dr. Kuntz join our faculty."

"One further announcement, the girls' locker room will be closed today for repairs. Have a good day students."

Justin Lafayette shouts out the question that is on everyone's minds, "How come we're not getting a day off to mourn the death of Sister Margaret?" He's right. We got one when Mr. Apgar died, the precedent has clearly been established – we get one day off for each Latin teacher who decides to drop dead during class.

O'Reilly realizes he can't be too insensitive to the traumatized students. "All right, all those who feel they need a day to mourn and recover may do so. Although we recommend that you go to classes, those who choose to leave will not be penalized."

Justin would be the most popular kid in Clayton High if there were any kids left in school to vote.

I go back to my house and mourn the passing of Sister Margaret by ordering a four by five foot poster of Nina. Lucretia has always told me never to send cash through the mail, so I borrow her credit card. I add an extra $2.00 for special delivery.

Nina must have sensed me thinking of her, because while I'm sealing the envelope she rings me on the phone.

"Hi Ric, it's Nina. I was wondering how you were getting to Sister Margaret's memorial service?"

I hadn't planned on going to the Mass, but I'm not going to admit it to Nina. "I was planning on using my mother's car, how about you?"

"Would you mind taking me? Funerals freak me a little, I get so emotional, I'd feel better if I were there with you."

I've heard of people taking dates to restaurants, movies, shows, bowling, and sleazy motels – but I think this is the first time that anyone, much less me, was making a date to go to a funeral with the girl of his dreams. "I'd love to go with you, shall I pick you up at 5:30?" I'm hoping Stephan has learned his lesson and isn't using Lucretia's car.

Since it's an evening date with Nina, which means picking her up at her parents' house I want to make a good impression. I go down to the library and check out a copy of *Amy Vanderbilt's Complete Book of Etiquette* to see what I'm supposed to wear. All it seems to say is wear something black – and make sure it's clean. I should be safe with the clothes I wore to Apgar's funeral.

Being that a funeral Mass is a formal affair I figure this is a formal date. I look up 'formal date'. According to Vanderbilt one is supposed to bring his date a corsage. I stop off at the florist on my way home.

The sky may be overcast, but it's a sunny day in my world. Lucretia's Pontiac LeMans is in the garage. I feed the dog and put Bowie's *Hunky Dory* on the record player. I jump in the shower and wash my hair. I apply Clearasil to the zit on my nose, and use deodorant. *Changes* is blaring full blast while I get dressed in my black pants, black turtleneck, and black jacket. I look in the mirror. I'm Johnny Cash, the Man in Black.

I turn off the stereo and remember the Quaaludes. I debate whether it would be okay with God if I take one with me in case I get lucky on my date. I decide He might understand plying her with a 'lude, but would probably frown at my bringing one with me to a funeral mass for one of His nuns. I think He might sanction it if we came home afterward and picked it up. I don't take the Quaalude with me. Theology is very confusing. I guess that's why there are so many religions.

I knock on Nina's door and her mother answers it. Mrs. Pennington looks at me strangely. "What's in the box?"

"A corsage for Nina."

"You're giving her a corsage for a funeral Mass?"

"It's a formal occasion, I looked it up in Amy Vanderbilt at the library and it says you're supposed to bring your date a corsage when you go to formal events." I start to sweat. Did I fuck up, and is my deodorant working?

Mrs. Pennington lets me off the hook. "If Amy Vanderbilt says it's okay, it's fine. I'm glad Nina is going out with a boy considerate enough to consult a manners book. It shows breeding; your parents must be quite proud of you. Come on in." What shows is that Mrs. Pennington has no mind reading capabilities whatsoever.

A few seconds later Nina comes down the stairs looking somber in a sexy way, or is it sexy in a somber way? All I know is my dick is beginning to act up again. Thankfully it doesn't itch.

I hand Nina the corsage, she seems surprised, and says it's very pretty. She wants to put it in the refrigerator so it doesn't get ruined. I could care less what she does with the flowers as long as I get brownie points.

We tell her mother we're not sure when the Mass will end, but that we should be back by eleven. It's beginning to rain, so Mrs. Pennington gives us an umbrella and warns us to be careful and drive safely. I'm still waiting for someone to hand me a set of car keys and tell me to be careless and drive recklessly.

The rain is turning to sleet as we pull onto Highway 40. There is a bad accident at the Ballas Road overpass and traffic is moving at a crawl. We exit on Woodsmill Road and stop at the traffic light a mile from the church. I hear the screech of brakes and look in the rear view mirror to see a blue Dodge Dart whose driver has obviously not had Mrs. Pennington's admonition and is not going to be able to stop. As I reach my arm out to hold Nina back against the seat we get clobbered. My head slams into the steering wheel and I'm a little dizzy, but strangely I don't feel any pain. Nina is screaming that I'm bleeding. I feel the blood trickling down my face; I don't think it's too bad – and Nina seems to be fine.

I get out and approach the car that hit us. It has five occupants and they are all nuns! They appear to be in the midst of some sort of rapid synchronized genuflection drill. I guess they're okay. It's bizarre; no one gets out and asks how we are or apologizes for plowing into us. They just sit there praying and watching me bleed. I take a look at my mother's car. The whole back end is fucked. Lucretia is going to pick up where the nuns failed...she's going to kill me.

A State Trooper is on the scene within a minute. He hands me a towel to hold against my head and asks me if I'm okay. I assure him I'm fine – better than the car. He says not to worry, he saw the whole thing and the other car is at fault. That's a relief.

He checks out Nina, she's calmed down and is okay. He then walks back to the nuns and questions them. "Are you all right?" They look at him and smile and genuflect. "Excuse me Sisters you have to answer my questions. Are you okay?" No answer. "Okay ladies, if you won't answer me, you understand I will have no choice but to arrest you. Please get out of the car."

FEED THE DOG

Finally, the driving nun tries to talk. It's a good thing that Billy and Roger Lefley aren't here because I'd probably be out some serious dough as it takes her at least six ahems and two false starts before her squeaky voice gets going, "I'msorryofficerwearejustfivenunsonaourwaytothefuneralof ourbelovedlateSisterMargaretandwehavebeensworntoavowofsilencewhichIdearLordhavejustbroken..."

"Slow down Sister one word at a time. I promise I won't go anywhere until you tell me what happened. Take a deep breath and try again."

She takes a few breaths, crosses herself again, and starts over, "Please forgive me Officer, we are Carmelite nuns, until just now I have not spoken a word in three years. We are sworn to a vow of silence, which I have just broken. I admit fault. We were on the way to Our Lady of the Sacred Assumption for the funeral Mass for our dearly departed Sister Margaret, when I hit some ice and skidded into the vehicle driven by this young man."

Nina tells her we were going to the same funeral and the nuns seem relieved. Two of them mouth "God bless you" to us silently.

The Trooper asks for our licenses and registrations. I hand him mine, and he asks me who owns my car.

"My mom."

"I remember when I was your age and got in a wreck. My mother nearly ripped my head off thinking it was my fault. You want to call her and straighten everything out?"

"Would you please?"

"Sure, what's her number?"

"She's in County General's Mental Hospital, I don't have the number, but she's not allowed to have calls until tomorrow."

"Wait, is she the one who left the 'While I'm Dead Feed The Dog' suicide notes?"

"You've heard of her?"

"Yeah, every policeman in the world has heard of her, it sounds like you've had a rough couple of days kid. I'm glad to see she lived. I'm sorry about everything... I'll give her a call if she, um, is coherent enough to understand it. At least you were luckier than that guy you passed on Highway 40 – he died."

Great! The Thibault name is now coupled with Dillinger and Oswald earning me celebrity kid status in every police station in the world. Nina wipes the blood from my face and hugs me.

The cop suggests I go to the hospital to get stitched up, but Nina is giving me such good sympathy that I want to be brave and milk it for what it's worth. "I'll go to the funeral first, then I'll get some stitches."

Our car is driveable, the nuns' isn't. Nina offers them a ride to the Mass. The sisters accept and we all pile in. We must look like a couple of smugglers with a full cargo of illegal wetback nuns when we pull up to the Cathedral in the dented Pontiac.

The service is conducted by the Archbishop of St. Louis and is all in mumbled Latin. It takes about an hour, but Nina holds me the whole time so it seems like only five minutes. When it ends the nun who already blew her vow of silence goes over and speaks to the Archbishop while Nina and I talk with Father O'Brien. A few moments later the Archbishop comes over and apologizes profusely for the accident. He insists that I go to the hospital immediately for my cut and escorts us to our wrecked car.

"Don't worry young man the Church will pay for all your medical and automobile repair bills. Father O'Brien will drive with you to the hospital and then see you home. God be with you."

The hospital gives me the V.I.P. treatment. The head of plastic surgery, Dr. Jirik gives me fourteen stitches to close my cut. He says I don't have a concussion and assures me the scar won't be bad at all, but I might experience some stiffness of the neck and lower back pain over the next few days. The doctor asks if I want any painkillers. I know I can always sell them to Jimmy Leach, so I say yes.

"Have you ever taken painkillers before?"

"Yes, my doctor prescribed something that worked really well once when I broke my leg," I lie.

"Do you remember what it was called?"

"I remember it was white and looked like a big aspirin, I forget what it was called but it made me forget the pain and sleep real well."

"Was it called a Quaalude?"

"That's it."

The Doctor gives me a soul X-ray stare, but I still have my lead shields on and he can't see anything. "Well, I don't like to prescribe Quaaludes as a rule; too many drug abusers take them, but since the Archbishop called and asked us to take special care of you, I'll write you a prescription."

I get a non refillable prescription for fifty 'Fuck Me biscuits' at the Archdiocese's expense. This

FEED THE DOG

must be a sign from God that he wants me to get into Nina's pants.

♪

My head aches and my back is kind of stiff but I'm feeling pretty good on account of Nina's fawning over me in Wednesday's Assembly. She tells me while holding my hand that her parents are really impressed that I had Father O'Brien walk her to her door last night. They think I'm a perfect gentleman and want to invite my parents and me to dinner some night. I tell Nina I would love to have dinner with her parents but it is not a good idea to have my parents together in the same room together with finely honed cutlery.

Basil O'Reilly is fidgeting while preparing for this morning's announcements. He probably knows how pissed off everyone is that he didn't call school on account of the two inches of snow that fell overnight.

"Ladies and gentlemen, I have some regrettable news. Clayton High is suspending Latin from our curriculum for the rest of the semester on account of the death of Professor Markus Kuntz in an auto accident on Highway 40 last night. We would love to continue Latin instruction but there is a shortage of qualified teachers in this field."

Justin Lafayette asks whether we get the day off for mourning.

"No, Professor Kuntz never actually taught here so you don't get a mourning day. We will however fly the flag at half-mast in honor of the three Latin teachers."

Kevin Micheletti complains that precedent clearly dictates that we get the day off.

O'Reilly is adamant, "Look you get days off when, and only when, you see a teacher die in front of you. That is my final word on the subject."

I raise my hand, "Nina Pennington and I were on Highway 40 last night on our way to Sister Margaret's funeral, and we saw the accident on the Ballas Road exit ramp. I feel traumatized."

O'Reilly throws up his arms. "Okay you have the day off, but we're going to have to elaborate an official policy on mourning periods for dead faculty members. I will have an announcement on this during tomorrow's assembly."

I need today off. I have to go visit Lucretia at the private mental hospital downtown to which she has been transferred. I also need to get her car fixed.

I call Father O'Brien and ask him if the Archbishop really meant to get my car repaired or whether I should call my mother's insurance company.

"Don't call the insurance company, they just slow everything down with their questions, adjusters and red tape. Archbishop Frontere has already set everything up and wants you to call him on his private line."

I don't have a pen handy to write the number down and ask him to hold while I get one. Father O'Brien tells me I won't need it, all I have to dial is "NO-SATAN".

I dial the number and a woman with a sultry voice answers. I hang up thinking I have the wrong number and dial again. I get the same woman. "Hello is this the Archbishop's number?" I ask.

"Yes, hold on a second," she puts the phone down and I hear a muffled "Gussy it's for you." I hear some whispering and she returns to the line to ask, "Who may I say is calling?"

"Ric Thibault."

A minute later Archbishop Gussy is on the line. "Hi, Ric, how are you feeling today?"

"A little sore but fine sir, I mean, Your Eminence."

"No, I'm not a Cardinal, I'm only an Archbishop so I'm an 'Excellency' not an 'Eminence'," he laughs. "Father O'Brien tells me good things about you, although he does think that you could improve your attendance at Confession. You haven't reported the accident to your mother's insurance company or talked to a lawyer yet have you?"

"No, Your Excellency."

"Good, they won't be needed. I've made arrangements for a friend of mine, Salvatore Veneruzzo, to fix the car. Salvatore will loan you a car to drive while he's fixing yours. Let me have him give you a call. What's your number?"

"Parkview 1-7830."

"Look son, I'm deeply sorry about last night's accident and Father O'Brien told me about your mother, if there is anything I can ever do for you please don't hesitate to call. Good-bye now."

Five minutes later the phone rings and the voice of a man who sounds like he gargles with razor blades says, "Let me speak to Ric Thibault." I tell him that I am Ric. "Ric, this is Sal Veneruzzo, the Archbishop told me to help him out and take care of you. So what's the problem with your car?"

I tell him the story of my encounter with the nuns.

"No problem, it sounds like it'll take a week to fix the car. In the meantime what type of car do you want?"

I'm not sure how to answer. I'd love to have a Corvette, but I can't exactly ask him for one. I play it safe, "I don't know."

"His Excellency told me to get you whatever you want, you must have a favorite car."

"I'll take anything, whatever is easiest."

"Come on kid, live a little, what type of car do you want?"

"A Corvette."

"What color 'vette do you want?"

"You're joking aren't you?"

"I never joke."

"Red."

Twenty minutes later looking as if he had stepped right out of *The Godfather*, a cigar smoking Salvatore Veneruzzo is at my front door. His face looks like he's been on the losing end of a knife fight or two and is perched on top of a neck which is too big for his shoulders. He even has the standard Mafia regulation issue gold chain with a Crucifix embedded in the hair covering his barrel chest. Behind him I see a brand new 1973 red Corvette convertible.

I hope he doesn't own any cigarette machines. I wouldn't look good on a meat-hook. Salvatore is smiling.

"Hey kid, whatcha think?"

"Is that really for me?"

"Yeah sure kid, compliments of the Archbishop, I bet you get laid in this car." He slaps me on the shoulder causing me to wince in pain. "Here's the keys. Now let's take a look at what the flying nuns did to your mother's car."

We walk into the garage, Sal spends maybe two seconds looking at the Pontiac and asks for the keys. "It'll take about a week, but it'll be as good as new. I'll call you." He gets into the car.

"Don't I need a receipt or something? My mom will kill me if I don't get one."

Sal looks puzzled. "I don't have a receipt on me but don't worry here's my card."

I read the card. Along with a phone number and address it says "Salvatore Veneruzzo, President, Ace Plumbing, Ace Record Distribution and Promotion, Ace Auto Repair, Ace Concrete, Ace Trucking, Ace Party Supplies." Nowhere does it say 'Ace Vending'. I breathe easier.

"Oh, you do party supplies too?" I ask.

"Sure kid, why?"

"We're throwing a party Friday night and I'm going to need to buy the usual party stuff."

"What type of party?"

"A bunch of friends are going to be over, you know?"

"Is it like a bachelor party?"

All my friends are single, so of course it is going to be a bachelor party. "Yeah, can we get what we need from you?"

"Sure kid, I'll provide everything, I'll call you later to make the arrangements. It'll be on the house, compliments of the Archbishop and me."

"You don't have to do that, I'll pay for it." I'm beginning to appreciate Ace Industries' one stop shopping principle.

"No you won't kid, it's the least I can do for a friend of the Archbishop's." Salvatore Veneruzzo drives off leaving me wondering whether there might actually be a Santa Claus, except this one must have a different fiscal year.

I call Billy and ask him if he wants to take a ride in my new car. He doesn't believe the Corvette parked right outside his window is mine. "Come downstairs and I'll prove it."

Two minutes later we're cruising listening to T-Rex's *The Slider* at full blast on the radio in the coolest car in Clayton. I drive slowly so everyone can see us, and so I can learn how to use a manual transmission. I only stall twice.

It's pushing noon when we return home. Marge Bender sees us in the car and wants to know how and where I got it and when she can go for a ride. After Billy goes inside she tells me Corvettes and stick shifts make her horny. I guess she's gotten over both the guilt and the crabs.

I tell her I have to go visit Lucretia. Unfortunately it's the truth.

The Malcolm Renard Pavilion of Barnes Hospital is the first lunatic asylum I have ever visited. I expect to see a guy who thinks he is Napoleon, a couple of catatonics, a few drooling schizophrenics, and a handful of straight jacketed psychopaths.

Reality is a letdown. It seems to be a very mundane place. I worry that this appearance of normalcy means I have been in a nuthouse all my life. I ponder this thought some more, it is profound; an almost existential paradox. I realize I'm only trying to avoid thinking about facing Lucretia. Nevertheless, I will have to find a way of working these philosophical discoveries into my next conversation with Nina.

I ask the receptionist where I can find Lucretia Thibault and she directs me to room 822 where I

FEED THE DOG

find my mother and a private nurse watching television. Lucretia looks haggard and hungover - in other words, normal.

"Hi, Mom."

"Did you feed Duke like I asked?"

"Yeah, but you're not dead anymore so I stopped yesterday. He's getting hungry so you better hurry back home," I try to humor her.

"I hear it's your fault I'm here."

"I didn't make you take the pills."

"Yeah, but you're the one who called 911 instead of leaving me alone so I could die in peace."

"You should know I'm opprobrious."

"Have you fucked Marge lately?"

"No."

"Did you bring me anything to drink?"

"No."

"Listen if you're going to insist that I hang around and live it's going to be done on my terms. I want to be shitfaced drunk so I can deal with all of you."

The nurse gives me a sympathetic smile while loading up a syringe. Before my mother knows what is happening the woman injects her with some sort of sedative. Two minutes later Lucretia is snoring. I wish I had had some of those hypodermic needles for the last few years. They should be issued to kids once they turn thirteen. It would restore the balance of power, they have their birth control pills we have our parent control shots.

"She'll be out for a few hours," the nurse explains, "and by that time visiting hours will be over, so thanks for coming by and we'll see you tomorrow."

Stephan is suspicious. He wants to know why there is a Corvette rather than a Pontiac in the garage. I tell him the truth and he doesn't believe me. I call Father O'Brien and put Stephan on the phone with him to confirm it. Now he's jealous.

"It's a loaner to replace Mom's car so it should be all of ours to drive."

"You can't drive it, I'm the only insured driver, but I'll make you a deal, you don't have to pitch in any money for the party if you leave the car alone," I offer knowing Stephan, greedy bastard that he is, will agree.

"So you'll buy all the beer and stuff?"

"Yeah, all you have to do is let me know how many people are coming."

Marge Bender is at the door and wants to go for a ride. Rather than run the risk of her embarrassing me in front of Stephan I agree to take her. "Where do you want to go?"

"Around the world."

It's forty degrees out but Marge wants to drive with the top down. "It's too cold," I complain as we head out on Highway 40 past the scene of the Professor Kuntz tragedy.

"I'll provide all the heat you need," replies Marge, trying to unzip my pants.

"Marge, we can't." I try to shove her away.

"Yes we can," she says reaching for the zipper.

"I won't, I made a deal with God and I intend to honor it."

"Which would you rather do, get a blowjob from a horny attractive woman in a Corvette, or explain to that woman's husband, who owns a whole store full of guns, how he caught the crabs?"

I believe God put me on earth to fulfill an as yet unfulfilled mission; therefore it would be stupid to allow myself to be killed before I make the world a better place. While a teamster in a Yellow Freight eighteen wheeler flashes me a grin and a thumbs up sign from the next lane, I sacrifice my virtue and some bodily fluids for a higher calling. God will understand.

Basil O'Reilly seems relieved at Thursday morning's assembly. I guess it's because every one of his teachers showed up at work alive. The new mourning procedures are announced. "Henceforth you will receive a day off only when a member of the faculty dies on campus in front of students. If he or she dies at home you will get a day off only if they have taught here for at least one full year. Any new teachers who die, either off campus or on campus, out of the sight of students will be mourned only by flags flying at half-mast and the wearing of black arm bands. The death of one or more students will earn a day off if it happens on campus, whether the demise is seen by their fellow students or not. Off campus student deaths warrant a group counseling session from either a chaplain or, if any court holds that this constitutes religious instruction and therefore is in violation of the Constitution, a trained psychologist. Copies of these new edicts have been posted clearly on all class bulletin boards."

Terry Borotsik asks if any provisions have been made for the deaths of school custodians or kitchen workers. O'Reilly pauses for a second and then announces that the new policy will undergo a revision and therefore we are to ignore the posted policy.

Roger Lefley asks what happens if someone dies today. O'Reilly refuses to consider the possibility and sends us off to class.

Mrs. Lukowich seems edgy during first period English. While grading our papers she noticed Roman numerals on page thirty-one of *Lolita* and is concerned that whatever evil spirit who has been dooming Latin teachers to premature deaths might misconstrue her as an ersatz Latin instructor and kill her. "I want you all to know I neither teach nor like Latin," she screams and breaks down into tears. She keeps crying, mumbling she never wanted to teach anything and wouldn't be here if she had only become a Las Vegas showgirl when she had the chance. It seems her parents did not approve of her career choice and forced her to go to Harris Teachers College instead of the showroom of the Flamingo Hilton. "You all get A's on your papers just please God get me out of here."

Her sobbing grows worse and she appears to be having a complete nervous breakdown. Nina summons the school nurse, who escorts the now hysterical woman out the door. I have a feeling Lucretia may be getting a new roommate when Basil O'Reilly arrives to officially cancel the class.

I ask O'Reilly if Clayton High has an official nervous breakdown policy. The veins in his neck are bulging as he tells me to get the fuck out of his sight before he is forced to formulate a policy on faculty murdering students.

Second period biology is no fun at all. My attempt to point out that the common toad of North America is officially known by the Latin 'bufo vulgaris' is met with apathy by Mr. Hucul. "I'm not some weak pansy English teacher who is going to go bull goose loony because of a few colleagues dying. Death doesn't bother me, I dissect frogs all day." He then gives us a pop quiz on the heart rates of amphibians. There are no questions on the heart rates of teenagers in love. I fail miserably.

Johann has always stated that a person's job must challenge their intellectual capacity for them to achieve their full potential. Emily Wheldon, the big titted bleached blond whose job as receptionist at KDNA involves her being receptive to Clyde Zanussi, the program director, is certainly challenged enough to maximize her potential.

Seeing me pull up to work in the Corvette, Emily wants to go for a ride. She makes me put the top down. "Corvettes make me horny," she says proceeding to make me happy for the second time in two days that I did not take Salvatore Veneruzzo's bet.

When we return Jimmy Leach is furious. "How dare you neglect your job to go for a ride with a kid who makes fifty cents an hour?" Emily shrugs causing her already taut jersey to tighten further around her breasts. Jimmy remembers how she dares.

I go back to the record library and file the albums from Jimmy's show. While putting away records by Three Dog Night, The Grassroots, and Sir Lord Baltimore I realize why Jimmy's ratings are so low – his taste in music sucks. He doesn't play enough Bowie.

I'm putting the last of the records away when I feel a big slap on my shoulder. I turn to find Salvatore Veneruzzo smiling and carrying a bunch of records. "Hi ya kid, whatcha doing here?"

"I work here."

"Oh yeah? Cool, come with me I'm just going to see Clyde about this new record I want you guys to play."

"What record?"

"It's by a new band called Suckerpunch."

"I saw those guys at my doctor's office, can I hear it?" Salvatore hands me a copy and I take it out of the dust jacket. A one hundred dollar bill falls out. "Mr. Veneruzzo, look what was in the record."

"Whoops, I gave you Clyde's copy, here's another one for you kid, and from now on call me 'Sal'. How's the Corvette?"

"Great, you were right."

"You got laid huh? Good kid, and you'll get even luckier at your party," Sal slaps me on the back while I marvel how he knows about my plan to slip Nina the Quaaludes.

Clyde Zanussi looks very happy to see Sal. Five minutes later Jimmy Leach debuts the new supergroup, Suckerpunch, on the radio for all of St. Louis to hear. I think Brother Theodore's ratings just went up.

I glance at the clock and see there is only an hour of visiting time left at the hospital so I race downtown. It is a well known fact that red sport cars possess some sort of special remote control which activate speed traps. I'm cruising past Big Bend Road when I find myself being pulled over by one of Missouri's finest. The cop asks me for my license and registration. I tell him I'm driving a borrowed car from a body shop and I don't have the registration. He doesn't believe me. He asks me to step out of the car slowly and assume the position. I obey and he searches me for weapons. Finding nothing he escorts me back to his car to call in and check what crimes I'm wanted for and if the Corvette is stolen.

I wait nervously to see if the Missouri police are any smarter than the Illinois cops back at the diner. Is he going to take me to some back room and interrogate me? "Boy, we have a sworn statement from Homer Featherstone of Edwardsville, Illinois. He says he saw you feloniously assault a cigarette machine. We also have a deposition from Elmer Affleck at the Pekin Days Inn, who says you checked into his motel with a female juvenile from Missouri. You're going to the big house, boy."

A few minutes later, the report comes back. "2XTE309, a red Corvette car belongs to Salvatore Veneruzzo, a/k/a 'Laughing Sal' of Ace Auto Body. Veneruzzo has been arrested seventeen times for assault, attempted murder, loansharking, and pandering. He has no convictions. There are no wants or warrants for Richard Alouitious Thibault. However, he is the boy whose mother tried to kill herself and left the note 'While I'm dead feed the dog', and he's the kid who was hit by the car full of nuns." My fame is growing.

The trooper hands me back my license. "How did you get 'Laughing Sal's' car?"

"It's a loaner. He's the guy who's fixing my mom's car."

"You're having the Mafia fix your mother's car?"

"No, Archbishop Frontere is having the car fixed."

"The Archbishop of St. Louis sent you to the Vespucci family's enforcer's body shop?"

I tell the cop how I ended up with the Corvette and that Sal is a nice guy. He laughs and lets me off with a warning ticket. "You're lucky kid, when my wife got into an accident she got a lousy Chevy Vega from the insurance company. I like your insurance better although the premiums might be a little high if you know what I mean. You're free to go but be careful." I remember the last time someone warned me to be careful. I decide to drive cautiously and slowly. I get to Lucretia's room with only fifteen minutes of visiting time left.

Lucretia has her martyr's cross prominently on display, "You get here with fifteen minutes left of visiting time. Is that all I am worth to you, well thank you so bloody much for saving my life."

"I would have been here earlier but the police stopped me."

"For what?"

"Speeding, I was trying to get here faster so I could spend more time with you."

"You're lying."

"I'm not, I can prove it. Look," I hand her the warning ticket.

"It says here you were driving a Corvette. Why didn't you take the Pontiac, and where did you get a Corvette?"

I figure that Lucretia is in a lunatic asylum where there are lots of doctors and nurses itching to shoot her full of sedatives if she gets the least bit out of line – so I tell her I crashed her car.

"I'll kill you," she screams at the top of her voice – causing a nurse to appear within seconds.

"Mom, I got hit by some nuns. No one was hurt and a policeman saw the whole thing and says it was their fault." If you don't believe me, you can call Father O'Brien and he'll tell you what happened. I can't tell if she hears me finishing the story because a needle is shoved into her arm and she goes limp.

"I got plenty more of these," the nurse says holding up the syringe, "so, I'll see you tomorrow."

"Mrs. Lukowich will be on sabbatical for the rest of the semester," Basil O'Reilly announces at Friday's Assembly. "Her classes will hereinafter be taken over by Miss Laura Stumpf. Miss Stumpf is known by many of you as the girls' gym teacher."

"Second, I have drafted a comprehensive mourning procedures policy. Any teacher or employee who dies on campus in front of any students will result in cancellation of the remainder of that day's classes. If the deceased is a teacher with five or more years tenure you will receive the next day off as well. If either a teacher with less than five years service or a non faculty employee of the school district dies on campus but out of sight of the student body we will lower the flags to half mast and be issued black arm bands. If a student dies on campus, regardless of whether anyone sees it or not, you get the rest of the day off as well as the next day. Any students dying off campus will be mourned with flags at half mast and black arm bands, but school will be open on an optional basis – unless it is during final exam week in which case tests will be administered on schedule."

"I believe this is a comprehensive policy; are there any questions?"

"What happens if the principal has a heart attack in his office out of sight of students?" I ask, having spotted a potential loophole.

Basil O'Reilly glares at me with an 'if looks could kill we'd all be getting a day off' stare. "If I die, regardless of how and why, there will be no time off."

Billy whispers, "He's trying to lower the incentive for anyone to kill him."

"Finally," our beloved principal continues, "I want to congratulate Kristen Thibault who won a full scholarship to Stanford. I have heard through the grapevine that there is going to be a party tonight to celebrate this and I want to remind you it is illegal for anyone under the age of eighteen to drink alcohol in the state of Missouri. Any violations of this law will result in academic disciplinary hearings. Let's have a good day in and out of school ladies and gentlemen."

Walking to class Billy revises his opinion on the incentive to assassinate O'Reilly. I remind Billy that any harm inflicted by him on Basil might be viewed unfavorably by the court in his upcoming trial for the Shady Oak riot.

Laura Stumpf is a muscular woman in a tweed suit with short cropped brown hair, and just a hint of a mustache. She announces she is changing our reading list. Hemingway's *A Farewell To Arms* is out and Gertrude Stein's *Autobiography of Alice B. Toklas* is in.

Ms. Stumpf is on a soapbox. "Ernest Hemingway was a misogynist. He was also a philandering, whoremongering, drunken, second-rate writer. Gertrude Stein, although a nominal friend of Hemingway, is the catalyst for most 20th century art and literature, a person whose lifestyle serves to this day as a beacon to each and every truly emancipated woman."

Nina raises her hand and asks, "Is it true that Gertrude Stein was a lesbian?"

This strikes a raw nerve with our new English teacher. "Society has brainwashed you by making 'lesbian' a pejorative term. Yes, she was a truly liberated homosexual woman. My mission here is to convert you and every other woman in this class from being cute little slaves to the male dominated fashion industry with your Revlon makeup and tight femme clothes to free thinking individuals. As for the men in this class perhaps you will learn how ridiculous this male myth of macho conquest is. You will no longer be able to oppress us by virtue of the useless appendage you have swinging between your legs."

"It sounds like you want us to read *A Farewell To Dicks*," I suggest.

Miss Stumpf is not amused. "I cannot put up with sarcasm from some hooligan male with an overdose of testosterone. You and the rest of the male chauvinist pigs in the class are trying to oppress me and all women with such outrageous comments. I want all the males out of this class. I want you all to report to Principal O'Reilly's office at once."

So my comrades, the ten other would-be tyrants in the class, and I go to O'Reilly's office. Basil is suffering from the same lack of amusement as our English teacher, "You've been in Miss Stumpf's class for only ten minutes and you guys have already been kicked out?" He looks nervously at his desk and then without so much as looking at me he asks, "Thibault, I assume that you're behind this, what happened?"

"Picture this," I say stressing the word 'picture' and giving Basil a quick stare, "Miss Stumpf kicked us out for having penises. I get the feeling she is not too fond of men."

O'Reilly understands. He mutters, "I knew I shouldn't have trusted the dike," and then asks us to come with him back to class. On the way up I ask Kevin Micheletti what Basil means by 'dike', I mean, who goes around placing trust in embankments? Kevin informs me that Basil said 'dyke', a derogatory word for lesbian. I guess my mental picture of a Dutch boy sticking his finger in a dyke to save his town needs a slight bit of revision.

When we get to the classroom Basil tells us to sit down and shut up while he and Miss Stumpf have a conference in the hall.

"Okay sisters, I'll be back in a moment after I deal with this male oppressor," she says. We can't hear the actual words but can make out the two arguing in the hall. Evidently our beloved principal is considering amending the dead teacher's policy to include a clause on what happens when an administrator murders an instructor on campus out of sight of students.

Tammy Sue Edestrand offers to bet that Miss Stumpf castrates O'Reilly. I consider taking the bet, but realize it would be hard to get Basil to drop his trousers in order to determine the winner.

Five minutes later Basil returns with an announcement, "Miss Stumpf has decided she is unable to continue as your English instructor, due to her decision to relocate immediately to San Francisco. Therefore, I will be taking over as your teacher commencing Monday. Your assignment is to read Hemingway's *A Farewell To Arms*. I apologize for any confusion and thank you for your understanding."

Salvatore Veneruzzo's party supplies are to arrive at five o'clock which makes it impossible to go see Lucretia. I figure I can tell her tomorrow that I came today and then, when she says I didn't, I'll tell her she's crazy which is why she's in the mental ward in the first place. It might fly, and if it doesn't, she'll work herself up into such a dither that I'm sure she'll convince a nurse to give her a magic shot. Sedatives and Quaaludes – I'm glad to live in the age of pharmaceuticals.

I go upstairs and plot my seduction of Nina. Jimmy Leach told me I need only one 'Fuck Me biscuit' to turn her into a raving nymphomaniac, and I have sixty-five Quaaludes to work with. All

I have to do is figure out how to get her to take them and I'm in like Flynn. I decide to conduct a scientific experiment. I take a glass of water and throw a Quaalude in it to see if it will dissolve. I wait five minutes. The pill turns pasty but remains intact. In my mind's eye I can see Jimmy Leach crying as I pour my failed experiment down the bathroom sink. I still have sixty-four 'ludes.

I go downstairs into the kitchen and take another tablet and try to crush it into little pieces. I sprinkle the Quaalude dust on top of a Stone Wheat Cracker with brie. I hear the doorbell. Kristen answers it and in walks Marge Bender.

"Billy tells me that you guys are throwing a big party tonight. I've got two questions, does your mother know and am I invited?"

Kristen gives in to Marge's implied threat and assures Marge she is welcome to come. My plans to come have been fundamentally altered. My nightmare is unleashed in full fury when Marge grabs my experiment and eats it. She chews and swallows. "You shouldn't serve this brie tonight – it's too powdery." She throws the rest of the cheese along with my fantasy of seducing Nina down the disposal.

Salvatore Veneruzzo's delivery guys knock on the door. They have five kegs of beer, a bunch of chips, a huge punch bowl and a lot of paper cups. They tell me the girls will be here at nine. I'm not exactly sure what they mean by 'the girls' but I guess Sal must be sending some women to help serve and clean up. He's an incredibly nice and thoughtful man.

I can't get rid of Marge. She insists on helping set everything up. At least she's not throwing a tantrum about the beer.

About half an hour later Kristen goes to take a shower. She's not gone two seconds before Marge grabs my hand and shoves it under her skirt. I'm not sure whether it is Marge Bender the nymphomaniac or Marge Bender the Quaaluded nymphomaniac who says, "Feel this, I'm not wearing any underwear."

The phone rings and I escape from Marge's clutches to answer it. It's Johann.

"Hi, Dad, how you doing?" I ask while our friendly local neighborhood slut reaches for my zipper.

"Okay, how's your mother doing?"

"She's her normal crazy self," I respond as Marge pulls down my underpants and giggles.

"Who is that laughing?"

"It's the television," I lie, not wanting to explain that Billy's mother is giving me a blowjob.

"Ric, I've decided I can't give in to your mother's emotional blackmail and I'm filing for divorce."

"Great," I sigh to both Johann and Marge.

"This time I'm going through with it," Johann tries to convince me.

"I'm sure everything will come out fine," I say to both parties.

"What do you mean, everything will come out fine?"

I pull away from Marge so I can allow my full brain to function. "Uh, you're always threatening to get a divorce but you never do, so I'll believe it when and if it happens."

My father launches into his patented 'this time it's for real' speech as some intense moaning crescendos from the floor. I look down to find Marge has pulled up her skirt and is busy masturbating. "Ric, you can't tell me those noises are coming from the television, who is that and what's going on there?

"I was in the middle of a business meeting when you called," I try a lie out of Johann's own book while signaling Marge to be quiet.

"You're a student, you're not in business; what the hell's going on there?"

I'm not convincing him, so there is only one thing to do, act like there is trouble with the phone, "Hello?"

"Ric, I'm still here."

"Hello? Dad if you're there I can't hear you."

"I can hear you fine. Can you hear...?"

"Hello?"

"Ric I can hear you..."

I hang up on him and zip my pants. "Marge you can't be doing this, my dad heard you, and besides Kristen's here."

"Fuck me."

"Marge, I can't."

"Fuck me right fucking now."

"Isn't that your husband who just pulled up?" I try a variation of the old Three Stooges 'look behind you' trick.

"Fuck him." She doesn't fall for it.

"Why don't you?"

"Why don't I what?"

"Fuck him."

Billy chooses this moment to come traipsing through the door. From the look on his face he has apparently never seen his mother lying on the floor with her skirt up before.

Marge titters and Billy punches me in the nose.

"What did you do that for?" I ask for some stupid reason.

"You better not be fucking my mother."

"I'm not," which is the truth because Billy used the present indicative tense, rather than either the imperfect (I was fucking), past (I fucked), or pluperfect (I had fucked), tenses. I silently thank poor crazy Mrs. Lukowich for all those boring grammar lessons. Education is good.

"Then what is she doing on the floor like that?"

"Ask your mother, I didn't do it."

"Mom, what are you doing?"

"I slipped and fell."

"Then why were you moaning?"

"Because she hurt herself stupid," I say while punching Billy.

Billy groans.

"See, if you get hurt you moan too," I attempt to convince my moronic friend.

"I feel kind of strange," Marge says getting up from the floor, "where do you keep your aspirin?" Before I can answer Marge sees my bottle of Quaaludes, and mistaking them for Excederin, grabs two tablets. If I tell her she's taking Quaaludes she'll kill me, so I remain quiet. Besides I still have sixty-one left.

"Billy, why don't you take your mother home, I think she needs to lie down for a while. I'll see you in a couple of hours."

They leave and I quickly call Jimmy Leach who is raving about a Suckerpunch song, *Can't Keep Us Down*. Knowing Jimmy's taste in music is as bad as everything else about him I cut him off by changing the subject and asking him, "how long do Quaaludes work for?"

"It depends. Why?"

"This woman I know took three by accident and she's trying to fuck me."

"What's wrong with that?"

"Because I'm throwing a party tonight and I've invited my girlfriend, Nina."

"I see. Well, she's going to either pass out in a few minutes or be really horny for the next six to ten hours – one or the other. What does she look like?"

I've read the Bible. I know most of the Ten Commandments. I don't remember any codicils saying, "Thou shalt not pimp thy best friend's mother off on a deejay." I'm sure any court in the world would rule that my conduct clearly does not fall under the "Thou shalt not covet thy neighbor's wife" doctrine. However, if I were God I might want to close this loophole in my upcoming sequel, *The Brand New And Improved Testament*.

"She's got huge tits and she's married but she seems to have an open marriage. You'll think she's beautiful," I say, knowing Jimmy believes any woman who will go to bed with him is gorgeous. "You want to come to the party?"

"What time does it start?"

"In an hour."

"Have the chick's 'ludes kicked in yet?"

"They're starting to."

"Shit, I've got an hour still to go on my show, and it will take fifteen minutes to get to your place. I guess I could play a live tape of the Grateful Dead doing *Dark Star* – it's about thirty minutes long. I'll see you in about forty-five minutes."

There are not many reasons for celebrations in Clayton, Missouri. The town council recently refused to pass a resolution calling for the creation of a holiday to honor our suburb for being the most boring place in America. It was a shame – the sponsors had already secured a commitment from Spiro Agnew to act as the Grand Marshall of the Boredom Day Parade.

However, we do have a few galas such as the Third Annual Frankie Dzierwa Memorial Bowlathon, held to commemorate man's eternal quest for perfection as exemplified by the late bowler who killed himself rather than face the ignominy of not achieving the paragon of a 300 game. There is also the yearly Stanley Komadoski Memorial Hemophiliac Ball to honor the late patriarch of Clayton society. Mr. Komadoski tragically bled to death as the result of a wound suffered when his daughter, Mabel, stabbed him during a game of pin-the-tail-on-the-donkey at Mabel's fourth birthday party.

Beyond that it's a steady diet of monotony. Consequently Kristen's college acceptance party is the social event of the year. Every kid in Clayton is here.

FEED THE DOG

Kristen's friends are divided into two groups. In one corner are her classmates, the future housewives of America, pimple-plagued girls in Pappagallo shoes and cardigan sweaters. Then there is the second, more interesting crowd, her stripper friends from Gaslight Square. They are long-legged girls in halter tops and short skirts. I like them better.

Stephan's fraternity crowd is in another corner bringing down our property values. They all look and talk alike. All twenty of them are the same pompous snot-nosed dork in a letter jacket. A frightening thought races through my mind, maybe some mad scientist has been cloning Stephan. I remind myself to enlist Stephan in the Marines tomorrow, maybe they will actually remove him from circulation before he can serve as a role model for any other assholes.

My friends are all cool with the exception of Jimmy Leach. He keeps grabbing my arm and telling me that whichever girl is standing in front of him at the moment just gave him the eye and wants him. "She's so horny I won't even have to waste a 'lude on her," he states. I watch him make his move and a few moments later he returns rejected mumbling about dykes.

A graveyard of empty bottles have given their lives to create a lethal mixture of Boone's Farm Apple Wine, Southern Comfort, vodka, gin, Ripple, Wild Turkey, Jack Daniels and Hi-C Orange Drink. This is the center of the party, where all groups seem to intersect. Stephan and Justin Lafayette engage in a contest to see who can drink the most without throwing up. The fraternity guys are giving two to one odds on my asshole brother, so I put two bucks on my classmate. After three drinks Justin is staggering and Stephan is drooling but no vomit has been detected. It's going to be a race to the wire.

My attention is ripped from the match by the entrance of Nina Pennington. Spotlit by the front hall's track lighting she's like one of those old paintings of the saints with the halos. Brother Theodore must use those same lights at his house to fleece money from the faithful.

Nina looks spectacular. She's wearing a black sequined dress with a plunging neckline revealing the sacred Twin Peaks of Pennington. She hugs me and gives me a quick slip of the tongue kiss. I might not even need the Quaaludes, I think while leading her to the punchbowl. I pour Nina a drink and put my hand on her ass. She smiles. I stare into her eyes. They smile. I move in to give her another kiss – and the next thing I know my jaw is sore and I'm lying on the floor.

I'm not quite focusing as my eyes travel up the female legs standing over me. High heels, stockings, garter belt, no underwear – it's Marge doing her Mohammed Ali imitation.

Evidently I'm Sonny Liston. But Marge isn't going to a neutral corner and the referee has already been committed to the cuckoo's nest downtown.

"I told you not to mess around with any other women," she mutters in a strange slurred, subtract-one-hundred-points-from-your-IQ voice.

I'm stunned.

Nina's stunned.

Billy, who appears from behind the newly crowned heavyweight champion of Clayton, is stunned.

Jimmy Leach helps me to my feet, "That isn't the chick you gave the 'ludes to is it?" he asks.

"Yeah, she gets aggressive when she's horny," I say trying to figure out why there are two Jimmy Leaches standing in front of me.

"I like that in a woman. Aren't you going to introduce me?" he inquires, while over my shoulder the now unstunned Nina throws a hard right uppercut into Marge's jaw dropping her to the floor. "Leave my boyfriend alone bitch."

Jimmy helps Marge to her knees, but the combination of the Quaaludes and the blow cause her to fall back down dragging Jimmy on top of her.

With my best Amy Vanderbilt manners I perform the introductions, "Marge Bender may I present Jimmy Leach, Jimmy Leach meet Marge Bender."

I can see Billy getting ready to slug me when Roger Lefley comes over with three extremely attractive girls who are barely dressed in five inch stiletto heels, fishnet stockings, and assorted lingerie. "Ric, these girls are asking for you."

Billy freezes and gives me a pleading 'you can fuck my mother all you want if you fix me up with one of them' look, while Nina shoots a 'who are these sluts?' stare in my direction. The brief moment of elation caused by Nina publicly acknowledging me as her boyfriend evaporates while I try to figure out what is going on.

"I'm Ric Thibault, may I help you?"

"Hi, I'm Cherie. Sal Veneruzzo sent us here to entertain you for your party, but there must be a mistake 'cause this is the first coed bachelor party I ever have been to," a tall redhead with an overbite responds.

"Bachelor party?" Jimmy questions excitedly, jumping off Marge.

"Bachelor party?" Nina echoes in an offended tone.

"I'll cut your balls off," Marge screams.

"This is a bachelor party, no one here except for Mrs. Bender is married," I say honestly.

FEED THE DOG

Kristen is drawn over by the commotion, "Laura?" she asks in a surprised voice of the girl identified as Cherie, "what are you doing here?"

"We were sent here to entertain some guys at a bachelor party, what's going on Bambi?"

Kristen embarrasses me by telling the girls I'm too naive and don't know what I'm talking about. She further explains that this is a party to celebrate her getting into Stanford, and welcomes them to stay as guests rather than performers. "Do me a favor though," she adds, lowering her voice, "a lot of these people don't know I strip so could you change back into street clothes, and call me 'Kristen'?"

"I like what you're wearing now don't change," Jimmy Leach begs. "Did she mention there's plenty of booze and Quaaludes?"

Cherie and her friends decide they have already been paid by Sal so they may as well hang around and have some fun.

Marge cries out from the floor, "Those bimbos don't have anything on me," as she pulls down her dress and passes out. Everyone at the party stares at Marge's boobs and then at Sal's girls. The general consensus seems to be that Marge spoke the truth. The lone dissenter is a rather confused Billy Bender, who is torn between taking care of his mother and trying to get laid by one of Salvatore Veneruzzo's girls.

I ask Jimmy and Billy to help me carry the comatose Marge into Lucretia's room and put her to bed. While Jimmy tucks her in Billy pulls me aside and plaintively asks "Did you fuck my mom?"

"I'm in love with Nina Pennington," I respond truthfully.

Billy buys it.

I hope Nina will too.

Coming out of the bedroom Jimmy solidifies his reputation as a pervert by whispering in my ear, "Did you know Billy's mother shaves her pussy? She isn't wearing panties – I checked."

Kristen is talking with Cherie a/k/a Laura. Kristen laughs and asks me if I know yet what a bachelor party is. Embarrassed, I reluctantly admit I may have been laboring under a misconception concerning the term and ask for details. Cherie summarizes the duties she and her friends perform. From what I gather they are much like a condemned prisoner's last meal – you get one last fuck before execution. Cherie is extremely sexy. I debate whether it is proper etiquette to ask for her phone number in case I should ever need her professional services.

I see Nina angrily heading for the door. I run and grab her. "How could you invite me to a bachelor party and what's with that Mrs. Bender woman, are you going to bed with her?"

"Until two minutes ago I didn't even know what a bachelor party was. I truly believed it was a party for single people. As for Mrs. Bender, she's my best friend's mother and I think she's high on something so you can't pay attention to anything she says," I answer with the same skill and honesty exhibited by a politician running for office.

She's buying. *Hello Mr. Arafat, the three tons of sand you ordered are here... That will be three million dollars...We only take cash...You're a little short on bucks? May I recommend you hijack another jet?...Yes, we do take marked bills.*

I get an apologetic hug which turns into our imitation of Siamese twins joined at the tonsils. Life is good. Nina excuses herself to go to the bathroom and I wander back to where Jimmy, Billy, Kristen and Sal's girls are congregated.

"If you haven't wasted all those 'ludes yet slip her a couple and I guarantee you'll be in her pants," Jimmy whispers and then adds, "Does your sister have a boyfriend?"

Meanwhile, Billy is trying to put the moves on Cherie. Feeling a little bit guilty about Marge, I offer him a 'fuck-me biscuit' to abet his seduction of the stripper. I ask him quietly if he knows anything about Quaaludes. "Yeah, Quaaludes make you want to fuck," he announces for everyone in the next few counties to hear.

Cherie and Kristen ask in unison, "Who has 'ludes?"

I feel trapped like the kid caught in school with chewing gum who is forced to share with everyone. I admit to having a few and find myself doling out a tablet to each of Billy, Kristen, and the three strippers.

"Don't I get any?" asks Jimmy.

"What happened to the thirty-five you got from the doctor the other day?"

"They're all gone."

"In four days?" I inquire incredulously.

"Some were for me and," Jimmy winks, "I got laid a lot."

If a pill could get Jimmy laid it must be pretty damn effective. Unless she was being paid a lot of money no woman in her right mind would go to bed with Leach. But since I would never have heard of, much less gotten, this magical aphrodisiac without him I feel obliged to give Jimmy one. I've already used nine Quaaludes and still haven't pumped any into Nina. On the bright side I've got fifty-six left and Nina called me her boyfriend.

Nina returns from the bathroom as a gigantic groan erupts from Stephan's fraternity brothers. They are not the only ones to erupt because Stephan just puked all over the dining room carpet. On his fourth glass Justin Lafayette has triumphed, but he doesn't have too much time to celebrate because he passes out during a victory toast. I'm not too concerned – I'm up four dollars.

I cheerfully refill Nina's punch glass. Judging from Justin's reactions two more cups and she ought to be putty in my hands, even without pharmaceuticals. I fill a glass for myself and toast my beautiful companion, "Bottoms up." We clink our glasses together and she takes a big gulp. I take a sip and when no one is looking pour the rest back into the punchbowl. "Want another?" I ask.

"Everybody freeze."

I turn around to see Basil O'Reilly armed with a pen and a spiral notebook standing over Justin's prostrate body.

"I told you this morning that anyone caught drinking alcohol would be suspended. I am writing down names and you will all be before the disciplinary committee Monday morning," our beloved principal states.

"What are you going to do – suspend the whole school?" inquires Roger Lefley.

"I will do whatever is necessary to maintain discipline."

Kristen is worried that Stanford might reconsider her acceptance if she is suspended. While O'Reilly walks around writing down names I formulate a plan. "I know this is a lot to ask but would it be possible for you and your friends to resume work and designate our friend O'Reilly as the bachelor?" I ask Cherie.

She agrees to come out of retirement, "Honey, for ten more Quaaludes we'll show him the time of his life. Just put some danceable music on."

To the strains of Bowie's *Suffragette City* Basil's jottings are interrupted by the three girls' bumping and grinding. Cherie and her coworkers remove their tops to the applause of the party. "I'm going to suspend you girls for lewd conduct if you don't stop this instant," our beleaguered educator threatens.

"Sorry, we don't go to your school darling," replies the now nude Cherie before sticking her tongue in his ear.

"Stop this at once. I insist."

"What's the matter honey don't you like girls?" asks the blond stripper, shoving her boobs in his face.

"I like girls, but everything has its place and time," a muffled voice says from behind the blonde's chest.

Over his muted objections, the girls remove Basil's clothing while I go get a camera. I return with Lucretia's Polaroid. The girls are sitting on the now naked Basil who is lying on the floor. "Say cheese everybody," I request. *Click*. Only the strippers comply with my instructions, so I feel obliged to snap another picture.

"*Wham bam thank you ma'am*," sings Bowie in the background.

"What's this sticky stuff, Mr. O'Reilly?" questions Cherie reaching between his legs. I move in for a close-up. *Click*.

The girls get off of Basil and gather around the photos to watch them develop. The old adage about a picture being worth a thousand words is an understatement. I think it's worth a lot more. "Bas, you take a real nice picture. I think I'll send this one to Mrs. O'Reilly for your family photo album."

"Are you trying to blackmail me?" O'Reilly blusters.

"Yes," at least twenty kids say in unison.

I'm getting proficient at deal making. Maybe someday I'll write one of those self help books. It will be entitled *Ric Thibault's How To Get Anything You Want Through Negotiation and Photography*. I'm willing to bet five dollars it will make all the bestseller lists. In exchange for the photographs O'Reilly agrees to sign a note exempting us from any disciplinary action for the rest of the year.

We all salute Basil's departure with a glass of punch. I discover human beings shouldn't mix Quaaludes and alcohol as Kristen, Billy, and the three strippers have all passed out. Jimmy Leach gives further proof to those who maintain deejays don't qualify as people because he is still ambulatory. He shows concern for the plight of the sleeping drug consumers by insisting on listening to their heartbeats. He puts his head to Cherie's chest. "She's okay." He leans over the brunette stripper and places his head on her torso. "This one's okay too." He repeats the process with the blonde dancer, pronouncing her fit. He then gives Kristen a more extensive examination. "She's fine." I ask him to check Billy. "I don't need to," Jimmy says, "I'm sure he's all right, but I think I had better check your sister every few minutes or so throughout the night, okay?"

I tell him to get fucked...but not here.

What with my siblings and neighbors all reposing and Nina beginning to show the effects of

FEED THE DOG

three glasses of punch, I decide to make my move. I lead her upstairs to my room and we make out. I get her dress off. She puts up no resistance. She climbs on top of me and we kiss passionately while I successfully wrestle her bra off her. We break the kiss. Nina sits up giving me my first unobstructed live view of her glorious breasts. Trembling with excitement, I reach up to fondle the sacred mounds. They are the most sensuous objects I have ever touched. Nina sighs with pleasure. She smiles, and leans forward for what promises to be the most romantic kiss of my life. Her mouth opens. My mouth opens. Milliseconds take hours as we move inexorably toward each other. Her tongue emerges from behind coral lips prepared for action. My tongue is prepared for a duel. She pauses, I think, to savor the momentous occasion. She makes a cute little sexy gurgling noise... and pukes all over my face.

Nina is extremely embarrassed and apologetic, while trying to clean up both me and the bed. I attempt to resume our amorous explorations but she claims to not be in the mood anymore and gets dressed to go home. She won't even kiss me goodnight when she leaves. I now understand why men are always protesting that women have too many mood swings. They certainly are fickle.

I'm too depressed to rejoin the party so I lock my door and work on my masterpiece *Talkin' Nina Pennington Blues*:

> Got puked on by my beautiful girlfriend
> Nina you're so lascivious
> Got puked on by my beautiful girlfriend
> Nina you make me lecherous

I fall asleep bemoaning the fact that I have learned the true meaning of the blues.

Someone is trying to rob me. I awaken early Saturday morning to the sound of my dresser being opened. I can see two figures searching my drawers with a flashlight. I look at the clock. It's 4:45. I reach for the hockey stick by my bed and slam it as hard as I can on the closest burglar, who collapses in a heap on the floor. I'm getting ready to highstick the second robber when Stephan yells that he surrenders.

I flick on the light to find Jimmy Leach lying on the floor and Stephan with his arms up holding my Quaalude bottle.

"What the fuck are you doing?"

"We only wanted to borrow a couple of Quaaludes to give the girls," my brother, the thief, says.

"Why didn't you ask me?"

"We didn't want to wake you."

"Who is still here?"

"Just Cherie, Tawny, and Kristen."

"Who is Tawny?"

"The blonde stripper."

"I thought they passed out."

"They came to an hour ago."

"Where's the brunette stripper?"

"She left."

"What happened to Marge Bender?"

"Billy and I carried her home, and Mr. Bender is pissed off that she's so fucked up."

I think back. Marge never knew she swallowed any 'ludes and Billy doesn't know anything so I should be okay.

"Who are you trying to give the 'ludes to?" I ask Stephan.

"Cherie."

"And Jimmy?"

"You'll have to ask him, if he's still alive."

Jimmy moans that he's not dead yet.

"Who were you trying for?"

"Your sister is pretty cute."

I'm really pissed at Stephan for even thinking of assisting in the seduction of our sister by a scumbag like Jimmy.

I'm not sure whether Jimmy is woozy from the drugs or the blow on the head, but he manages to stagger back to his feet. He claims to be okay.

I'm awake, and there are three girls downstairs awaiting Quaaludes. Tawny is pretty sexy. Nina left me hanging. Kristen is older than me; she can fight her own battles. I sell Jimmy and Stephan two tablets each for ten bucks apiece, and then accompany the inept brigands downstairs.

The girls have split. Written in lipstick on the punchbowl is "Suckers."

"Dyke bitches," says Jimmy.

Stephan tries to get me to refund his twenty dollars. I tell him to fuck off and go back upstairs.

I realize why Nina is flirting with existential philosophy. This is a perfect example of existentialism at work. Jimmy and Stephan are struggling in a purposeless and hostile universe that is only going to get more hostile as the result of them waking me up seeking help in their fruitless struggle against reality. I'll have to drop this deep concept into my next conversation with Nina. She'll think I'm enigmatic. Enigmatic teenagers get laid a lot by sensitive intellectuals. I know. I read it in *How To Pick Up Girls*.

The phone rousts me from a deep slumber. The woman's voice on the other end asks me to hold for Archbishop Frontere. Who the hell does he think he is waking me up at 8:15 and then putting me on hold? I hang up. The phone rings again fifteen seconds later. This time it's the Archbishop himself.

"Hello Ric, I must have cut you off I'm sorry," he apologizes. "How's your mother?"

"About the same."

"I pray for her everyday; but that isn't why I called. We have a little problem and I think you can help us out. I was hoping you could come and meet with me this morning."

"What type of problem?"

"I can't discuss it over the phone, but could you be here at noon?"

I agree to the visit and try to determine what sort of problem the Archbishop could have involving me. I compose a list:

1. Getting blowjob yesterday from Marge. Technical violation of "Thou shalt not covet thy neighbor's wife" commandment. However, I wasn't the one doing the coveting. I should get off.

2. I am somewhat vulnerable on the "Thou shalt not commit adultery" commandment. But, under Missouri law I'm still a minor, and therefore I think I can get off on a technicality. A few Hail Marys should have me covered.

3. I did take the twenty-one bucks from Lucretia's purse and have violated the "Thou shalt not steal" rule. I decide to put the money back before my mother gets out of the asylum. Otherwise Stephan would probably steal it anyway – so in a way I'm holding the money in trust for her protection. No foul. Worst case scenario – a few more Hail Marys.

4. The tenth commandment says "Thou shalt not covet thy neighbor's wife, nor his manservant, nor his maidservant, nor his ox, nor his ass, nor anything that is thy neighbor's." I do covet Nina's ass. But she lives two miles away, so she isn't exactly a neighbor. A good lawyer should beat the rap.

5. Being a friend of Jimmy Leach. It doesn't violate any commandment, but I'm sure that it is a damnable sin which could cause me to rot in Hell.

I figure it like this – if you are a coal miner you don't change your clothes every time you get dirty; you wait until the end of the day when you're really filthy before you take a shower. Therefore, if I'm going into the Archbishop's for Confession, I should make sure I've gotten all my sins under my belt. This way I'll get a blanket amnesty at my One Stop Absolution Center. I go upstairs and sneak into Stephan's room. He's asleep. I find his wallet and borrow his driver's license and drive down to the Marine recruiting center.

No kid in his right mind wants a job where you get shot at and in return you get paid less than minimum wage. Consequently Sergeant Markell, the Marine's recruitment representative, has one of the loneliest jobs in St. Louis. He looks up from his copy of *Soldier of Fortune* and seems genuinely pleased to see me when I walk in.

"What's your name son?"

I try to impress the Sergeant. I snap to attention, stomach in, jaw down, shoulders rigid, "Stephan Thibault, sir."

"How old are you?"

"Nineteen, sir."

"You look a little young, do you have any identification?"

"Yes sir," I hand him Stephan's driver's license.

He reads it and hands the license back to me. "Okay, why do you want to join the Marines?"

"I want to serve my country sir."

"I admire your patriotic spirit son, just sign here." I sign Stephan's name, carefully imitating the signature on his license. "Son, I want you to go down the hall for a physical."

I walk down the hall and strip to my underwear. A doctor listens to my heart and pronounces me fit to be shot at. He instructs me to get dressed and go to room 113, telling me all I have to do to be admitted to the Marines is pass the psychiatric test.

I go to the proper room, open the door and find a nervous looking man in a captain's uniform sitting at a desk alone. He stares at me without saying anything.

"I'm here for the psychiatric test sir," I finally say.

He ignores me.

I'm paranoid. He may have figured out I'm not Stephan. My criminal history has caught up with me. I'm going to be the subject of the next *Dragnet* episode except they aren't going to change any names – there aren't any innocent to protect. Maybe I should do a quick runner and head for the nearest French Foreign Legion recruitment center. They give you a complete new identity after you finish your enlistment. There's only one small hitch – each tour of duty is five years. I stand at attention waiting for the proverbial other shoe to drop.

He says nothing.

I sweat.

He's breathing, so he hasn't croaked like Sister Margaret. Maybe he's gone catatonic and is another future roommate for Lucretia. I try again. "Excuse me sir, I'm here for the psychiatric exam."

He picks up a pen and writes something on a piece of paper, but remains silent.

I wait two minutes. "Are you deaf?" I ask loudly.

He looks up, smiles, says nothing and resumes writing.

I wait another minute or two and finally decide to provoke the shrink. I walk behind his desk and yell as loudly as I can into his ear, "Hello, Captain Shrink."

He grabs me by my shirt collar and pulls me down so that I can taste his incredibly bad breath when he erupts, "Don't you ever yell at me shithead," and lets me go. "Get back over there and wait for me to get to you."

I improvise. Wouldn't it be cooler to get Stephan a black mark on his permanent record by getting him kicked out of the Marines before he even got in? I jump on top of the shrink's desk and goose-step about wildly.

"Get off my desk at once."

I break out into a full out dance and scream, "Armageddon is coming unless you let me join the Marines. Give me a gun and turn me loose on the heathen so I can get the Antichrist before it's too late."

The shrink runs out the door, and returns a few seconds later with Sergeant Markell. They drag me off the desk.

"This guy is a Section Eight case. He's a paranoid schizophrenic if I ever saw one, we can't take him," states the Captain. Stephan has just been officially certified as crazy.

For good measure I confirm the shrink's diagnosis, "Sergeant give me a gun and I'll make the world safe for democracy. Let me get the whole satanic empire, in fact give me your gun right now and I'll get started here," I babble.

Sergeant Markell seems disappointed as he shoves me out the door. "I'm sorry Thibault. You've got the right spirit, but we you're not quite what we're looking for in the Marine Corps. Try the Army – they'll take anybody."

It's only 10:45 and I still have time to kill before my meeting with the Archbishop, so I drive down to visit the original lunatic in our family, Lucretia. She's distraught.

"What happened to my car?"

"You don't want to get upset again, you remember what happened last time we talked about it," I say, not too convincingly, fondly recalling my mother being sedated.

"Didn't you say you crashed it?"

"Yes, but it wasn't my fault. The Archbishop is having the car fixed at this very moment. It'll be as good as new by the time you're home."

"That's not what the police said this morning."

She really is suffering from delusions. "What are you talking about?" I ask looking for the nurse with the magic syringe to come to my rescue.

"The police said they found the bodies of two dead people in my car last night. They wanted to know what I know about it," she claims.

I try to calm her by changing the subject, "I fed Duke this morning."

She doesn't fall for the diversion, "The police want to talk to you – and if I find out you had anything to do with it I'll take you out of my will. I'll disinherit you faster than you can say Jack Robinson."

"Aren't you forgetting your will has to start with the phrase 'I, Lucretia Garbo Thibault, being of sound mind and body'? I don't think you quite qualify for the will amending sweepstakes right now," I respond, dismissing the potential tragedy of not inheriting the genuine Brother Theodore plastic Jesus with matching prayer cloth.

Her wrath is momentarily interrupted by a nurse who plops a thermometer down her throat. I consider how nice it would be if I could gag her by shoving something down her gullet every time she goes off on one of her diatribes. The nurse pulls the instrument out of her mouth bringing the

FEED THE DOG

respite to an all too swift conclusion.

"Ninety-eight point six – all normal," she proclaims.

She's wrong. There is nothing normal about Lucretia Thibault.

♪

I never knew that nuns wore short skirts, tight sweaters, makeup, and high heels; but evidently they do, judging from the attractive woman who opens Archbishop Frontere's door.

"I'm Ric Thibault and I have an appointment with the Archbishop."

She escorts me into a Victorian waiting room and tells me to make myself comfortable while she gets him. I sit down and look at the magazines on the coffee table. There are copies of *Catholic Youth*, *The National Enquirer* and a dog eared *National Geographic*. I take the *National Geographic* and read the story on some tribe of Indians in the Amazon. I come upon a few pages which are stuck together. Separating the well worn pages I find pictures of topless native women cooking a pig on a spit. I wonder if their husbands mind that men all over the world are jerking off to their wives' pictures.

"Gussy, we can't now... you have a visitor downstairs," the nun's voice disturbs my reading.

A minute later His Excellency Gussy appears. "Ric, it's so good of you to come, may I offer you something to drink – how about a glass of milk, or a soda or would you care to join me in a glass of wine?"

"No thank you."

"It's not that horrible sacramental garbage. This is Chateau Lafite-Rothschild 1959. It costs over a hundred dollars a bottle. You really should try it."

"Your Excellency, I'm only sixteen, I'm not supposed to drink."

"I'm the Archbishop. I can get you a dispensation from the Pope. Have a drink." He pours me a glass and toasts, "Salut." I take a sip. "An excellent wine, don't you think?" he asks.

I don't want to insult the Archbishop, so, even though it's not as sweet as Ripple I try to be polite, "Yes, it's very good, well worth a hundred dollars."

"Ric, the reason I asked you to come visit is I have a slightly tricky predicament which I was hoping you could help me with. Last night my friends Salvatore Veneruzzo and Louis Palazarri were murdered and their bodies were found in your mother's car."

"You mean my mother isn't crazy and was telling the truth?" I ask in shock and disbelief.

"What are you talking about?"

"I went to see my mother this morning and she told me the police had come and questioned her about two dead guys they found in her car. I thought she was making it all up."

"So what was your mother saying?"

"I don't know, she asked me what I had to do with it."

"What did you tell her?"

"I didn't tell her anything, I thought she was crazy, why?"

"Ric, the Bible tells us 'judge not lest you be judged'. My duty as Archbishop is to minister to both the rich and the poor, the educated and the illiterate, the good and the less than good. There are all too few saints in this world – most men, even me, have strayed a few times in their lives. What I'm leading up to is this; some people claim my friend Salvatore Veneruzzo belonged to the Mafia. I don't know if this is true or not and frankly I don't care. He was always generous to the Church with both his time and money. If it were not for the bingo games he organized the Saint Stanislaus Kotska orphanage would have been closed years ago. Salvatore was a good man, perhaps, like all of us, capable of evil deeds; but I am sure that the Lord has a place at His table for him. I considered Sal a true friend. At the same time it could reflect poorly if the Church were seen to be close to reputed criminals, even if the allegations had never been proved. Do you understand what I'm saying?"

"That you and Mr. Veneruzzo were friends and you don't want anyone to know about it?" I guess.

"Father O'Brien told me you were perspicacious. Yes, I would prefer that you refrain from telling anyone that the Church had anything to do with Salvatore."

"May I ask a question, your Excellency?"

"Sure."

"Are you and the Church one and the same?"

"How do you mean?"

"You said you don't want me to tell anyone that the Church had anything to do with poor Mr. Veneruzzo. Does 'the Church' mean you?"

The Archbishop sips his wine and smiles. "Has anyone ever suggested that you become a lawyer when you grow up? I think you could make a fine attorney one day. I was referring to myself in my capacity as an official of the Church."

"So what do you, I mean the Church, want me to do?"

"I would like you to tell the police that you took the car to Sal's garage on your own. I would prefer you forget I was involved with your choice of body shops."

"In other words you want me to tell a lie?"

He refills my glass and pours another glass for himself, "Yes."

"Isn't lying a sin?"

"Not always," he says, lighting up a cigar, "you know this is a genuine Cuban cigar. They're hard to find here but I have them shipped by a friend from the Vatican, you should try one."

"No thank you. Could you explain how lying isn't sinful?"

"Okay, let's say you have two married friends who you like a lot. You discover the husband is being unfaithful to the wife. You know it will break the wife's heart if she finds out that her spouse is cheating. One day while you're out you run into him with his girlfriend. When you get home you run into his wife who asks you if you know where her husband is. You can either tell the truth and break her heart, maybe even cause her to commit suicide, or you can tell a white lie and say you don't know. This is not a sin. The Church condones this sort of fib to protect the vulnerable in the hope of promoting the greater good – the goal of reconciliation between husband and wife."

I understand the concept fully. My next Confession will not take as long as I thought it would. I'm fibbing not lying and thereby sparing Kevin Bender's feelings.

"There's one small problem. When I got a speeding ticket the day before yesterday, I told a policeman how I got the Corvette from Mr. Veneruzzo."

"Do you know the policeman's name?"

"No, but I have the ticket with me. I think his name might be on it." I open my wallet and pull out the ticket. It is signed by State Trooper Kelly O'Shea.

"O'Shea, sounds like a good Catholic name to me." Archbishop Frontere rings a bell and the nun enters the room. "Sister Marie, would you please get me Captain Beaudin of the Missouri Highway Patrol on the phone?"

A few moments later Sister Marie tells him Beaudin is on the line. The Archbishop asks me to excuse him for a moment and goes into the other room to talk in privacy.

I sip some wine and read the *Enquirer*. It's chock full of news. Hitler is still alive and working as a shepherd in Australia. Also, some guy in Lafayette Indiana has had the misfortune of his father undergoing a sex change operation and subsequently marrying his former brother in-law. There is now some confusion as to whether the kid should refer to his father as 'Dad' or 'my sister in-law'.

My problems pale in comparison.

His Excellency returns smiling. "I've spoken with Trooper O'Shea, and it's all set, he doesn't remember you saying anything about how you got the Corvette. It's now entirely in your hands."

"What are the penalties for perjury?" I inquire.

"A lot less severe than eternal damnation," he replies quickly. "And I think you should be rewarded for your piety and concern for the greater good in this matter. I am the Executor of Salvatore Veneruzzo's estate, and I will arrange for you to receive the title to the Corvette as a token of the Church's gratitude for your selfless devotion."

I'm pretty sure there are no Nina Penningtons in Hell. Eternal damnation is not an attractive proposition. I elect to affirm my spiritual commitments by accepting the Archbishop's generous offer of the car.

The poster has arrived! Sitting on the kitchen table is a cardboard mailing tube from Ace Photo Labs. It must be another division of the late Salvatore Veneruzzo's Ace Industries empire. I take the tube to my room and unroll the four by six foot poster of Nina Pennington as captured by Basil O'Reilly's hidden camera.

Nina is gorgeous, she looks even better than she did last night. I think it has something to do with her not vomiting on me in the photo. I tape the poster to the ceiling above my bed. It will be inspirational. She'll be the first thing I see each morning when I wake up and the last thing I see before going to sleep.

I'm admiring Nina's portrait when I hear the doorbell. Kristen answers the door and a second later yells that the police are here and want to talk to me. An adrenaline rush races through my veins. It's showtime.

I go downstairs.

The doughnut cop and his partner are standing in the foyer. "We would like you to come downtown to answer some questions."

"Questions about what?" I ask, reviewing my recent criminal activities.

The corpulent cop takes great delight in not letting me know. "I'm not allowed to tell you. The Chief is waiting for you at headquarters, I'm sure he'll clue you in. But let me give you something to think about. Until your mother tried to commit suicide nothing has happened in Clayton since the

Frankie Dzierwa incident. Now every day we have somebody turning up dead or dying, your mother, Sister Margaret, and now these two mobsters – and you're always involved..."

"Ronnie, you weren't supposed to tell him," says the other cop.

"I didn't tell him anything about the Veneruzzo murder," officer fat Ronnie responds.

"You just did twice stupid," his partner asserts.

"I did not."

"You did too, tubby."

They bicker the whole drive downtown. According to Amy Vanderbilt proper etiquette dictates that one should try to mediate any dispute between friends in a way that each side doesn't lose face. However, I don't recall if there is a footnote covering what happens when you're in the back seat of a police car and everyone has a gun except you.

I elect to stay out of the argument.

Miraculously we arrive at police headquarters without either of the cops shooting each other. Apparently Seymour Stankiewicz, fat Ronnie's partner, is incensed that nepotism has permeated the Clayton police department's ranks. Officer Ronnie Watt disagrees vehemently.

If I had to take sides, I would probably agree with Officer Stankiewicz as the Laurel and Hardy of Clayton law enforcement escort me through the double doors of Chief of Police Harold D. Watt's vacant office. They order me to sit and then continue quarreling.

"Silence," a shrill voice screams from behind me.

I turn around. The city of Clayton must have reckoned that it was imperative to hire a big man for the big job of Chief of Police. The rather irate sweaty five hundred pound figure of Harold D. Watt lumbers through the double doors.

"Daddy, will you tell Seymour to stop picking on me in front of the suspect?" begs Ronnie Watt.

"I wasn't picking on you, I merely told you not to tell the suspect what was going on."

I look around. There are three policemen, none of whom look bright enough to be suspected of anything other than stupidity, and me. I deduce I must be the suspect, but I'm still unsure which of my crimes I've been pinched for.

Chief Watt settles the argument by sending both of the officers to their desks. They close the door leaving me alone with their boss. He collapses onto the overstuffed purple sofa which is the only seating receptacle capable of handling his bulk.

"Tell me about your mother's car," he wheezes.

"I'm sorry but I heard the word 'suspect' used in reference to me. What am I suspected of?" I ask.

"I'll let you know after I finish questioning you."

"Don't you have to read me my rights?"

"Yeah, I guess so. You have the right to remain silent...um...a...how's the rest of it go?" he stutters for a second and then tries to reach into his pocket which is impossible due to his amazing obesity. "I have my Miranda card in my wallet, and it's a little hard for me to...um...get it right now. Would you mind going outside and asking one of the officers to read you your rights?"

"Yes I would mind. If you're going to arrest me for something, you're going to have to do it without my assistance."

"I wasn't going to arrest you yet. You're only a suspect," he differentiates.

"If you tell me what I'm suspected of then maybe I'll help you."

He points a fat finger at me menacingly, "Listen kid, I've been waiting five years for a murder case to come along. I've stayed up late at night studying all the great detectives – Sherlock Holmes, Hercule Poirot, Charlie Chan, Dick Tracy, I've done them all. I know every interrogation technique in the book, and this is going to be my first opportunity to prove to the world that I am an expert. So don't make it any more difficult on yourself – go get one of the officers to come in here and read you your rights."

"No," I remain defiant.

"If you don't I'll sit on you," he threatens.

His technique is good. Very good. I'm intimidated. I go find Seymour Stankiewicz.

Stankiewicz accompanies me back into the Chief's office. Seymour is no Joe Friday; he stumbles through the Miranda warnings. When it gets to the part asking me whether I understand my rights I am tempted to say "I understand them, but I don't think you do," but I chicken out.

"Okay Thibault, tell me about your mother's car," Chief Watt demands.

"It's a blue Pontiac with a crummy radio, no eight track player..."

"I already know that. I want to know what was your mother's Pontiac doing at Ace Auto Repair last night?"

"It was parked there," I respond truthfully.

"I already know that too," the Chief snorts, "why was it parked there?"

"It was being fixed."

"Why did you take it to Ace rather than some other repair shop?"

"Because I looked in the Yellow Pages and they were the first body shop listed. I called them and they said they could do the work quickly."

"Did you know Salvatore Veneruzzo?"

"Yes."

"Did you know that he was found shot to death in your mother's trunk?"

"Yes."

"How did you find out?"

"My mother told me."

"Where were you last night at midnight?"

"At home."

"Do you have any witnesses?"

"About one hundred. My sister and I had a party."

"I need names," he demands.

I give him names. While Seymour Stankiewicz copies them down Chief Watt yawns and stretches causing his uniform shirt to ride up above his gargantuan stomach. I sit aghast, looking at his grotesquely fat body. How did he manage to get near enough Mrs. Watt to create his moronic offspring, Officer Ronnie? Did the sex act require the assistance of a crane operator who hoisted him above his wife in order that he didn't crush her to death? Is there still a Mrs. Watt, and if not would the Chief like to meet his female counterpart, Cousin Julie?

My daydreaming is rudely interrupted by an immense belch from Chief Fatty. He has another question, "Where did you get the red Corvette?"

"Mr. Veneruzzo gave it to me."

With great difficulty he manages to get back to his feet and waddle over to the chair in which I'm sitting. He leans forward until his perspiring fat face is right in front of mine.

"Why did he give the Corvette to you?" he demands.

My mind lingers on his threat to sit on me and every pore in my body commences oozing water as it's time for the official Church sanctioned fib. I know I have to make it really good or he will squash me like Nero did to Poppaea. Hold on a second, I say to myself, I had nothing to do with Sal's murder. I'm innocent. All I have to do is deflect his attention in another direction and I'll be rid of him – just make the fib plausible. I have an idea, Johann is in France and therefore has an airtight alibi. "Mr. Veneruzzo said it was a gift in honor of my father."

His mouth opens revealing a half chewed piece of lettuce clinging to his heavily decayed teeth. "What did your father do to earn such a gift from a gangster?"

"I don't know."

"What does your father do for a living?"

"He's a management consultant."

"Where is he now?"

"At the Hotel Georges V in Paris."

"Paris as in France?"

I nod.

Watt is momentarily stunned. He then lurches forward and rambles, "My God, I think I've stumbled onto an international Mafia conspiracy. I can see the headlines – 'Clayton Chief of Police Howard D. Watt smashes Mafia cartel.' I'll be famous. They'll make a movie. Paul Newman could play me or maybe Robert Redford..."

"How about Marlon Brando?" I suggest bewildered as to how he has deduced the birth of an international Mafia conspiracy from anything I have said. I have a feeling the middle initial in Chief Howard D. Watt's name stands for 'dim'.

"Get me Interpol on the phone," he yells to Officer Stankiewicz, "and also the William Morris agency."

Clayton cops are creeps. They drag me downtown thinking that I'm a suspect in a Mafia murder and then after finally concluding I've got nothing to do with it they won't give me a ride back home. Somehow Chief Dim Watt has figured that Johann is involved. I'm sure my father will prove himself innocent, but it is out of my hands – it's not my problem.

As long as I'm downtown anyway I may as well stop in at Big Dick's Head Shop to see if they've got any new David Bowie posters. If I can find a good one I'll pick it up as a present for Nina. That will give me an excuse for calling her.

I leaf through the normal collection of posters featuring Hendrix, the Who, the Stones, a couple of those insipid nature scenes with Rod McEuen sayings printed on them. There are none of Bowie.

I ask the sales clerk if she has any posters other than the ones on display. She says they received a new shipment this morning which hasn't been put out yet. She is really nice and lets me go through the new stuff.

There is one of Elvis Presley. Who in their right mind would want Elvis's washed up face staring at them from their walls? The guy is a loser. The only people who like him are Richard Nixon and fifty year old blue haired women in Las Vegas. I thumb through to the next one – it's a semi-nude Raquel Welch. I gaze longingly at it before moving on to the next one.

I'm dumbfounded.

Staring out from the poster rack is Basil O'Reilly's photographic masterpiece of Nina. It's an exact copy of the one taped to my ceiling. The only difference is at the bottom of the picture – this one says, 'Copyright 1973 – Ace Industries'.

I'm pissed off.

It's bad enough they used the photo to make more posters – but this one costs only four dollars and ninety-five cents. I paid twenty bucks plus two dollars extra for special delivery. I've been ripped off.

I debate how angry I would be with Salvatore Veneruzzo if he were still alive. After all he did give me the Corvette, but taking my girlfriend's naked picture and marketing it all over the world is not right...especially when I paid eighteen dollars extra. Maybe he deserved to be bumped off. It's a tough call. I guess that's why there are priests and archbishops around to make the really difficult moral judgments.

Following considerable soul searching I forgive Sal. I even buy an extra copy of the poster in his memory. It will give me a spare in case something ever happens to the original.

I call Nina. She's hungover and still unaware of her new found celebrity. She remembers coming to the party and slugging Marge, and watching Basil O'Reilly get his comeuppance, but she has only vague memories of our making out. She wants to know what happened. I utilize the Archbishop's white lie approach and omit any mention of her retching all over me.

She asks me if she had a good time. I assure her she did, and ask her if she would like to go to the movies this evening. She tells me she can't – her parents grounded her the rest of the weekend for getting home late.

I go upstairs and close the door so I can look undisturbed at my ceiling art. I imagine that I'm the Pope admiring the Sistine Chapel roof. It is a religious experience. I wonder if he gets a hard on too, and if he does, what he does to get rid of it, which reminds me I better get the hell to Church tomorrow. I don't think God will feel my trip to the Archbishop's constituted a proper Confession.

My daydreams are interrupted by Billy Bender's pounding on the door. He's carrying a rolled up poster.

"You're not going to believe what I just bought for ten bucks," he unravels his poster. Billy overpaid. It's Ace Industries' photo of Nina.

I point to the ceiling. Billy is dejected. "You always have to be the first kid on the block to have everything," he complains.

Other than the poster, the crabs, and his mother, who in actuality has been had first by Kevin Bender, I think he is wrong, I'm usually the last one to get anything,

"Has Nina seen it yet?" Billy inquires.

"I don't think so."

"Do you think O'Reilly had anything to do with the poster?" Billy asks.

"Well, it was his camera which took the shot," I say allowing Billy to draw his own conclusion without any lying on my part. We discuss the ramifications of our principal being involved in pornography and agree that his tenure as an educator may be in jeopardy. Alas poor Basil, I knew him well, I paraphrase Shakespeare.

Billy tells me his trial is scheduled for Tuesday and that Marge has hired a lawyer to defend him. He asks me if I will be a witness on his behalf.

"Why do you want me as a witness? You're guilty, I saw the whole thing."

"You're my best friend, can't you just tell a lie or something? I'd do it for you," he snivels.

I agree to talk to his attorney and see if I can be of any help to his defense.

There is a definite air of gloom at KDNA. Clyde Zanussi is in mourning. Jimmy Leach probably is too, although he may just be hungover. Even Emily Wheldon is depressed because she flunked the 'Does Your Man Think You Are Stupid?' test in the new issue of *Cosmopolitan*.

I notice the Suckerpunch album has been taken off the playlist and is now residing in the trash. I try to find out why from Clyde, but he answers by asking if I know anyone who wants to buy either his Rolex or his time share in Aspen. He has suffered a sudden reversal of fortune and needs to raise some cash.

While we are talking he gets a phone call and excuses himself for a moment while he speaks with his lawyer about a personal matter. I go outside and wait. Clyde forgets to close his door all the way and I overhear his end of the conversation.

"Why would Veneruzzo have kept books identifying who he gave the payola to?...Do you think the police have them?...She didn't say she was eighteen, but she sure the hell looked it...What Grand Jury investigation? ...Do you know if any radio stations in Costa Rica need a program director?..."

My attention is distracted by Jimmy Leach's complaining. He's got a huge bruise on his face from last night's run in with my hockey stick, but it is not the cause of his despondency.

"Where the hell does Zanussi get off telling me to play records solely by the virtue of how they 'test'? Can you believe the guy? He says we're gonna contract with some idiotic bastard in Texas who attaches a machine to the palms of a scientifically selected group of people. The idiot bastard then plays a song and measures how much each person sweats. Whatever song makes them sweat the most – we're supposed to play. That's bullshit. I didn't get to where I am today by studying the perspiration patterns of random Texans," he rants.

I decide against mentioning that his ratings are so low that picking records solely by seeing how far an orangutan could throw them would be an improvement. Instead I ask the zero king of the ratings book if he has found out yet which records have tested well.

Jimmy tosses me the new list. For once in his life he is right. KDNA is going to a new format titled 'Sincerely Yours – Sincere music for sincere people.' It sucks. We are now going to be playing the Carpenters, Jackson Browne, the Partridge Family and Joni Mitchell – there is no mention anywhere of Bowie. I'm pretty sure the reason the test group was sweating so much is that they were frightened by the prospect of having to listen to these records over and over again.

"How the fuck am I supposed to play sincere music?" Jimmy asks before quickly changing the subject. "Do you have any more Quaaludes I could borrow?"

I drive home to find the house surrounded once again by reporters. Billy Bender is in the front yard being interviewed by Channel 3. Marge is talking to a guy from Channel 7. Even our mailman, Sam Wensink, is holding court with a couple of guys from *The Globe Republican.*

Upon stepping out the car I am engulfed by the media horde. My position is akin to that of a worm in the middle of a school of fish during a feeding frenzy. "What did you tell the police about your father's involvement in the Salvatore Veneruzzo slayings?" shouts out the dwarf reporter from

Channel 6, Brian Savage.

Before I can answer a woman from Channel 3 yells, "Can you describe what it's like growing up with your father being in the Mafia?"

I pause to think. Johann in the Mafia? I always thought the Mob hired Sicilian thugs with bushy eyebrows and cute nicknames in parentheses followed by pasta-sounding surnames ending in vowels, like Vito (Vic Flowers) Rigatoni. To my knowledge the Cosa Nostra haven't been subject to any affirmative action sanctions and aren't recruiting middle-aged German management consultants. It's too bad, Johann (Joe the Lover) Thibaultiano has a nice ring to it.

Before I can respond another reporter screams out a question, "According to police sources the Corvette you are driving was furnished to your father by Sal Veneruzzo who was found dead in your mother's car. Is your father involved with the Mafia?"

"If my father is involved in the Mafia, I don't know anything about it. Now please everyone get off our property and go away."

I walk back to the house leaving the media to pounce on the other potential interviewees. I hear Sam Wensink accusing Johann of being a bad tipper at Christmas, and Billy Bender denying that his actions during the Shady Oak Riot had anything to do with some secret Mafia initiation rite conducted by my father.

A woman who introduces herself as Mary Ecclestone, Chief Investigative Reporter For Channel 7 grabs my arm. In a throaty seductive voice she purrs, "Mr. Thibault, I'd like an exclusive interview. I promise to make it extremely worth your while."

I look at Mary Ecclestone. She has deep blue eyes, long red hair, great legs, and judging from her taut red sweater, huge breasts. I ask her how she is planning to make it worth my while.

"I can't show you here, but," she runs her hand over my crotch, "let's go in the house and negotiate terms."

I decide to accommodate the press. I open the door and hear a piercing scream. I turn around quickly. Mary Ecclestone is sent careening out of control past me.

Marge Bender has gone berserk.

"Get away from him you slut," she screams at the reporter who is sprawled out on the floor.

Mary Ecclestone gets up and punches Marge. She lands a left hand blow to the mouth but leaves herself open to a right upper cut thrown by the heavyweight Queen of Clayton, and falls back to the floor. Mary Ecclestone's cameraman tries to grab Marge. Brian Savage thinks that Channel 6 might be trying to scoop him and kicks the cameraman in the knee sending him crashing into the woman from Channel 3. She retaliates by punching the midget and within seconds the entire St. Louis press corps is involved in a full scale melee. Cameras, microphones, and Brian Savage's toupee are all flying through the air.

Brian Savage is pissed at Terry Madigan from Channel 12. "You can't get away with this you bastard. You stole my wig and now there's going to be a quid pro quo." He jumps up and grabs Madigan's hairpiece. Terry Madigan chases after the midget reporter as the police arrive to quell the disturbance. Seymour Stankiewicz and Ronnie Watt are the first patrolmen on the scene. The peace officers survey the battlefield and decide not to enter the fray directly. Instead Ronnie Watt draws his service revolver and fires a warning shot into the air to secure everyone's attention.

Unfortunately, Officer Watt failed to notice there is an electrical line running right above him. The bullet neatly severs the fully powered wire, which comes crashing down with a light show worthy of Bowie upon Brian Savage.

He is dead. He should have known better than to say anything in Latin. It will kill you every time.

However, Ronnie Watt has been successful at garnering the full and undivided attention of everyone present who is still alive.

Marge Bender and the entire Saint Louis press corps are under arrest and in the Clayton jail! Chief Howard D. Watt is pressing charges against them for inciting a riot and involuntary manslaughter. For some unknown reason no charges are being brought against Ronnie Watt for firing the shot that led to the death of Brian Savage.

I would be in jail too had it not been for Sam Wensink's eyewitness testimony that I was an innocent bystander. Chief Watt had no choice but to let me go after hearing the postman and viewing the video tape from some of the confiscated cameras. I can be seen clearly asking the reporters to leave and was merely opening my door when the riot broke out.

So Billy and I head into the kitchen to try and figure out how to break the news to Kevin Bender that Marge is in need of both a bail bondsman and a lawyer. The phone is ringing off the hook. I pick it up. It's Nina.

"My parents and I just saw you on television," the love of my life says.

"How?"

"Channel 3 was televising the whole thing live. I didn't know your dad was in the Mafia; and what's with Marge Bender she's always picking fights with any woman who goes near you. Are you sleeping with her?"

"My dad is not in the Mafia and, as I told you last night, Marge Bender is my best friend's mother." I figure this totally truthful explanation worked last night – and hope it will work again.

It does. While Billy looks at me quizzically Nina continues expressing her concern about my family's Mafia ties. "My parents say that the press would never intimate anything unless it was one hundred percent true. The media thinks your dad is a Mafioso. Therefore they told me I'm not allowed to see you anymore."

My heart sinks. I'm so low I'd have to jump up just to reach the floor. *Talkin' Nina Pennington Blues* is going to be an epic. I swallow hard and ask, "What are you going to do?"

"Ric, I really like you, in fact," she drops her voice to a whisper, "I think I may even love you..." I feel like Tinkerbelle making her comeback in *Peter Pan*. Nina continues, "Have you ever read *Romeo and Juliet*?"

"You mean you want us both to commit suicide?" I ask, quickly reassessing how much I value Nina's love.

"No, I only mean the part where the parents are against the relationship between Romeo and Juliet. The lovers still see each other only they do it behind their parents' backs."

I feel relieved. "So you want us to keep seeing each other?" I ask tentatively.

"Of course silly, I'm in love with you."

"I love you too."

Billy is being an asshole. "Can you stop your cooing and get off the phone so I can get my fucking mother out of jail?"

I reluctantly say good-bye to Nina and hang up.

The phone rings again as soon as I put it down. It's the Archbishop. He has seen the riot on television too.

"Ric I'm proud of the way you handled both the press and, from what my sources say, the police. I want you to know that I'm here to help you if you need anything."

"Can you get my friend's mother out of jail?" I ask.

"What's she charged with?"

"She's the one who started the fight with the reporter who touched off the riot."

FEED THE DOG

"Oh the infamous Marge Bender? Let me make a few calls and see what I can do. I'm sure it won't be too difficult."

I hang up and tell Billy the news. He's relieved.

The phone keeps ringing and ringing. Without being able to put the phone down even for a second, I have already received calls from Lucretia ("I always knew your father would come to no good when he left me for his bimbos"), Kevin Bender ("Why is my family always inciting riots, and how much bail money do I need this time?"), Roger Lefley ("Hey man, you saw Brian Savage fry and should ask Basil O'Reilly to let you miss a day of school"), Basil O'Reilly ("Listen you little prick blackmailer, I'm not going to let you out of school for this one – no matter how hard you try"), and Jimmy Leach ("Do you still have any Quaaludes?...Can I borrow them?").

I finally take the phone off the hook. Due to the downed power line we don't have any electricity for about an hour. The lights come on at five fifty-five and I turn on the television in time to see Walter Cronkite and the six o'clock CBS evening news. The lead story is the electrocution of Brian Savage and the subsequent arrest of St. Louis's media. The dwarf's death is shown in slow motion and from several angles.

"For an in depth report on the events leading to the death of our colleague, Brian Savage, we take you to Sonny Odrowski, who is the weatherman on our affiliate in St. Louis," Cronkite intones.

They cut away to Sonny Odrowski live in front of the Clayton police station. "It all started when the press attempted to talk to sixteen year old Ric Thibault, whose father Johann Thibault, according to Clayton police sources, is linked to the slaying of Vespucci family enforcer Salvatore Veneruzzo and his bodyguard Louis Palazarri."

I am a celebrity! My face takes up the whole screen as CBS shows me being interviewed in my front yard. "My father is involved in the Mafia, I don't know anything about it. Now please everyone get off our property and go away," I say.

The bastards started the tape one word too late. They left off the qualifying "if" which started the sentence. I have been edited to accuse Johann of being a criminal in front of the entire country.

I put the phone back on the hook long enough to dial the local CBS affiliate to complain. No one is in at the news department. They are all in jail.

I open the front door to let Duke out in the morning. He sees Sunday's *Tribune* lying on the front steps and pisses all over it. His soaking of the newspaper has rendered it unreadable. I think it may be an editorial comment on the dog's part.

I go next door and borrow the Bender's paper. Marge wasn't bailed out until four in the morning, so they are probably going to be sleeping late and won't miss it.

I'm disappointed. The main headline screams:

LOCAL CRIME BOSS COLLARED IN PARIS BORDELLO!

I was certain that the Brian Savage death and media riot would be the lead story. Instead it's in the second column, which I read first:

> In a related story Channel 6's Brian Savage was electrocuted when Clayton Police Officer Ronnie Q. Watt fired his service revolver into a power line causing it to strike the diminutive reporter.
>
> Savage was attempting to interview Ric Thibault, the youngest son of suspected organized crime figure, Johann Thibault (see adjacent story for details of Thibault's apprehension)...

Thibault's apprehension? I look at the adjacent story. According to the *Tribune* Johann was arrested early this morning (French time) in a Paris whorehouse by French police acting on an Interpol A.P.B. He is suspected of running the Vespucci family's international prostitution ring. Johann has waived extradition and is being brought back today in handcuffs to face questioning about the two dead mobsters found in Lucretia's car.

Two thoughts come to mind. First, I probably should put the phone back on the hook. I bet Johann may have tried to call. Second, he probably won't need me to pick him up at the airport.

I look through the paper's special photo section on yesterday's riot. There's a pretty good picture of me standing at the front door with Marge Bender and Mary Ecclestone. However, it's not the most flattering picture of either of the two women. Besides the fact that Marge's slip is showing, Mary's tongue is hanging dog-like from her mouth and her eyeballs are bulging from her head. I think it has something to do with Marge trying to strangle her.

I finish the newspaper and decide that I really should go to Confession. I've got a few things to get off my chest.

I look at the confessional while waiting my turn and realize why everyone, myself included, is always skipping the Sacraments. The booth is too small, too drab, and too depressing.

If I were the head of production at Chrysler I wouldn't be manufacturing dark brown cars with tiny interiors and uncomfortable seating. No, I would be making cars with lots of leg room and bucket seats. I'd use leggy blond models with big breasts in all the advertisements to entice buyers. It's basic marketing.

If I were the Pope there would be big changes in the Catholic Church. Instead of cramped claustrophobic confessionals we would have spacious booths with plush sofas. There would be a big neon sign flashing the word 'Confess' in blue light over a red crucifix. Nuns wouldn't be wearing any loose black robes either. Except for the old and ugly ones, who would be shifted to back room operations, the new and improved ultra-modern nuns would be wearing hot pants, tight sweaters and patent leather knee high boots with five inch heels. I know Archbishop Frontere will agree with me. I must remember to tell him my suggestions next time we talk.

I enter the booth. "Forgive me Father for I have sinned. It's been three months since my last Confession." I wait for Father O'Brien's response.

"Ric it's been at least four months."

He's right. I start over. "Forgive me Father for I have sinned. It's been approximately four months since my last Confession."

"Tell me about your sins."

"I told a few lies."

"Why did you lie?"

"I wanted to win the love of Nina Pennington so I told a few stories which stretched the truth a little bit."

"That's not a mortal sin, anything else?"

I decide I've covered mendacious behavior enough in my Confession so I move to another topic skipping over the lies I told for Archbishop Frontere. "I've had sex a few times."

"Masturbation?"

"No, sex with girls."

"I need names."

"First I had sex from this groupie Dominique, and then later I made it with her friend Boom Boom."

"I see. These are venial sins, serious nonetheless but not mortal."

"I'm not done yet, I got a blowjob from Emily Wheldon and I've been having sex regularly with Mrs. Bender."

"Marge Bender, Kevin Bender's wife, and your best friend Billy Bender's mother?" I can sense the invisible penance scoreboard spinning out of control. I've never heard so much agitation in Father O'Brien's voice. "Get out of here right this instant before I do something contrary to my sacred vows of the priesthood."

"But I'm not through yet."

"I'm not a prison chaplain – that's who you should be talking to. You're excommunicated!"

I leave and drive home feeling confused and upset. I had always thought the purpose of Confession was to come clean with God and own up to your sins. I told the truth and now I'm out on my ass.

Maybe it's time for a new religion – time for a new Martin Luther to come and nail a manifesto to the Church door. I could implement all my marketing ideas. We wouldn't have some dead boring name like 'Methodist', 'Presbyterian', or 'Baptist'. We'd get something sexy, like 'Church of the Amazingly Big Breasted Former Virgins'. We would use all the same holidays as everyone else and add a few of our own. There would be Nina's birthday, my birthday, and a day off for the 'Feast of the Dead Latin Teachers'. This holiday would be scheduled to coincide with any exams forced upon the oppressed student masses in Clayton.

It could work. We would be the fastest growing religion in the world in no time flat.

I'm upstairs looking at my ceiling when I hear a commotion coming from next door. I hear a man yelling at Marge but I know it isn't Kevin because he and Billy have hockey tickets for this afternoon. I run downstairs and go outside so I can hear better. I can barely make the man's words out.

FEED THE DOG

"How could you?...with your best friend's son...corrupting a minor...blowjob...Jezebel...my standing in the community...burn in Hell."

I hear the sounds of pots and pans being thrown and then Marge's voice, "...me feel like a fulfilled woman...hypocrite...my husband's guns...burn in Hell."

Marge screams and there are sounds of a struggle. This is shortly followed by the door flying open and an older man tumbling down the steps. He seems to be in a daze while crawling on the ground searching blindly for his glasses.

It's Father O'Brien!

I do the Christian thing and hand him his spectacles while helping the shaken priest to his feet. Father O'Brien cleans the glasses and thanks me for my assistance. He puts them on. He takes a look at me, realizes who I am, and punches me in the stomach.

"What did you do that for?" I gasp.

"Character development, you little shit."

Capitalism reigns supreme in the Thibault household. The phone is constantly ringing. It's as if *Dialing For Dollars* is stuck on our number as reporters try to buy the inside scoop on our family's nefarious gangster. Everyone is unquestioningly accepting Johann's guilt and trying to cash in on the windfall. Each ring of the phone causes my brother, sister and me to fight to answer it first. After nearly killing each other we finally agree to take turns answering. No matter who calls it counts as one turn.

Stephan gets to answer the first call. It's the *Midnight Sun* and he sells them his exclusive story on 'My Father the Mob Enforcer' for one hundred bucks.

Kristen goes second and talks to some guy from *Penthouse* who offers her ten thousand dollars if she will bare all, literally, for a pictorial in *Penthouse* entitled 'Daughter of the Mob Exposed'. She's not sure if she'll do it or not because she's worried that people will think she's a slut. I don't see why she's bothered – from all reports anyone who has seen Bambi Bosoms' act already knows she is one.

I get the third call. Life is unfair. It's my mother. Lucretia is calling to tell me that she is wheeling and dealing from her hospital bed. For a thousand dollars she has told *The National Enquirer* that Johann forced the Seconal tablets down her throat causing her to be locked away in the nuthouse.

The fourth call is Stephan's. It's *True Detective*. He sells them his exclusive story of 'My Father the Mob Enforcer' for two hundred fifty dollars. I ask Stephan if he has any moral problems with selling his exclusive story twice. "No," he says succinctly.

The next call is picked up by Kristen. *The Star* is willing to give her a hundred dollars for incriminating pictures of our private Mafia chief. Kristen offers them a picture of Johann and Lucretia dressed as Bonnie and Clyde from a Halloween party five years ago, replete with our father holding a toy submachine gun, for a mere five hundred bucks. They accept and their representative will be over with the money for the picture in an hour.

I eagerly await my turn. The phone rings and I dive to pick it up. It's Father O'Brien. He wants to apologize for hitting and excommunicating me. "You just cost me money for that?" I shout, angrily slamming the phone down.

Stephan fields the next call. It's Mike Wallace from *60 Minutes*. He wants to interview me about last night's riot. Stephan asks him for money before any interviews can happen. Wallace hangs up on him. Stephan calls him a cheap bastard and throws the phone down.

Kristen gets the next call and agrees to sell her diary for four hundred dollars to some newspaper in England. "I never knew you had a diary," I remark.

"I didn't, but I do now," she replies handing me the phone.

So far everyone has made money except me. I'm the one who told the cops to look for Johann. I'm the one who saw Brian Savage die. Where's my share? I cross my fingers and wait impatiently for the next call.

The phone rings. I say a little prayer under my breath as I answer it. God is not listening. It is Johann calling from jail. I may have to rethink my religious beliefs.

My father can't understand why he has been brought back in chains from France to be questioned about Salvatore Veneruzzo's murder. The police have no evidence, only an anonymous underworld source who claims Sal gave me a Corvette as some sort of payment for a Mafia rubout.

I change the subject and ask him how the cops caught up with him.

He doesn't want to talk about it.

Two months ago when Johann disagreed with a *Globe Republican* editorial condemning fluoridation as a communist plot to undermine the moral fabric of American society, he canceled our subscription. Regrettably no one bothered to tell Duke, whose job it had been to retrieve the morning paper. On the six days a week that the arch-conservative rag is published our dog has tried to rectify the delivery man's apparent mistake by taking a copy from one of our neighbors.

I am particularly glad Duke has secured today's edition because in the center of the front page, under the caption:

REPUTED MAFIA DON QUESTIONED

is a picture of a handcuffed Johann being escorted into Clayton police headquarters. Accompanying the photo is an interview with a Parisian gendarme, Jacques Belanger, concerning the apprehension of my father. According to Belanger the French cops, acting on a tip from Interpol, found Johann in Madame Claude's infamous brothel. The initial identification of the suspect proved difficult since he was disguised as a scantily clad woman.

Next to the interview is an article in which Chief of Police Howard D. Watt admits that there is at the present time insufficient evidence to link Johann to the Salvatore Veneruzzo execution. Therefore, Watt had no choice but to release my father, albeit reluctantly. However, the Chief stresses, Johann is still considered a prime suspect and the investigation is continuing. In further developments Watt reveals that the police have recovered a few shell casings from the crime scene which have been sent to the FBI's laboratories in Washington D.C. for analysis.

In a front page editorial the editors of *The Globe Republican* decry the Clayton Police's handling of the melee which claimed the life of Brian Savage:

> *The First Article of the Bill of Rights says "Congress shall make no law...abridging the freedom of speech or of the press; or of the right of the people peaceably to assemble and to petition the Government for a redress of grievances.*
>
> *The conduct of the Clayton Police on Saturday evening culminating in the death of the crusading reporter, Brian Savage, is a direct affront to our sacred and fundamental rights as guaranteed by the Constitution. It is a sad day indeed when reporters are butchered and led in chains to jail. Our Founding Fathers would certainly share our dismay at the brutal response of Chief Howard D. Watt's minions to the disturbance outside the home of gangster Johann Thibault.*
>
> *We, the supposedly Free Press of America, cannot condone such outrageous behavior from those whose sworn duty is to protect our rights – not to trample them. Having lost faith*

in Chief Watt's ability to act with proper restraint we must strongly urge the Federal Justice Department to intervene and launch an investigation into this blatant affront to our cherished Civil Rights.

The community is up in arms. We cannot be silenced on this matter.

I turn on the television. Channel 6 is eulogizing Brian Savage as a 'giant among men' who died defending the American constitution. Repulsed, I switch to Channel 7 where Mary Ecclestone, nursing a black eye, is talking about her humiliating experience in jail. "I spent four hours locked up with the foul mouthed deranged woman who started the riot by attacking me," she complains before I can change stations. Channel 3 is also decrying the brutal suppression of the media. "The whole nation is up in arms," news anchor Darren McTavish claims. "To sample the angry mood of the public we go to our reporter, Ernie Skidmore, in front of the Clayton court house."

"Thanks Darren. I'm standing here in the extremely irate community of Clayton. The barbarous treatment of the press is a hot topic here and the citizenry is outraged. Let me stop this gentleman and ask him for his opinion." He shoves his microphone in front of a conservatively dressed middle aged white man. "Sir, could you tell me what your reaction is to the inhuman treatment of the press during the Johann Thibault riot?"

"The press had it coming. It's too bad they didn't off a few more of those pompous assholes," the man replies before an embarrassed Ernie Skidmore can pull the microphone away from him.

"There's one in every crowd," Skidmore laughs tensely and grabs an elderly black woman, "let's ask this lady what she thinks."

"They should have finished the job, they should have shot the whole lot of you..."

I'm glad I'm watching color television, because I can see Skidmore's face becoming red with vexation.

"Let me try someone else, Darren," he stops a hippy looking guy with a peace sign around his neck and asks him for his reaction.

"Wow man, it was cool, they should have wasted the whole press while they had a chance, except for Mary Ecclestone, 'cause she's got great knockers. I'd like to fuck her."

"Don't you dare talk about my girlfriend like that," Ernie Skidmore reveals his love life by slugging out the hippy. While the cameras roll we get to see the whole Clayton community pull together as they come to the hippy's defense and beat the shit out of Ernie Skidmore.

The Clayton police must have been reading the newspaper. They decide to use proper restraint

FEED THE DOG

and refuse to suppress the enraged citizenry.

It's too bad I have to go to school. I'm sure I would learn a lot more about the United States Constitution as it relates to our everyday life through television than I would by attending Mrs. Ogilve's sixth period Social Studies class.

♪

Having a reputed Mafia crime boss as a father has its rewards. Kevin Futterman, whose vocational tests came back showing him as suited only to becoming a member of a motorcycle gang, is suddenly extremely solicitous. Also, Mr. Hucul catches me before assembly and tells me he has determined last week's biology quiz was culturally biased against gangsters' children, and therefore the results have been thrown out.

I'm actually looking forward to assembly. Although I've been staring at her poster practically every waking moment, this is the first time I've seen Nina in person since Friday night. We hold hands and I manage to accidentally brush my arm against her breasts several times while a harried looking Basil O'Reilly motions everyone to quiet down.

"Ladies and gentlemen, the St. Louis chapter of the American Red Cross will be conducting it's annual blood drive today on campus. I am sure you all know the importance of this event. Each year thousands of lives are saved by blood transfusions which would not be possible without the gift of life from people such as yourselves. But this year there is an added reward for your contribution. The Missouri Association of Liquor and Cigarette Distributors, in conjunction with the Stanley Komadoski Memorial Hemophiliac Foundation, is granting a twenty-five thousand dollar endowment to the school district which gives the most blood. I want to win this award for all of us, so I'm adding a little bit more incentive by giving today off from school to every student donating a pint of blood."

Needless to say every kid wants to be a great humanitarian and help the Clayton school district win the award. Even Rachel Collyard, who recently got over hepatitis, joins the queue around the bloodmobile. Poor Rachel, the Red Cross won't accept her tainted blood. It looks like she's going to be the only kid in Clayton going to school today.

While I stand in line with Nina a nurse comes around and asks if I want to be an organ donor. All I have to do is complete and sign the form she hands me. I fill it out, and forge Stephan's signature thereby donating his eyes, lungs, kidneys and liver to medicine. I write on the bottom that they can come around to our place any time to collect.

After about a half hour wait it's our turn. Nina and I are instructed to lie down on beds along side of each other. I've never given blood before and I'm not sure what part of the body they draw it from. I ask Nina, and she says they take it from your arm. Too bad, I was hoping it would be from somewhere where she would have to take off her sweater.

It doesn't hurt that much, they give me an orange to suck on and say I might feel dizzy for a while. That's cool with me because it will give me an excuse to lean on Nina if I should feel faint.

I ask Nina what she wants to do with her day off.

"I want to get the new *Crawdaddy*. I hear it has a cover article on Bowie." So we walk to the newsstand which is right down the street next door to Elmer's House of Doughnuts. We can't find the issue so Nina asks the clerk when he's getting the magazine.

"You're her, aren't you sweetheart?" the heavily tattooed man asks Nina.

"I beg your pardon?" Nina says.

"You're this girl, aren't you? Can I have your autograph?" he asks, handing Nina a pen and Ace Industries' best-selling poster. "Will you please sign it 'To Al, thanks for last night'?"

"Where did you get that?" Nina cries.

"I bought it for ten bucks like everyone else," the clerk says, unaware that you can get it for only four-ninety-five at Big Dick's record store. "So honey, won't you sign it – please? All my friends will be in awe of me."

Nina is neither as awed nor as appreciative as Al is upon her first viewing of Basil O'Reilly's masterpiece. She reaches into her purse, pulls out a canister of mace and sprays the man. He screams and drops the poster. Nina grabs it and runs out of the newsstand smack into Officer Ronnie Watt, who just happened to pick this moment to emerge from next door carrying a cup of coffee and a sack of doughnuts.

Nina has been hit with a two count indictment. The first is for felonious assault with intent to cause grave bodily injury for the mace attack. The second charge is a misdemeanor for malicious destruction of city property. She is alleged to have destroyed the two dollar fifty-seven cent bag of doughnuts which was owned by the City of Clayton Police Department.

Since Nina's parents have banned me from seeing her I can't call them to throw her bail. Lucretia

FEED THE DOG

is in the hospital, Johann is God knows where, and Marge Bender has enough problems already and besides would probably kill me for hanging out with her rival. There is only one place to turn for help.

I put a dime in the pay phone and dial N-O-S-A-T-A-N. Sister Marie answers.

"Hello, this is Ric Thibault calling. May I please speak to Archbishop Frontere?"

"He's, um, all tied up at the moment, can he call you back?"

"It's an emergency, I'm at the police station."

"Oh, hold on a second I'll get him."

I hear some whispers and then what sounds like the rattling of chains accompanied by the sound of someone literally hopping toward the phone.

"Sister Marie says you're at the police station; are you under arrest? You haven't talked have you? What's going on?" questions the panicking Archbishop.

"I'm fine, it's my girlfriend, Nina Pennington, who has been arrested. She maced some guy because he wanted her to autograph a poster of her naked."

"Your girlfriend posed naked for some poster and now she's upset? That's common in my line of work. You get a young girl sucked into the evil world of pornography and then, when confronted with her evil deeds, she sees the error of her ways and is embarrassed..."

"No, that's not what happened. This picture isn't posed. Some pervert secretly photographed Nina in the girl's locker room at Clayton High. He must have sold the film to a company called Ace Industries and now they're selling it all over town. Nina never knew anything about it; that's why she maced the guy."

"You said Ace Industries?"

"Yes. Wasn't that Mr. Veneruzzo's company?"

"Um, yes I believe it may have been. Listen I'm coming right down there as soon as I get dressed. Don't you or Nina say anything to anybody until I get there. I'll straighten everything out."

I hang up wondering why the Archbishop would need to get dressed if he's already in the same room with Sister Marie. The Church sure operates in mysterious ways.

All charges have been dropped against Nina and her criminal record has been expunged. All she has to do is make restitution to the City of Clayton for the two dollar fifty-seven cents worth of destroyed doughnuts.

Nina is not calmed by the outcome. I offer to pay for the doughnuts, but that doesn't cheer her up. She says she is traumatized.

Upon leaving police headquarters the Archbishop is approached by a frumpy man with a camera. "I beg your pardon Your Excellency, I'm Neil Posavad, the crime reporter for *The Evening Tribune*. May I ask you what brings you here?"

"Nothing really son, I just wanted to pay a parking ticket," he fibs demonstrating to me the proper usage of a white lie.

Neil Posavad asks the Archbishop if he can take a picture of him paying the ticket.

"I'm sorry, but I've already paid it."

"Well then, can I just get a picture of you outside the parking violations bureau?" Archbishop Frontere agrees and walks back across the hall to accommodate the reporter.

Nina is still distraught while we wait for the Archbishop to return. She leans on my shoulder and sobs, "Welcome to the worst day of my life. What kind of pervert would take pictures like that? What am I going to do?"

"Only an asshole could have taken that picture," I answer firmly while trying to soothe her with a hug.

The Archbishop returns and asks us to ride back to his office with him so that we can figure out what to do about the posters.

We get to his house and His Excellency has Sister Marie get us some brandy to 'fortify our spirits'. While Sister Marie is pouring the liquor Nina breaks down again in tears, "I can't look anyone in the face again knowing that they've seen me naked, it's embarrassing. I'm going to have to withdraw from society...maybe I should become a nun."

I drop my glass at this devastating idea. It doesn't break, but I've spilled brandy all over the coffee table. I hope Nina's not serious – nuns take a vow of chastity and can't have sex with their boyfriends. Sister Marie doesn't seem too happy either as she helps me soak up the liquor with a couple of napkins, I hope I didn't ruin the table – it looks like one of those antiques you always see in snotty magazines like *Architectural Digest*. Archbishop Frontere seems too preoccupied with the possibility of having a new recruit to notice. He puts his hand on her knee, "That's an excellent solution. The Church always has a place for a girl of your moral caliber..."

Sister Marie reaches for the bottle, takes a swig directly from it and interrupts, "Let's not be too hasty. My dear, cloistered life is not for one as young and beautiful as you. I'm sure the Archbishop can solve this problem without you doing anything as drastic as turning your back on both the outside world and your loved ones."

If looks could kill there would be two members of the clergy pushing up the daisies from the way Archbishop Frontere and Sister Marie are glaring at each other.

Finally the Archbishop stands up and asks if Nina and I would mind excusing Sister Marie and himself for a moment while they discuss some urgent Church business.

Sister Marie follows him upstairs. I hear a door slam, and then some indecipherable conversation. Nina chugs down her brandy and I pour her another glass. A few moments later a somewhat cowed Archbishop Frontere and a steel-faced Sister Marie return.

"Sister Marie has had an idea. I'm the executor of the late Salvatore Veneruzzo's estate; so I might have a little bit of sway over at Ace Industries. I think we should be able to nip this problem in the bud and stop any more posters from being distributed."

Nina is still emotional. "You mean you're friends with the people who are trying to ruin my life?" she bawls. "How can I trust you?"

"Nina, I work for God, which means my job is to be the friend to all creatures – whether they are good or bad. If the Ace Industries people did something wrong and I can convince them of the error of their ways it will be a service to everyone concerned. If you can't trust me, then who can you trust?"

"I'm sorry, Your Excellency. I trust you," Nina snivels.

"No apology is necessary my dear, I know how you must feel." he says patting her knee again while Sister Marie develops a sudden coughing fit. The Archbishop jumps up and goes over to where the nun is sitting. He grasps her hand and her coughing stops immediately. I think to myself the power of the Catholic Church is truly awesome. Brother Theodore and his faith healers couldn't cure her any faster. Neither could Robitussen.

"What am I going to do about the ones that already have gotten out? My parents will kill me if they ever find out about them." Nina asks.

"We can get Ace Industries to recall all the unsold posters, but I'm afraid there's nothing I can do about those that have already been sold. As for your parents I'll talk to them for you. Meanwhile, I'm going to have my new head of security, Kelly O'Shea, investigate how this filth got into circulation."

A feeling of dread engulfs me. I hope they can't trace the poster back to Lucretia Thibault's credit card. My mother has enough problems already.

Kristen tells me that Billy has been looking for me about something important, so I go over to his house. I find him in the living room with Marge and a weaselish looking man in a three piece suit. Billy introduces him as his high priced lawyer, Julius Rotter.

Billy is excited, "You're not going to believe this. You remember that guy in the seersucker jacket at the Shady Oak who said he saw everything? Well, guess what, Mr. Rotter told me that he was Louis Palazarri the guy who got killed with Sal Veneruzzo in your mom's car! Now all we have to do is convince Stephan not to testify and I'll be home free."

"Stephan is a creep and he hates your guts, so how are you going to convince him?" I ask.

"I don't know, maybe I can bribe him," Billy says,

"Billy, it is my sworn duty as an officer of the court not to permit you to indulge in such behavior," admonishes Rotter.

"I thought I was paying you to get my son off," Marge says, agitated.

"Mrs. Bender, I'm going to be frank with you. Your son is incredibly guilty and everyone knows it. If my alimony payments weren't so high and my insurance company hadn't just raised my malpractice rates I wouldn't touch this case with a ten foot pole. Now, I understand that you are paying me good money to defend your boy – and I appreciate it. But I am not going to violate legal ethics by being party to illegal acts just to keep your little juvenile delinquent out of the jail cell he so richly deserves."

"What if I give you a bonus if you get Billy off?" Marge inquires.

"Excuse me," I interrupt, "but did you know that Stephan has been certified as crazy by the United States Marines?"

"What?" Rotter and Marge exclaim in unison.

"Well I happen to know that if you talk to a Sergeant Markell at the Marine recruiting center he will tell you Stephan has been classified as mentally unbalanced and unfit to serve in the armed forces."

"If this is true it means they have no credible witnesses and no case, doesn't it?" Marge asks.

"Exactly how much of a bonus are we talking about?" Rotter wants to know.

Marge tells him to fuck off and use the kitchen phone to call Sergeant Markell.

A few minutes later a smiling Julius Rotter returns saying the Marines will provide an affidavit swearing that Stephan is a paranoid schizophrenic.

While Billy escorts the lawyer to his car, Marge grabs my crotch and tells me she feels eternally in my debt and wants to start paying me back in the most meaningful way she can think of as soon as possible.

I think I'd rather have cash.

♪

"I want to speak with Ric Thibault." a heavily British accented voice demands over the phone.

"This is Ric Thibault."

"Oh jolly good. Ric, my name is Derek Irons, I'm the manager of Suckerpunch and I got your number from my friend, Jimmy Leach."

Alarms are going off in my brain from Irons saying he's a friend of Jimmy's. Disaster must be close at hand. But against my better judgment, which says to hang up immediately, I elect to be polite and hear what he has to say.

"We've got a couple of big shows coming up opening for David Bowie. The band and I have decided we need to fill out our sound by adding a rhythm guitar. Jimmy tells me you're a pretty good guitarist, and I was wondering if you'd be interested in coming down and auditioning for the band."

"I've heard their album and know all their songs," I say, omitting the fact that they suck.

Irons tells me to meet him at Opus Studios tomorrow night at eight. "We'll have you meet the guys and run through a few songs," he says.

I hang up having visions of riding in limousines with Bowie and Dominique while throngs of adoring long legged, big breasted groupies in short skirts compete for my attention. I'll be destroying hotel rooms, throwing up in public places and getting named in paternity suits by famous models.

I go upstairs to my room and get my guitar. I look up at the ceiling and see the poster, thereby revising my daydreams to include my love of life. Nina and Dominique are shopping at Tiffany's and I'm waiting for them in the limo with Bowie. David is saying how jealous he is of me that I have a goddess for a wife, "I'd give it all up for the love of a perfect woman like your Nina. Does she have a sister, and could you get her to autograph this 'To Dave, thanks for last night'?" he asks, unrolling a copy of Ace Industries' best-selling poster.

I put the Suckerpunch record on the turntable and play guitar along with the first song, *I'm Stupid And So Are You*;

I really hate your girlfriends,
they hate me too
I wanna call and tell them
I'm stupid and so are you

The tune is not as bad as I remember. I might have found the ticket out of Clayton. I'm on the verge of escaping the most boring place in the world where nothing ever happens.

I call Nina to inform her of my upcoming audition. If things go right she might finally get to meet Bowie.

"Hello?" Mr. Pennington answers the phone.

"May I please speak with Nina?"

"May I tell her who is calling please?"

"Ric Thibault."

"Listen you little bastard. I don't want your type ever calling here again. Do you understand me?" *Click*.

I go to bed staring at Nina's poster. I fantasize of someday getting even with Zachary Pennington. I'll be the worst son-in-law he could ever have.

Mr. Harlow from down the block is at the door asking if I have by any chance mistakenly taken his copy of Tuesday morning's *Globe Republican*.

"First of all, I haven't even been out yet, as you should be able to tell by my standing here shivering in my pajamas. Second, stealing is a sin, and I resent the accusation."

He apologizes and retreats to look for his paper, which he won't find because Duke brought it in half an hour ago.

I examine the front page and find that my celebrity status is intact. My father has managed to get himself in the headlines again. Under the banner:

POLICE PROBE MAFIA BOSS
THIBAULT'S NEIGHBOR

is the latest on the Veneruzzo rubout:

FEED THE DOG

> *According to Federal Bureau of Investigation spokeswoman Geraldine B. MacEarchern, tests conducted by the F.B.I.'s lab on shell casings found near the bodies of Salvatore Veneruzzo and Louis Palazarri have been linked to a sporting goods store owned by Kevin Bender. Bender, whose next door neighbor is prime suspect and reputed Mafia boss Johann Thibault, is also the father of Billy Bender, the alleged instigator of the Shady Oak Riot, whose trial is set to begin today. Clayton Police refuse to identify the elder Bender as a member of the Thibault crime family, but will state only that they are pursuing their investigation into possible links between the two men.*

Meanwhile the muckrakers are working overtime. Next to the story on my father's latest dealings with the police, under the caption:

WHAT'S HE HIDING?

is a picture of Archbishop Frontere standing outside the parking violations bureau. Neil Posavad's accompanying story tells how he was merely doing a routine human interest piece on a famous person paying a parking ticket when:

> *After snapping the cleric's picture this reporter talked to a parking fines department clerk who claimed that the Archbishop was never there. Upon further questioning* The Globe Republican *has learned that Frontere was actually at the office of Clayton Police Chief Howard D. Watt. According to an anonymous source the Archbishop was successful in having felony charges against a clearly guilty criminal dropped. A city already terrorized by Judge Irving Heinz's release of Billy Bender now faces the prospect of another thug lurking about its streets preparing to continue vicious assaults on a defenseless community.*

Albeit for different reasons I agree with Johann's decision to cancel our subscription to *The Globe Republican*. Clearly the paper is prejudiced against both our friends and family.

However, the front page is not without its good news. The results of a Harris poll taken yesterday are in. Asked their opinion of the Clayton Police's treatment of the press during the Johann Thibault riot, eighty-seven percent of those responding felt that the police acted properly. Six percent felt that the police used too much restraint and four percent had no opinion. Only three percent of the population felt that the press were wrongfully treated. I fall into the latter minority group. I don't think Mary Ecclestone should have been arrested immediately. She should have been allowed to complete her interview with me before being jailed. The poll has pissed off the local media.

According to the paper all radio, television and print journalists are mounting a one day strike to protest the death of Brian Savage and the subsequent jailing of the Saint Louis press corps by Chief Watt. There will be neither newspapers nor television news tomorrow. We will have to suffer without our vigilant guardians of civil liberties for one day. We will also have to forego the comics and the sports page.

There is further good news. On page six, adjacent to a two sentence Reuters report on the death of seven thousand people in an earthquake in Bangladesh, is coverage of yesterday's blood drive. The bloodmobile collected more blood from Clayton High than had ever been gathered from any previous location in its history. The Missouri Association of Liquor and Cigarette Distributors will present a twenty-five thousand dollar check to Basil O'Reilly today in recognition of our school's achievement.

It's reassuring to know that the Missouri Association of Liquor and Cigarette Distributors cares so much about the health of our community.

There is another knock on the door. While Kristen answers it I hide the newspaper just in case it's Mr. Harlow again. He can be persistent.

My fears are allayed. Billy Bender comes bounding in the kitchen with a present. He hands me a subpoena for his trial. "Don't worry, no one is going to call on you to testify. I got a whole bunch of these for all my friends so they can get out of school today."

I ask him if he got one for Nina. He did. Today is going to be a good day. I can feel it.

Outside the courtroom the betting line favors Billy being convicted on at least one count. I am able to get two to one odds on ten dollars from Justin Lafayette that Billy will walk free. Roger Lefley wants to bet me too, but he wants to call it a push if Billy gets probation. I think I should win in that event so we're unable to book a wager.

We go inside and wait for the trial. Nina, Roger, Kevin Micheletti and I all sit down behind the defense table in a show of solidarity with our classmate. Justin sits with us but since he has money riding against Billy, I don't think his motives are as pure. Maybe he should be sitting with Stephan over on the prosecution's side of the aisle.

Like a handicapper at the track inspecting the horses before a race I check out the lawyers. Julius Rotter looks both sleazy and confident in his three piece sharkskin suit. I can't see the prosecutor, so

FEED THE DOG

I lean forward and ask Billy in a whisper where he is. He points to a red haired woman in a black dress who is sitting at the opposite table. "That's the bitch," he whispers as the bailiff orders us to rise in honor of Judge Irving Heinz's entrance.

If I were on the jury I'd vote to convict Billy. Assistant District Attorney Annette Stratton-Osborne has the best legs I've ever seen. Even Nina is looking at them, but she claims she's only paying attention to the prosecutor's Charles Jourdan pumps which she says would make anyone, even cousin Julie, look good. Roger Lefley checks out the Jourdan patent leather shoes too, and whispers in my ear that Annette Stratton-Osborne isn't wearing any underwear. "Look at the reflection," he says.

I check it out but I can't see anything. Nina wants to know what I'm staring at and I tell her I really like the prosecutor's high heels. I ask her if she has any Charles Jourdans. She says she can't afford them. They cost over a hundred bucks a pair, and she only gets two dollars a week allowance. Just then I catch a reflection, although I can't make out exactly what it is that I'm seeing. Roger could be right. I decide that if I can sell my story to *The National Enquirer* I'll buy Nina a pair of Jourdan patent leather pumps.

The jurors are transfixed by Annette Stratton-Osborne's opening statement. Roger and I aren't paying too much attention to what she is saying but we're transfixed nonetheless.

"The prosecution will prove beyond a shadow of doubt that Billy Bender, with malice aforethought, launched a wanton attack not only upon the patrons seated below the Shady Oak's balcony, but upon the fundamental moral fabric of our society. No civilized community can function when the basic right to sit unmolested in a movie theater is challenged by hooligans armed with soggy corn flakes. We have a witness, and," Stratton-Osborne holds up a clear plastic bag full of a yellowish brown goo, "we have the evidence."

Stratton-Osborne holds the bag up so the jury can see Billy's lethal mixture which was painstakingly gathered from the scene of the crime. She turns and starts back to her seat when she somehow drops the bag. It falls to the floor breaking open and oozing its foul-smelling contents all over the place. "Oh fuck," Stratton-Osborne mutters, bending down and trying to gather up the evidence. As she reaches down her skirt rides up exposing her garter belt.

"I object. The District Attorney is deliberately trying to sway the jury with her lurid invitation to commit fornication, and her suggestive striptease, plus she's tampering with the evidence," Julius Rotter shouts.

"Counsel approach the bench," Judge Heinz demands.

Stratton-Osborne abandons her efforts to gather up the spilled evidence and walks toward the Judge. Enroute, she slips on the slimy corn flakes and tumbles to the floor.

Roger is right. She isn't wearing any underwear.

"She's doing it again Your Honor," complains Rotter.

Judge Heinz eyes the prosecutor sprawled in the corn flake slime doing her imitation of a fish out of water. "Objection overruled." I try to cancel the bet with Justin Lafayette, but he says a bet is a bet and I'm welcome to pay up anytime.

Stratton-Osborne gets up and confers with Rotter and the Judge in hushed tones. I ask Roger if he knows what they are talking about. He thinks Judge Heinz is ordering her to go get some underwear. I offer Roger two to one odds on a dollar that he doesn't. Roger takes the bet. Nina says we're being sexist pigs and refuses to hold hands with me anymore, which is probably good anyway from the way Marge Bender is glaring at us.

"We will declare an hour recess for the District Attorney to get cleaned up and properly attired," Judge Heinz declares.

I pay Roger the two bucks.

We've got an hour to kill. Nina and Justin want to go across the street to Nedomansky's coffee shop and talk about tonight's Suckerpunch audition. We get up to leave but my path is blocked by Stephan who is acting friendly.

He must want something.

"Ric, I want to introduce you to Jasper Gilbertson of *The Midnight Sun*," he pushes me in the direction of a balding guy with his shirttail hanging out. "Jasper is writing a story on the anguish we're going through with our father being in the Mafia."

"Hello, I'm Ric Thibault, and our father is not in the Mafia – and no one I know is anguished," I add heading for the door to rejoin my friends.

While walking out I hear Stephan and Gilbertson arguing about my brother hustling *The Midnight Sun*. "You better not be making this up or I'll get more than my hundred dollars back," the reporter threatens.

I think today isn't going to be one of Stephan's better days.

In the hall I run into Clyde Zanussi. He's coming out a door with a sign saying 'Do Not Disturb - Grand Jury In Session'. I invite him to accompany us across the street, but he says he can't – he has to go home and get all his bank statements for the last three years.

Annette Stratton-Osborne calls her first witness, Stephan Thibault.

Roger leans over and whispers that the District Attorney is still not wearing any underwear. I scrutinize her shoes, but she's changed to a pair of red suede heels which don't reflect anything. Nina babbles something about them being made by some trendy Italian guy named Fiorucci while I ponder how Roger knows so much about the state of Stratton-Osborne's undergarments.

"Do you solemnly swear to tell the truth, the whole truth and nothing but the truth so help you God?" asks the bailiff.

"I do," Stephan swears.

"Mr. Thibault, can you please explain what happened at the Shady Oak Theater on the evening preceding Easter?"

"I was watching *Love Story* with my girlfriend when I heard someone making vomiting noises from above me. I looked up and saw the defendant, Billy Bender, dropping soggy corn flakes from the balcony."

"You're positive that it was Billy Bender?"

"Absolutely."

"No further questions, Your Honor."

Julius Rotter walks slowly over to the witness stand like a coyote stalking his prey. I'm jealous. It's not fair that a stranger like Rotter should have all the fun of making my brother squirm.

I imagine it's me up there cross-examining Stephan. *"Mr. Thibault, you have been sworn to tell the whole truth so help you God correct? You know that this sacred oath means you will rot in Hell for eternity if you lie. So please tell the court about the money you stole from Lucretia's purse, your magazines in that stupid hiding place behind the bookcase, and the time you dumped thirty dollars worth of Jell-O in Clayton High's swimming pool."*

My daydream stops when Rotter moves in for the kill. "Mr. Thibault, I have here an affidavit from the United States Marines which says you are, and I quote, 'a paranoid schizophrenic walking time bomb, with no firm grounding in reality'."

Stephan has a look of total confusion on his face while Stratton-Osborne jumps to her feet, "I object. Stephan Thibault is not on trial here, Billy Bender is."

"The defense feels Thibault's mental health is of great importance to this trial Your Honor. We have psychiatric evidence proving he is suffering from a form of mental illness which impairs his ability to distinguish between fantasy and reality. Therefore we contend his testimony cannot be accepted as credible."

"I object too," Stephan complains, "are you trying to say I'm crazy...and what is this about the Marines?"

"You're only a witness, you can't object," Judge Heinz states, "now be quiet while I rule on the matter. Counsel approach the bench."

"He's saying I'm a lunatic like my mother and you expect me to be quiet? That's bullshit."

"If you don't settle down, I'll hold you in contempt of court," warns the Judge.

"I'm not in contempt of court, I'm in contempt of him," Stephan points to Rotter.

Judge Heinz has had enough, "I find you in contempt. The bailiff will remand you into custody as soon as you finish testifying."

Rotter hands Judge Heinz the affidavit. He reads it and passes the document to the prosecutor. She glances at it and grimaces. The two attorneys and Heinz confer briefly and the Judge motions them to return to their tables.

"The objection is overruled. Due to the lack of credible witnesses and the prosecution's destruction of physical evidence I am prepared to entertain a motion for dismissal on all counts."

Julius Rotter makes the motion and it is quickly granted. Billy Bender is a free man. Stephan Thibault, on the other hand, isn't. Judge Heinz sentences him to eight hours in jail for his outburst. Poor stupid Stephan, if he was smart he could have pleaded insanity and probably gotten off.

I give Nina a good long celebratory hug and then go settle accounts with Justin Lafayette. He claims my organized crime family's friends somehow managed to fix Billy's trial, but he pays me the twenty bucks anyway.

Jasper Gilbertson wants to know what my reaction is to seeing Stephan thrown in the slammer. I see no reason to give him free quotes to use in order to sell more of his scuzzy tabloids. However, for a thousand dollars I offer him my exclusive perspective on the agony of belonging to a cursed family ripped apart by the twin scourges of mental illness and crime.

Gilbertson agrees if I will permit my picture to be taken for the story.

Julius Rotter cheerfully volunteers to draw up a quick one page handwritten contract for Gilbertson and me to sign. The lawyer charges me one hundred dollars, payable upon my receipts of

FEED THE DOG

payment from the *Midnight Sun*.

I pose for the camera outside the courthouse. "You're supposed to be tormented – so quit smiling," Gilbertson directs.

I will probably never be an actor. It takes two hours and ten rolls of film before I finally manage to wipe the grin off my face.

♪

I drive to the mental hospital. I can't wait to tell my mother that she's not the only one in our family capable of making a thousand bucks selling a story to the tabloids.

Walking down the hall I can hear Kristen in my mother's room stealing my thunder. She's explaining she has accepted *Penthouse's* ten thousand dollar offer for the pictorial.

Our mother isn't impressed with my sister's business acumen. "I cannot believe that the Almighty would curse me like this. How could I have raised a harlot?"

I share Lucretia's disappointment with my sister. Anyone who knows anything about negotiating knows better than to accept a first offer. Kristen should have held out for more money.

My mother notices me entering the room. For the first time in a long while she actually seems pleased to see me, "At least I have two sons who know the difference between right and wrong."

The task of shattering Lucretia's perception of my brother's moral integrity is left to me. "Stephan's in jail, but the good news is I made a thousand dollars selling my story to the *Midnight Sun*, and I won twenty bucks from Justin Lafayette."

"You mean Billy Bender's in jail, don't you?" my mother interrupts.

"No, Billy was acquitted. Stephan's the one in jail."

"What happened?" an upset Lucretia demands.

So I relate the trial's highlights, my bet with Justin, Stratton-Osborne's legs, her destruction of the evidence, and my deal with the *Midnight Sun*. I gloss over my bet with Roger regarding the prosecutor's lack of underwear.

"I don't care about any of that. Why is Stephan in jail?"

I spare my mother the trauma of discovering her eldest son has been publicly branded as crazy by an agency of the United States government. "Oh, he refused to listen to the Judge when he was told to shut-up and got hit with a contempt of court citation; but don't worry. He's only in jail for eight hours, he'll be home in time for dinner."

Lucretia looks depressed. It's my filial duty to try to cheer her up. "I saved the best news of the day for last. I've been asked to audition for the band Suckerpunch. Their manager called me and said he heard I was a really good guitar player. Isn't it cool? Did you know they're going out on tour with Bowie?"

Lucretia reaches over and presses the intercom button to summon a nurse. "My family is going to hell in a hand basket. I need a shot of something," she shouts, "I don't care whether it's scotch or Thorazine just bring me plenty and be quick about it."

A few seconds later my friend the nurse shows up with a magic syringe.

Lucretia passes out quickly.

Kristen and I walk out trying to figure out why, with so much good news, our mother is so despondent. My sister thinks it has something to do with the shock treatments Lucretia is getting.

I think it's that Mom is just plain crazy.

I arrive at Opus studios with my guitar and Marshall amplifier at exactly eight o'clock and am directed into Suckerpunch's rehearsal room. Other than a roadie, who is on the drum riser making out with a pudgy girl in a fringed mini-skirt, no one from the band is here.

"Excuse me, I'm Ric Thibault and I'm supposed to meet Derek Irons and Suckerpunch."

The roadie withdraws his tongue from the girl's mouth and looks at me. "I'm Billy Jo Brackenbury, you're the celebrity guitarist, huh? Well, the guys aren't here yet. They're always late so feel free to hang out and wait."

The girl says she needs to go to the bathroom and fix her makeup. I ask Billy Jo where I should set up my amp.

"It doesn't matter. You're not going to be plugged in anyway."

"How is anyone going to hear me?"

"They're not."

"How will they be able to tell if I'm playing the songs right?"

"Didn't Irons tell you you're playing air guitar? You're just here as another one of his publicity stunts."

"What are you talking about?" I ask, fearing I should have listened to those alarms when Derek Irons told me he was a friend of Jimmy Leach's.

FEED THE DOG

"All Irons cares about is publicity. He thinks getting a kid like you, whose father runs the Mafia, will get Suckerpunch written up in all the papers."

I'm caught in a dilemma. I covet standing on the same stage as David Bowie (When I get home tonight I'll have to check whether there is anything in the Bible about coveting sharing a stage. I don't think there is, however I'd rather be on the safe side when dealing with God), but I don't want to be an idiot playing air guitar. If Bowie hears me play he might want me to join his band, or at least jam with him. Then Nina will love me forever, not to mention Dominique and Boom Boom.

I have an idea.

"You said you've heard of my dad?" I ask the roadie.

"Yeah, it's pretty hard not to in this town. Is all that Mafia stuff true?"

"I only know what I read in the newspapers. But I'll tell you this – my father won't be happy if he discovers your band is trying to embarrass our family by having me play air guitar. From my experience you don't want to make Johann Thibault angry. I remember the last time I saw him mad – it wasn't a pretty sight," I say truthfully, recalling the look Johann had on his face upon discovering me in Pekin, Illinois.

"Let me set up your amp," Billy Jo offers, "and then I'd be happy to change strings and tune your guitar for you."

Derek Irons shows up about half an hour later with Jimmy Leach in tow. Irons is a stereotypical Englishman – thin, pale, bad teeth, trendy shoes, limp handshake, and breath smelling like Jack Daniels rents a room inside his mouth.

Both Irons and Jimmy must have caught colds, they are sporadically wiping their noses and sniffling. I think it's gross, especially since Jimmy has a white blotch of something hanging from under his left nostril. I try to hand him a Kleenex from the box on top of the mixing console, but he looks at me like I'm crazy, "I don't have to fucking blow my nose stupid."

I confront Derek Irons about his plans, "When you called me this morning you said you wanted to fill out the sound by adding a rhythm guitarist. You didn't say anything about me playing air guitar."

Irons claims he doesn't understand what I'm talking about.

"Billy Jo told me I wasn't supposed to plug into an amp, and that you brought me here to cash in on my father's purported ties to organized crime."

He scowls at the roadie for a second and asks if he can talk to Billy Jo outside. While they are having their conference I try to pump Jimmy for information. Jimmy asks me if I still have any Quaaludes.

"I'll give you one if you tell me what the fuck is going on. Is Irons just trying to use me as a publicity gimmick?"

"When do I get the 'lude?" Jimmy asks.

"I don't have any with me, but I promise to give you one tomorrow."

"Okay. Here's the deal. Derek Irons manages Suckerpunch but Sal Veneruzzo owned the band lock, stock and barrel. Everyone knew Veneruzzo was in the Mafia. Whores, drugs, and money are what make the world go round, and Sal was using everything at his disposal to get the record played. Now that Sal's dead no one is paying for airplay, and every station in the country has dropped the band like a hot potato. Since everyone knows your dad is a Mob boss, Derek figures you joining Suckerpunch will get radio to think they'll start getting payola again if they put the album back in heavy rotation. Do you understand what I'm saying?"

"That Irons is out of his mind?"

"Yeah, but he has great drugs to get him there, speaking of which, when do I get..."

"I told you, tomorrow."

Derek Irons returns without Billy Jo. "I'm sorry Ric, I had a talk with Billy Jo and there appears to have been a minor misunderstanding. I had asked him to make sure that I could hear you, and he thought I said to make sure that I couldn't hear you. It was an innocent mistake. So now everything's cool, right?"

I'm pretty sure he's lying, but it's probably one of those Church sanctioned fibs the Archbishop was telling me about. Besides I want to go on tour opening up for Bowie. So I forgive him. "I've got no problems."

"Good," he puts his arm around my shoulder, "Before the band gets here I want to give you a little background on the lads. Suckerpunch's leader is Mick Masters. Mick is a great singer, but not exactly a rocket scientist. The reason we print the tour dates on all the merchandising items is so Mick can stop any fan or roadie around, read the T-shirt and find out where he is supposed to be. Rico 'Bam Bam' Ross is a tremendous drummer, but he's strictly low IQ, high r.p.m. The bass player goes by Simon Q. Picasso, but his real name is Herbie Paruszkiewicz. Simon is a damn good bass player but he's a trifle, no, actually he's extraordinarily insecure. The only reason he joined the band was to make enough money to pay for his daily sessions with his analyst. The only one who's right in the head is Bernie Hrechkosy, the guitarist. His parole officer is right, Bernie is a good guy and I don't understand how he could have been involved in that unfortunate incident with those twelve year old twins. I'm sure it must be a case of mistaken identity..."

Whomp! The walls shake and cacophonous voices announce a fight taking place in the hall. "Would you like to meet the band?" Irons asks opening the door. Like bad television wrestlers two people engaged in a hair pulling contest tumble across the threshold.

"Don't you ever call me Herbie, my name is Simon Q. Picasso," screams the smaller of the two combatants who I presume to be the former Herbie Paruszkiewicz.

"Then don't fucking tell me your goddamn analyst says I have to rewrite our lyrics," expresses the other fighter, whom I recognize to be Mick Masters, while head butting Simon Q. Picasso.

"Dr. Caley is right. Your lyrics provoke violence not only in the community as a whole, but in me as an individual," explains Picasso aiming a left jab at Masters' jaw.

Irons and Billy Jo Brackenbury attempt to pull the two apart, but Simon escapes the roadie's grasp long enough to deliver the deciding blow via a solid knee to the singer's groin.

While Billy Jo tends to the groaning Masters, Irons introduces me to the three standing members of Suckerpunch. Rico 'Bam Bam' Ross explains the fight is quite normal behavior for the band, "Nothing like a good brawl to get us going in the morning."

Derek corrects 'Bam Bam' pointing out that it's nine-thirty at night, not in the morning, but the drummer doesn't seem to understand the concept and looks confused.

"Rico's a drummer and therefore has never been required to count beyond four. He can't be blamed for failing to comprehend big numbers like nine," says Bernie Hrechkosy. He pauses a moment, "Didn't Mick and I see you at Dr. Tudor's?"

I admit that he did.

"It's great to have you in the band," Bernie winks and slaps me on the back.

"Don't you want to hear me play first?" I ask.

"If you're a patient of Dr. Tudor's we like you already; but if you insist," states Masters from the floor. "Just let me have a sip of something and we'll jam."

Mick takes a few swigs of Southern Comfort and downs a couple of Budweisers as chasers before pronouncing himself properly fit to begin the audition. We run through a couple of cover songs to warm up. I have no problem with a breakneck version of The New York Dolls' *Pills*. We then do Iggy & The Stooges' *I Wanna Be Your Dog* before settling into Suckerpunch originals.

We start off with *I'm Stupid and So Are You*. I do a pretty good job catching all the chord changes and even add a few background vocals during the choruses. We follow that with Suckerpunch's anthem *Can't Keep Us Down*, and a somewhat out of tune rendition of *Let Me In* on which I get to play a few bars of lead guitar. We then launch into the band's new single, *Looking Up At Her Thighs*:

> *Been caught drinking in a river of lies*
> *Well I'm sitting on her bed*
> *yeah looking up at her thighs*
> *searching for an answer*
> *but my river has run dry*

Unfortunately the song is halted at the beginning of the second chorus when Simon trips over a guitar cable and crashes head first into Bernie's Marshall cabinets causing them to come unplugged and topple onto the fallen bass player's head.

The sight of Simon Q. Picasso sprawled unconscious with his scalp split open cheers Mick. "It makes it easier for his shrink to get inside his brain," he chortles.

Simon comes to a few minutes later, and Derek has Billy Jo take him to the hospital for stitches. Probably sensing the possibility of painkillers being prescribed, Jimmy volunteers to drive.

Derek asks if I will excuse him for a moment while he confers with the remaining musicians. I don't even have time to pack up my guitar before a smiling Mick Masters comes over and congratulates me. I'm the rhythm guitarist for Suckerpunch.

"Let's go have a drink and celebrate," suggests Rico.

"I'd love to but I'm only sixteen so I can't get served in any bars, and besides, I have to take my guitar and amp home."

"No problem, we'll stop off at a liquor store, pick up some booze, and go back to the hotel," says Derek Irons solving the problem. "As for your gear, leave it here since we need a few rehearsals before the Bowie dates."

Out in the parking lot Bernie admires my Corvette and I offer to take him out for a spin. Bernie takes me up on my offer and tells the guys we'll meet them at the Chase Park Plaza Hotel.

"I'm really excited to be joining Suckerpunch," I tell Bernie, "I can't wait to get up on stage."

"You're not half as happy as we are," Bernie says, "Now that you're in the group we'll be able to get the tour support money from those cheap bastards at Slipped Disk Records."

"How does my joining the band have anything to do with you getting money from your record company?"

"I'm not sure if you're supposed to know this – so don't tell Derek I told you – but the reason Slipped Disk used to give us money was they were scared of pissing off Sal Veneruzzo and the Mafia. Slipped Disk cut us off after Sal was killed. So Derek figures if word gets out that the head of the Mafia's kid is in Suckerpunch the record company will trip all over themselves to make us happy campers."

We drive in silence while I ponder the situation. Billy Jo was right. I'm just a bargaining chip in Irons negotiations with Slipped Disk. Finally I have to ask Bernie, "Not that it matters but tell me the truth, was I any good?"

"You won't have me killed or anything if I tell you?"

"I promise."

"As a guitarist you suck, but let's face it so does everyone else in this band. None of us are exactly artists. Artists are poor unappreciated bastards who die alone with needles in their arm in seedy fifth floor walkups. Me, I'm an entertainer."

"What's the difference between an entertainer and an artist?"

"Entertainers die with needles in their arm in the company of a couple of half-naked fashion models aboard a yacht on the Mediterranean."

We pull up to the Chase Park Plaza and have the valet park the car. In the elevator I ask Bernie whether Suckerpunch destroy hotel rooms like all the other rock stars do.

"I've discovered one should never trash one's own hotel room for two reasons. One, the hotel always makes you pay for it, and two, I prefer sleeping on an intact bed and watching a working television."

Before I can let Bernie know how disillusioned I am with his wimpy attitude he adds, "I prefer to take out my juvenile aggression differently by making everyone else suffer. In fact allow me to be the first to initiate you into senseless rock and roll vandalism."

The elevator opens on our floor and Bernie asks me to hold the door open. From his leather jacket he produces a screwdriver and takes off the plate covering the control panel. He disconnects all the wires leading to the floor selection buttons, and then reattaches them to different buttons, before screwing the plate back on.

"We have now rewired the elevator. When someone pushes the button for the eighth floor they will go promptly to the third floor. When they try to go to the lobby they will find themselves dispatched to the ninth floor. Totally untraceable mayhem – that's real rock and roll for you. Now let's walk downstairs and be rude to everyone like proper rock and roll stars."

I like Bernie Hrechkosy.

It's Wednesday and Duke is perplexed. No one bothered to tell him the *Globe Republican* has gone on strike and he is running up and down the street in a vain search for a paper. I finally go out in the trash and roll up an old one and throw it into the Harlow's front yard. The dog proudly retrieves it and returns home. I reward Duke for his dedication by supplementing his regular breakfast with the turkey sandwich my ex-convict brother had put aside for his lunchbox. Lucretia should be pleased. Despite the fact she's not even dead – I have continued faithfully to feed the dog.

Stephan is in a foul mood looking for his sandwich. "It's bad enough that Billy's lawyer framed me and that fucking asshole Heinz threw me in jail, but then I find out you stole Jasper Gilbertson."

"I didn't steal Gilbertson. He approached me for an interview after you abandoned him."

"I didn't abandon him, I was thrown in jail."

"It's not my fault you don't know when to shut up; and besides you got a hundred bucks from him."

Stephan isn't placated, "Yeah, but if it wasn't for me you would have never made the thousand."

"A thousand dollars isn't worth having you as a brother," I reply, "and furthermore, now that I'm in Suckerpunch you'll probably make a fortune giving interviews about what it's like having such a famous brother. So you should be grateful."

Stephan changes the subject, "I'm going down to the Marines to find out where they come up with this bullshit about me being crazy."

"I read somewhere that mental illness is hereditary. It usually strikes the first born. From what I remember it has something to do with the father being so horny and excited when fucking his wife the first few times that the sperm go berserk thereby creating lunatic kids. By the time the second and third kids are made it's gotten to be old hat and you get calm sperm and therefore normal children."

"That's bullshit."

"Mom was the oldest child," I remind Stephan.

"It's still bullshit."

"You want to bet five dollars?" I bluff.

Stephan thinks about it for a moment before declining and resuming his search for the missing sandwich.

I turn on the TV. Channel 3 is showing *Let's Make A Deal* in place of its regularly scheduled local newscast. I switch to Channel 7. They have replaced their news coverage with the debut of Brother Theodore's *Send Your Money To God Television Extravaganza* show. This is the first time I will be able to actually see Brother Theodore. I had always figured him to look like Billy Graham's slightly less photogenic brother, kind of the way Goober looked like Gomer Pyle when he replaced him on *The Andy Griffith Show*. My mental picture of Brother Theodore was well off the mark. He looks like Elvis Presley's tackier and slightly fatter brother with too much hair spray.

I watch a few minutes of the evangelist preaching fire and brimstone punctuated with a few sales pitches for his new line of plastic dashboard ornaments ("For just thirty-nine ninety-five of your tax deductible dollars you get not only an iridescent Virgin Mary but you will receive Jesus Our Lord and Savior on the cross. And, as a special bonus for the first one thousand callers, you will get a personally autographed poster suitable for framing of me, Brother Theodore...") before I change channels.

In place of its regularly scheduled news Channel 6 is showing a memorial retrospective on their dearly departed colleague Brian Savage. The announcer laments that the unforgettable Savage left big shoes to fill. He must have already forgotten his dearly departed colleague was a dwarf.

I switch to Channel 12. The station's management must not have supported the media strike. The regular newsmen have walked out on strike with their brethren from the other channels. But Channel 12 has hired scabs to replace them and we are not deprived of the news.

I watch as Yolanda Lopez covers the strike live from Clayton Police headquarters where the media is conducting a sit-in demonstration. Chief Howard D. Watt can be seen ordering the strikers removed and jailed. Mary Ecclestone is handcuffed and led off by Officer Seymour Stankiewicz. I notice her breasts look even bigger with her arms pulled back behind her. I wish I could understand what Yolanda Lopez is saying but she speaks in a thick Spanish accent which I can't comprehend.

The phone's ringing tears me away from the TV. It's Officer Ronnie Watt calling to let me know that the police have finished gathering evidence from my mother's car and are releasing it from the impound lot. We can pick it up anytime.

No sooner have I hung the phone up before it rings again. It's Derek Irons. *Rolling Stone* want to do a story on my joining Suckerpunch. I ask him how much they are willing to pay me.

"They're not going to pay you anything. We're lucky we don't have to pay them," he claims.

I reluctantly agree to do the interview, but I can't help wondering how good a manager Derek is. I'm sure I could have gotten at least five hundred bucks from them. Derek says he needs to get together with me and my lawyer tonight to discuss my contract.

"I don't have a lawyer," I say.

"Get one," he orders.

Billy Bender's acquittal is the hot topic of conversation within Clayton High's corridors Wednesday morning. Rumors have it that the absences of several individuals including Justin Lafayette and Mr. Hucul can be attributed to their having bet heavily on the wrong side of the verdict.

I don't have too much time to pay attention to such gossip because Nina is excited, having already heard from Billy that I got the Suckerpunch gig. She gives me a flying lip lock kiss with a tongue swabbing chaser before launching into a steady barrage of questions.

"Have you told Bowie yet?"

"I haven't had time."

"Am I going to be able to finally meet him?"

"If you can talk your father into letting you come on the road with me."

"Have you told O'Reilly yet that you're going to have to quit school?"

Ric Thibault, high school dropout – I hadn't even considered the possibility. I'm smart enough to know it's not as simple as 'good-bye Basil – hello Bowie'. Not every band is successful and few last more than two or three years anyway. Without an education to fall back on I could end up spending the rest of my life with bad teeth and tattoos pumping gas. Nina Penningtons don't hang out with guys who work in truck stops.

"I'm not going to quit school,"

"Then how are you going to go on tour?"

"I'll talk to Basil O'Reilly and work something out," I whisper as assembly begins. Nina smiles and takes my hand in hers.

O'Reilly acknowledges Billy's victory only in passing. "Due to the media strike you may have been unable to get the news of one of your less distinguished fellow students' legal proceedings.

FEED THE DOG

Much to my dismay I want to announce that a certain disruptive element of our student body has been allowed to remain within society by an all too liberal Judge. I want to use this forum to warn this particular disruptive element and his cohorts that a repeat of such behavior will neither be condoned nor tolerated."

After assembly I use the pay phone by the principal's office and call Julius Rotter. He says he can't represent me due to a conflict of interest. His new client, Zachary Pennington, has hired Rotter to foreclose on my father's mortgage. Rotter suggests I give Annette Stratton-Osborne a call. She was fired last night from her assistant District Attorney position and probably could use some clients.

I reach into my pocket and find I only have one dime left. I debate whether to call my father to warn him about Nina's father's plans or Stratton-Osborne. I figure Johann will find out soon enough what Zachary Pennington is up to and dial Annette Stratton-Osborne. She has better legs than my father.

"Hello may I please speak to Mrs. Stratton-Osborne?"

"This is Miss Stratton-Osborne," the former assistant District Attorney corrects me.

"Miss Stratton-Osborne, my name is Ric Thibault. Julius Rotter suggested that I call you."

"You're not related to Stephan Thibault are you?"

"Unfortunately."

"Is he out of jail yet?"

"Yes, but that's not why I called you. Julius Rotter recommended you as an attorney for a situation..."

"What are you in jail for?" she interrupts.

"I'm not in jail."

"So, they finally nailed your father?"

"No. As far as I know no one in my family is in jail."

"Then why are you calling me?"

"I need an attorney to negotiate a contract for me with the band I'm joining."

"Which band?"

"Suckerpunch."

"Wow! You're kidding, they're my favorite new group. I think *I'm Stupid And So Are You* is the best song this year. I bet it wins a Grammy."

"So will you represent me?"

"Sure, when would you like to meet?"

"How about after I'm done with school... say at five o'clock?" I ask while out of the corner of my eye watching Officer Ronnie Watt walking into Basil O'Reilly's office.

"Fine, only I don't have my new office set up yet, so would you mind if we get together at your house?"

"No problem."

I hang up and go to first period English class. This will be my first time with our new instructor, Basil O'Reilly, who is replacing Laura Stumpf who was in turn replacing poor crazy Mrs. Lukowich. Officer Watt seems to be delaying Basil. While we wait for the principal I ask Nina if she knows anything about her father canceling Johann's mortgage.

"Not really but I overheard my dad telling someone on the phone that he must protect his reputation for integrity at all cost. He said he doesn't want people thinking his bank does business with the Mafia."

Mrs. Babin, the school secretary, comes in and says she has an announcement. "Principal O'Reilly has been called away on emergency school business. Therefore today's class is canceled. Mr. O'Reilly has assigned no new homework but he wants you to be prepared for a test on *A Farewell To Arms* tomorrow."

I guess I better read it.

There are bright lights in the living room. I walk in and find all of Lucretia's remaining genuine Brother Theodore 'light this and get one step closer to God' prayer candles burning up a storm and a guy with a camera and a French accent taking pictures of Kristen. My sister is sprawled on a bear skin rug which I've never seen before wearing only a studded dog collar, garter belt, stockings and high heels.

"Tres bien, now cup your breast with one hand, pick up zat whip with ze other. Formidable! Give me a look like you always do zis. You know, natural."

Yeah, I think to myself, my naked sister looks real natural playing with herself in the living room while a French pervert takes pictures. I can't remember the number of times I've walked downstairs to catch her like this.

"Now smile longingly at the camera, c'est magnifique!"

FEED THE DOG

"Kristen can I talk to you for a second?" I ask.

"Oh shit!" Kristen jumps up knocking over a whole row of prayer candles each one guaranteed to have been blessed personally by Brother Theodore. If not for some quick stomping out of the flames on my part the whole place would have been on fire and we certainly would have been one step closer to God.

"Merde," exclaims the photographer, "you are trying to ruin my masterpiece. Who are you to interrupt ze great Jocelyn Dufour while he works?"

"I'm Kristen's brother, Ric. I'm sorry to disturb you but my lawyer is meeting me here in a few minutes and I was wondering if you could move your photo shoot into another room where you can have more privacy."

"Mais non, ce n'est pas possible," babbles the Frenchman with the camera, "I, Jocelyn Dufour, have chosen zis location and zis location it will be. Now go away little brother."

"Take your lawyer somewhere else in the house," my sister demands, "and stop staring at my boobs."

"Then stop showing them."

"They're paying me ten thousand dollars to show them," she replies.

"Well nobody is paying me to ignore your tits," I rejoin as the doorbell chimes.

I open the door. It's Annette Stratton-Osborne looking more like a fashion model than a lawyer in a red mini dress and a matching pair of snakeskin high heels which sadly don't reflect. My guess is they aren't Charles Jourdans.

I attempt to lead her past the living room into the kitchen but she notices the photographer's lights and asks who is taking pictures. Before I can stop her she peeks in and catches sight of the photo shoot.

"I know your father is in the Mafia, but I never thought he would run his pornography operations from his own home," she says aghast.

"My father has nothing to do with this. My sister is shooting a pictorial for *Penthouse*."

"Quiet you..." Jocelyn Dufour spins around all prepared to say something rude until he sees Annette Stratton-Osborne. He changes his mind and turns on the French charm which most women find irresistible. "Mon dieu! Vous êtes belle. Allow me to present myself. I am Jacques Dufour and je vous aime beaucoup. It is you I should be photographing for all ze world to see."

Dufour makes a great production of kissing my attorney's hand. It's a move he must have learned from all those old boring black and white Rudolph Valentino movies. Dufour probably read the French version of *How To Pick Up Girls*, because I can't believe how easily Annette Stratton-Osborne falls for his pompous gallantry. "Do you really think I could be a model?" Stratton-Osborne swoons.

"Certainement," answers Dufour caressing her hand.

"Really?" she sighs.

"It would be an honor and a privilege for me to shoot you," he responds.

Kristen, jealous at no longer being the center of attention, taps Dufour on the shoulder with the whip, "It might also be an honor and privilege for my father to shoot you if you don't finish this session."

"Quel dommage!" the photographer laments going back to work. I have to agree with him. I'd buy a copy of any magazine with topless pictures of Annette Stratton-Osborne.

My fantasizing is disrupted by a knock on the door. It's Nina. "My parents won't let me call you on the phone so I had to sneak out. You won't believe what I just found out – Principal O'Reilly was arrested for having a hidden camera in the girls locker room. Basil O'Reilly is the one behind that awful poster!"

Although I disagree with Nina's characterization of the poster as being awful I manage to say in a sympathetic and surprised voice, "what a scumbag," while trying to remember whether Basil was aware that I removed Nina's picture. I don't think he was so I don't panic too much. "How did they catch him?"

"The Archbishop told my dad what happened. He hired a detective who determined where the photo was taken. Then the police searched Clayton High and discovered an envelope full of pictures of naked girls in Basil's desk including one of your sister. That was all the evidence they needed."

"Did I hear you say that O'Reilly took pictures of me naked?" asks Kristen storming into the hallway.

"What is going on here?" cries Nina, uneasy at the sight of my mostly naked sister carrying a whip.

Before I can explain Dufour bursts into the hallway, "Yo! hold on a minute. You have an exclusive contract with *Penthouse* for ten G's. Guccione isn't going to like this one bit. Who is this O'Reilly guy you're doing photos for?"

"They're paying you ten thousand dollars?" both Annette Stratton–Osborne and Nina ask incredulously while I begin to suspect Monsieur Dufour of being a fraud. French people don't say 'yo'. Only gangsters from Brooklyn yell 'yo' – and how come he finally pronounced the 'th' in 'this' properly? "Hey, what happened to your French accent?" I demand.

"Uh, rien," Dufour answers glaring at me with a 'do you wanna bet five bucks whether you live until your seventeenth birthday?' look.

"Do all your models get ten thousand dollars?" Annette Stratton-Osborne inquires.

"Ones as beautiful as ze three of you do," he replies again pronouncing the 'th' in 'three', "now who is zis O'Reilly?"

"He's the asshole principal of our school," Kristen explains while Nina whispers to me she doesn't think Dufour is French either.

"Do you have a business card?" Stratton-Osborne asks in a tone of voice indicating her interest in possibly posing for him.

"Mais oui." Dufour reaches into his wallet and takes out a card. As he gives the card to my lawyer Dufour drops the wallet in front of me exposing his drivers license. I bend over and pick it up. The New Jersey license is for a Harvey Marvin Buynak from Paramus, New Jersey.

"Here's your wallet Harvey."

"My name is Jocelyn Dufour."

"Gee, it says here this is Harvey Buynak's wallet so it must not be yours," I say pulling it back.

"Give it to me you little bastard."

"I can't. Both this drivers license and this American Express Card are in the name of Harvey Buynak of Paramus, New Jersey." I show Stratton-Osborne the identification.

"Why the fake name and accent? Are you some sort of con artist?" she demands snapping back into her previous persona of a District Attorney.

"I'm legit, see Jocelyn Dufour is my professional name. You can call *Penthouse* – they'll vouch for me."

"You still haven't answered the question," Kristen says angrily, "do I need some of my father's associates to get the truth out of you?"

Harvey Buynak is sweating as he blurts out. "That won't be necessary. The truth is women don't take their clothes off for photographers named Harvey Buynak from Paramus, New Jersey. But if an American girl believes that I'm Jocelyn Dufour from Paris she goes nuts and does anything I want."

It makes sense to me. Harvey Buynak is a true existentialist. He's manipulating his past to gain control of his futile universe.

"You're pathetic," Stratton-Osborne says, tossing Harvey his wallet.

According to Buynak he already has enough pictures of Kristen for the pictorial. "Besides," he adds, "the vibes are no longer conducive to taking pictures." He packs up his gear and leaves.

While Kristen gets dressed and I blow out the remaining Brother Theodore prayer candles Annette Stratton-Osborne and Nina discuss the moral implications of women who pose naked for photographers. Nina claims it exploits women, while my lawyer feels it is okay as long as the woman is adequately compensated. I think it's perfectly acceptable unless the woman is fat or has really bad acne.

The doorbell rings again and I answer it figuring it is Derek Irons. I open the door and find Jimmy Leach instead. He has come to collect his Quaalude from last night. Upon seeing Nina and Annette Stratton-Osborne, the two best looking women in the St. Louis metropolitan area, Jimmy takes me aside and whispers, "You don't have to give me a 'lude – just slip one to each of the chicks and we'll have ourselves a real party."

Although the prospect of having two horny beautiful women in my living room is appealing I tell Jimmy to fuck off. I need Stratton-Osborne to be clear headed when dealing with Derek Irons and there is absolutely no way I trust Jimmy with Nina – even without her being under the influence of an aphrodisiac.

I excuse myself and run upstairs to get the bottle of Quaaludes from its hiding place in my bookcase behind *The Complete Works of Mark Twain*. I count them to make sure Stephan hasn't found my cache. He hasn't – I still have forty-two left.

"What are you doing?" Kristen's voice scares the shit out of me.

I spin around and find my sister standing in the doorway with Nina, Annette Stratton-Osborne and Jimmy.

"Uh," I stammer. If Nina looks up she's going to see her poster and my life as I now know it will be over. "I, um, was getting Jimmy aspirin for his headache." I need to distract Nina from looking up at the ceiling so I deliberately spill a few tablets onto the floor.

"It's a pretty bad headache I think I'm going to need at least two," Jimmy claims, diving to help pick up the spilled Quaaludes.

"All this stress has given me a headache too," Nina says, "so while you're at it could I also get a couple of aspirin?"

I manage to wrestle all but the two 'ludes which Jimmy swallows smilingly without water.

Kristen gives me an 'I know those aren't aspirin' look forcing me to quietly dole out an extra two pills to ward off a sudden outbreak of the great headache epidemic of 1973.

FEED THE DOG

I hear the doorbell ring again and usher everybody safely out of my room without either Nina noticing the poster or anyone hitting me up for any additional Quaaludes.

Derek Irons is standing at the door. He apologizes for being late, but he was delayed by a malfunctioning hotel elevator. He kept pressing the lobby button and ending up on the roof. He got so frustrated that he slammed the control panel thereby somehow knocking it haywire and causing the elevator to be stuck between the eighth and ninth floors. He was stranded for thirty minutes with a pregnant woman and a rotund television evangelist until the fire department was able to rescue him.

Jimmy takes me aside and whispers he wants to stick around and watch Kristen and Nina react to the Quaaludes. "I'm just thinking of the girls' welfare," he contends.

"Did I tell you I got a couple of new hockey sticks?" I threaten pushing him out the door.

I introduce Derek to Annette Stratton-Osborne, Kristen and Nina.

"I know I've seen the two of you before," Irons says to Nina and Kristen, "but I just can't place your faces. I'm sure it will come to me."

We go into the living room and sit down around the coffee table to discuss my deal with Suckerpunch. Derek proposes that I sign a contract which gives me a salary of four hundred dollars a week plus per diems, less his fifteen percent management commission.

I'm going to be rich. As soon as I get my first check I'm going to hire a limousine and take Nina shopping for black patent leather Charles Jourdan high heel pumps. It will be a classy thing to do. Her parents might even change their opinion of me and stop their hypocritical worrying about Johann's criminal associates. After all, Nina's an ex-con too, so how picky can they be?

Stratton-Osborne and Irons bicker back and forth about the length of my contract and the record royalty rate. All their legal mumbo jumbo is pretty boring. I'm far more interested in watching Nina for any signs of the Quaaludes kicking in. So far she seems unaffected.

I try to follow the conversation again, but I don't understand anything about indemnification clauses. However, I do notice that every time my lawyer uncrosses her legs Derek immediately concedes whichever point they are arguing.

After about twenty minutes of going back and forth Derek and Annette come to an agreement on the remaining terms. Irons puts the proposed contract down on the coffee table and picks up a couple of Polaroid test shots of Kristen which Harvey Buynak must have left behind. He examines them appreciatively.

"Now I know where I saw you. You're Bambi Bosoms," he points to Kristen, "and you're that hot new model from the poster which is sweeping the country."

I guess Nina's Quaaludes must be kicking in. In addition to making people horny the drug must also be some sort of tranquilizer because she doesn't even try to reach into her purse and pull out the mace canister. Instead she sits quietly on the couch smiling and playing with her hair.

Meanwhile Kristen recognizes Irons, "I remember you too. You're the guy who wanted to write a check and stuff it down my G-string instead of using cash like everyone else."

"The check was good. I don't see why you were so upset," says my manager.

Stratton-Osborne requests that part of her fee be a backstage pass for the next Suckerpunch gig. Irons has no objection. He even pays me a compliment as he is leaving, "I can tell you're going to be a great addition to the band," he says, "not only does your family name have publicity value, but I can tell you have sex appeal by the gorgeous women you surround yourself with. You're already a rock star – you've got a fashion model for a lawyer, a fashion model for a girlfriend, and a *Penthouse* pet as a sister. Bring all the women you want to our concerts, it's great for the band's image. I'll see you at nine o'clock at the rehearsal room."

I thank Stratton-Osborne for her help in conducting the negotiations. She says it was a lot of fun and she's going home now to finish the contracts. She'll have the whole agreement typed and ready to sign in a few hours. "Would you mind if I come by rehearsal tonight and hand deliver the contracts? Then, if it's all right with you, I'll be able to watch you play a few songs and meet the rest of the band."

I've got no objections and tell her I'll see her later. Rather than a handshake accompanying our good-byes she gives me a kiss on the cheek. Just like Dominique, Boom Boom, Marge Bender, and Mary Ecclestone – I sense Annette Stratton-Osborne is falling for me. Maybe Derek Irons was right. I might have a career as a sex object. Eat your heart out Paul Newman, there's a new stud on the scene – Ric Thibault. It's amazing considering I can feel a big pimple developing on my nose.

I look at my watch, it's seven o'clock which gives me two hours until rehearsal. It also gives me two hours to complete the seduction of Nina.

I go back into the living room where my Quaaluded girlfriend is reclining on the sofa. I bend over and kiss her on the lips. Being above her nothing will land on me if she throws up. All those boring physics classes I took last year are finally paying off. I've got it covered; this time I'm using gravity as an ally.

My heart beats faster as I reach under Nina's sweater for her breasts and get no resistance

145

whatsoever! I pull the sweater up over her tits revealing her bra and still get no resistance. Whoever designed the latching system for bras must have been firmly against sex, I think while wrestling with its hooks. They should have made some sort of push button quick release mechanism. Getting nowhere I finally yank it down her chest. Her tits are even more beautiful than they were the other night. I guess they improve with age, like a fine wine.

Remembering what I read in *The Joy Of Sex* I decide to slow things down a little. If I recall the passage correctly, and I'm pretty sure that I do, the book says to "soften her up with foreplay." So I move up her body again and stick my tongue as far into her mouth as I can. I again get no resistance; in fact I don't even get any response.

I don't recall Nina saying anything in Latin so I'm pretty sure she's not dead. I check her pulse just to be certain. She's still alive. Unfortunately she's also passed out.

I debate whether to proceed with my seduction. On the negative side:

1. Nina is my future wife. She might be pissed off to wake up and find out she's no longer a virgin.
2. Zachary Pennington might be even more pissed off when he finds out his daughter woke up no longer a virgin; this would significantly reduce our chances of getting valuable wedding gifts from him. I heard Kevin Micheletti's sister, Annica, got over twelve thousand bucks worth of presents from her in-laws. I don't want to be greedy and blow a potential good haul like those idiots on *Let's Make A Deal* who trade a new car for what is behind the curtain where Carol Merrill is standing. They always end up kissing Monte Hall after they wind up with a donkey and two cases of Purina donkey chow – which is equivalent to trading Nina for fat cousin Julie and kissing Father O'Brien in gratitude.
3. I want Nina to remember our first time as the best night of her life and it's hard to remember something when you're passed out.
4. Premarital sex is a sin – and if I'm going to get in trouble with God I want to make sure it's worth it. Sex is probably best when it's a shared experience. Fucking her while she is passed out would be closer to masturbation – and I certainly don't want to risk eternal damnation for something which could make me go blind.

I can only think of one reason on the positive side – I'm so horny that the crack of dawn had better watch out.

Consequently I decide to play with her breasts a little before putting her bra and sweater back on. Two Quaaludes are too much for Nina to handle at once. Next time I'll make sure she only takes one 'lude – which at the present rate of consumption is about all I will have left.

Clearly, I can't take Nina with me to rehearsal – and I can't exactly take her home either. I can see myself ringing the doorbell – "I have a special delivery package for Zachary Pennington from the Thibault crime family....What is it?...Oh it's your Quaaluded daughter, you know, the one who poses for dirty posters... Can you please sign here, sir?"

I decide to take her to my room and put her to bed and let her sleep it off. I'll take her home after rehearsal. Just in case she comes to before I return I take down her poster and hide it behind the bookcase.

Since I am now a rock star I figure I should be at least thirty minutes late for rehearsal. I arrive at Opus Studios at nine thirty and find I'm the first one from the band here other than Billy Jo Brackenbury. I guess I'll have to practice harder at being a rock star.

A few minutes later Derek Irons shows up with a bearded hippy wearing a Bay City Rollers tour jacket. The hippy is complaining that usually the record company flies him to exciting and exotic places like St. Tropez, Maui, or at very least Hollywood where he is plied with booze, drugs and hookers while he does his fluff pieces. Instead Slipped Disk has flown him to St. Louis and stuck him in a hotel where the elevators don't even work.

Irons assures the reporter, whom he introduces to me as Evan Montgomery from *Rolling Stone*, that everything will work out fine. "I've got the hottest girl in St. Louis on her way down here to take care of you; so all you have to do is concentrate on your interview with Ric."

God this guy is sleazy. Not only is he a scab for ignoring the local media strike, but, instead of paying me for an interview like every other journalist has, he expects to be bought off with hookers.

"Since the rest of the band isn't here yet you may as well do the interview now," Irons says, "this way you'll be able to split as soon as the girl gets here."

"Good idea," agrees Montgomery, "do you have anything to get me through this?"

"Like what?" Irons asks.

"Use your imagination," replies the writer.

Using my imagination I figure Derek should be getting Evan Montgomery a few Quaaludes, two hookers, and a suitcase full of unmarked bills.

FEED THE DOG

Montgomery starts the interview by asking me what it was like growing up in a Mafia family.

"I wouldn't know," I respond truthfully.

"It has been widely reported that your father is the capo of the Vespucci crime family, so how can you not know what it is like growing up in a Mafia family?"

"I'm sorry, but we live in a country priding itself on our judicial system which holds that all men are innocent until proven guilty. It has been alleged that my father is in the Mafia but never proven."

"Okay, let me rephrase the question, would you say you have had a normal family life?"

Unlike my brother I have morals. I've already sold an exclusive story on my upbringing to Jasper Gilbertson and *The Midnight Sun* for fifteen hundred dollars, so I cannot in good faith answer the hippy's question. "I'm not going to talk about my private family life. You can ask me anything about music but my family is off limits."

Montgomery isn't pleased. "Why am I here if you're not going to talk about your father and the Mob? It's not like I need to write about another misunderstood pimple faced kid with a guitar and a drug problem."

"I don't have a drug problem, I don't think I'm misunderstood and I only have one zit. As for the reason why you're here, I presume it is to justify whatever they pay you."

"I don't know if your manager fully explained to you the power of *Rolling Stone*. We can destroy your career with one bad review," Montgomery threatens.

Derek Irons looks alarmed.

If this hippy thinks he can intimidate me he's got another thing coming. Since Montgomery is gullible enough to believe I'm from a Mafia family I decide to fight fire with fire. "I don't know if your editor explained to you fully the power of the Mafia. We can destroy your life for one bad review," I bluff.

It must be awesome to have a father who really is in the Mafia – people become so eager to please you. "If somehow my words have been misconstrued please accept my most humble apology," Montgomery snivels.

So we do the standard fanzine interview in which I disclose my reasons for joining Suckerpunch (to have lots of long legged big breasted groupies), my influences (black blues players with colorful names like Muddy Waters and Howlin' Wolf, whom I've never heard – but I'm pretty sure there's a rule somewhere stating if you are a white guitar player from suburbia you must list them as your favorite artists), my serious goals in life (I invoke the standard platitude about trying to save the planet and helping people of all races to live together in peace), and tell Montgomery my lifestyle won't change one bit when I'm a big rock star – I'll be the same modest unassuming guy I am now.

Our conversation is interrupted by the arrival of the band, and Simon Q. Picasso's analyst, Dr. Caley. Simon is moaning about last night's fifteen stitch gash on his head, while Dr. Caley is explaining we have to be careful not to further traumatize our bass player's fragile psyche.

According to Dr. Caley, "every time we play *Looking Up At Her Thighs* we cause Simon's id to come into conflict with the social constraints from his superego thereby rendering him an angst ridden individual deprived of the hyperhedonia which naturally comes from the cathartic release of my valuable therapy – which all of you, especially Rico, should be undergoing in order to quell your antisocial behavior which is inimical to building a more perfect society through music."

"Huh?" responds Rico 'Bam Bam' Ross picking his nose.

"You're erecting hostile barriers thereby making it difficult for my spiritual soul to gain proper nourishment," explains Simon.

"Do you want to see a real hostile barrier Paruszkiewicz?" asks Rico hurling a drum stick at Simon Q. Picasso.

"Fuck all your psychobabble, I'm only trying to get laid and concurrently build my bank account," says Mick Masters aiming a wad of spit in Dr. Caley's direction.

Derek Irons shows his managerial skills by intervening and escorting the doctor from the rehearsal room before the psychological debate can be concluded.

Bernie Hrechkosy calms Simon down by giving him a crystal on a gold chain which the guitarist claims has psychic healing powers. Simon is moved to tears by Bernie's gift, "I'll cherish this as a sign of camaraderie and affection by my brothers in the band. Let me meditate a minute and I'll be ready to play."

"Fuck off," says Rico.

As I tune my guitar Bernie Hrechkosy walks over to me and whispers that the crystal is a fraud, "It's a necklace I found in my bed after getting rid of the groupie I fucked last night. I took it to a jeweler this morning and he said it was a worthless piece of glass on a cheap chain. Simon's such an idiot that he'll believe it has spiritual healing powers. Aren't you glad you're a member of this band?"

Simon tells us the crystal has already energized him and he is ready to jam. While Evan Montgomery jots down notes we play an energetic *Take It Away* and follow it with a rave-up

FEED THE DOG

rendition of *Can't Keep Us Down*. I notice Montgomery tapping his foot to the music. I think we've won him over as a fan.

Derek Irons returns with Annette Stratton-Osborne in tow. My lawyer has gotten dressed up for the occasion. She's wearing a red satin shirt with a plunging neckline, hot pants and patent leather stiletto heel knee length boots. Mick wants to play his ballad *Pulling A Train*. I guess in Mick's mind 'pulling a train' is a metaphor for something – but I'm not sure what. From what I know of our singer it's probably pretty stupid.

I feel silly singing the chorus' Mother Goosish lyrics in front of my lawyer:

> *We're all queued up*
> *'Cause Sally's pulling a train*
> *We'll all be used up*
> *'Cause Sally's pulling a train*

But Annette Stratton-Osborne doesn't seem to share my concerns about the lyrical content because she's dancing along with the music. When we get into the second chorus she really goes into action, shaking her body provocatively to the beat. Some of her body parts shake a little more than others and are extremely fun to watch.

Evan Montgomery gets up off the sofa, smiles and pats Derek Irons on the back. Reading his lips I can see him thanking Derek. The writer walks over to Stratton-Osborne and puts his hand on her ass and attempts to kiss her.

My attorney is apparently surprised by the writer's action and knees Montgomery in the groin, sending him reeling back to the sofa in pain with a confused look on his face. Irons goes over to console Montgomery and, if I read his lips correctly, says something to the effect that, "she's not the girl I ordered for you."

The rest of the songs go by rather quickly, especially with Stratton-Osborne's gyrations in front of us. After running through the set once, the now recovered Evan Montgomery asks me if I write any tunes. I tell him I've composed one song which I haven't shown the band yet. He asks if he can hear it.

So, I tune my guitar up and start with *Talkin' Nina Pennington Blues* I make a few lyrical alterations to make the song suit Suckerpunch's style a little better:

> *Got a girlfriend with a special purpose*
> *Nina be her name*

> *Gonna get her to pay me some lip service*
> *Nina scream my name*
> *Got a girlfriend with the cutest little cervix*
> *Nina moan my name*

I also improvise a new chorus:

> *Nina I wanna be on the tip of your tongue*
> *Can't remember when I've had so much fun*
> *Nina Wanna be on the tip of your tongue*

Evan Montgomery says he likes my song and Derek suggests we work it into our set opening for Bowie which, he reminds us, is only three days away. So we do another run through of *Talkin' Nina Pennington Blues* – this time with Mick singing.

During the second chorus a gum chewing girl wearing a halter top, hot pants and high heeled shoes enters and talks to Derek. He pulls out his wallet and hands her money. She nods and walks over to Montgomery who cautiously shakes her hand. Derek yells something into the writer's ear and a relieved look sweeps his face. He waves good-bye to us and disappears out the door with the girl in tow.

We finish the run through and Annette Stratton-Osborne tells me *Talkin' Nina Pennington Blues* is a masterpiece. "It's full of a youthful passion which refuses to be tamed," she says running her hand across my crotch, "although I'd like to try."

I ask her if she would excuse me for a moment while I use the phone. When I last saw Nina, my future wife and star of the masterpiece *Talkin' Nina Pennington Blues* was passed out on Quaaludes in my bedroom. I phone Jimmy Leach and ask him how long I should expect her to be unconscious.

"From my considerable experience you've got six hours provided no one disturbs her, why?" Jimmy asks.

I don't want Jimmy to know the reason lest he decide to go over and try to monitor my girlfriend's breathing. I protect Nina from the deejay by fibbing, "I wanted to know if I have time to do my homework before she comes to."

I hang up and rejoin Annette Stratton-Osborne who is sharing a bottle of Southern Comfort with Rico and Bernie.

"You know I always thought *Pulling A Train* could be about me," my attorney says handing me a pen and the contract to sign.

"Unfortunately it wasn't," remarks Bernie.

"It could be if you wanted," she says taking another swig of Southern Comfort.

Bernie and Rico are excited by the prospect, "Let's all go back to the hotel and rewrite the lyrics," Bernie proposes, "Are you going to join us Ric?"

"Of course he is," says Annette Stratton-Osborne grabbing me by the zipper.

I know you get publishing money for writing songs, so I'm not going to miss this opportunity, "Sure I'll go," I say handing Derek the contracts.

Annette Stratton-Osborne has drunk too much to drive and asks if she can ride over to the hotel with me. She grabs the open bottle of Southern Comfort and hops in the Corvette. "Don't worry about the booze," she says, "From my being a District Attorney the cops all know me and won't stop us."

She turns on the radio. Jimmy Leach is playing a wimpy but sincere Crosby Stills & Nash song so she switches to another station who are airing a live broadcast of the Kinks.

She gulps down another mouthful of Southern Comfort and licks her lips. "Do you think I could have been a model for *Penthouse*?" she asks.

"I'd buy at least one copy Miss Stratton-Osborne," I reply.

"Call me Annette. Do you really think I'm good looking enough?"

"Trust me, you're gorgeous."

"That's sweet. Did you know Corvettes make girls horny?" Annette asks, unzipping my fly.

I remember both Emily Wheldon and Marge Bender mentioning something about it, but I don't think this is the proper time to bring it up because Annette is demonstrating the real meaning of 'attorney-client privilege' while the radio blasts *You Really Got Me*.

We haven't gone two blocks when I notice flashing red lights in the rear-view mirror. I pull over hoping one of the fringe benefits of getting a blowjob from Annette is having my attorney with me when I most need her.

I reluctantly pull Annette off me and zip my pants as a fat policeman waddles toward the car carrying a flashlight. It's Ronnie Watt.

"Hello Mr. Opprobrious, step out of the car and let's see your license and registration," the fat cop demands.

"What's the problem Ronald?" asks Annette.

Fat Ronnie shines his light on the ex-District Attorney, "Shit," he mutters under his breath, "hello Miss Stratton-Osborne. I stopped your car because you were driving erotically."

"Did you mean erratically or erotically?" Annette inquires stepping out of the car.

"What's the difference?" the confused cop asks.

"Erotically is like this," Annette demonstrates by unzipping Fat Ronnie's pants and pulling them down around his ankles, "and erratically is the way you're breathing."

"Uh, I'm, uh, I'm not sure, are you, um, drunk?" Ronnie stammers.

"I don't know, wanna smell my breath?" she coos blowing into his face. While Ronnie Watt blushes Annette drops to her knees and yanks his pants off. She grabs them and runs back into the car. "Let's burn rubber," she yells leaving Officer Ronnie Watt bare assed and embarrassed in the middle of the road.

Upon arriving at the hotel Annette and I go up to Bernie's room. We knock on the door and are met by Rico, Bernie and Mick. "Simon's off with Dr. Caley, so it's just the four of us, not counting you. Is that all right?" Bernie asks Annette.

"Yeah, drop them," Annette says.

This time I don't say anything stupid like the last occasion I was ordered to remove my pants. Annette teaches me I still have a lot to learn, the most important thing being that you don't need a locomotive to pull a train.

It's one thirty in the morning and I'm exhausted. I walk up the stairs and don't even bother turning the light on before collapsing onto the bed.

Thump! I hit someone who is already ensconced in my bed. Assuming it is Duke I shove the body off the bed.

"Ow!" cries a groggy female voice from the floor.

I jump up and turn the lights on. What with the excitement of Annette's demonstration of the Kama Sutra I forgot Nina was still passed out in my bed – was being the operative word because she is now awake.

"Where am I? What time is it and what are you doing naked?" Nina questions.

"Oh my God, I don't believe it, I mean I forgot, I mean I'm sorry. It's one thirty... I just got back. Shit! You're in my room and I forgot you passed out. I went to rehearsal and then to a band meeting which was so exhausting that I forgot you were here," I stammer while trying to find my underwear.

"My father's going to kill us," Nina wails.

FEED THE DOG

"How's he going to know?" I ask, not really wanting to hear the answer.

"He comes into my room and says goodnight every night at eleven. He probably thinks I've run away and has called the police. I'm fucked."

"You're definitely not fucked," I assure her while putting on my pants.

"What am I going to do?" she wails.

"Give me a second to come up with a plan." I run through my mental list of plausible excuses. Finding nothing suitable I move into the slightly less plausible category. Still finding nothing to adequately cover the problem I am forced to delve into the 'in case of emergency – break glass' file of totally ridiculous justifications. I only find a few possible solutions in this classification:

1. Call Zachary Pennington and pretend to be a kidnapper holding his daughter for ransom. Positive side: Takes Nina totally off the hook and we might be able to turn situation into a profit deal. Negative side: We'd be breaking several federal and local ordinances, and could face the rest of our lives in separate prisons.

2. Call Zachary Pennington and tell the truth. Positive side: By the time I get out of jail for drugging her, Nina might be finished being grounded. Negative side: If I'm not immediately lynched, by the time I get out of jail I might be too old to care that Nina has finished being grounded.

3. Try to sneak Nina back into her house and try to convince Zachary Pennington she was there all the time. Positive side: I am no way involved. Negative side: It probably won't work.

4. Claim Nina went for a walk and was hit on the head by a falling tree branch. She suffered temporary amnesia and only now came to her senses. Positive side: I am no way involved. Negative side: It probably won't work. She doesn't even have a bump on her head...yet.

5. Claim she was with ex-District Attorney Annette Stratton-Osborne trying to learn about the possibilities open to a woman wanting to pursue a law career. Positive side: It sounds lofty and commendable. Negative side: She might find out I had sex with ex-district attorney Annette Stratton-Osborne.

I gamble and choose number five.

"How are we going to get Stratton-Osborne to go along with it?" Nina asks.

"I'll call Annette."

"Annette?"

"I mean, Miss Stratton Osborne."

"Now?"

"Uh, yeah, I guess."

I go downstairs and call the Chase Park Plaza and ask for Bernie Hrechkosy's room.

"Hello?" Bernie answers, half asleep.

"Bernie, it's Ric, is Annette still there?"

"Yeah, but she's busy."

"Doing what?"

"Rico."

"Can I talk to her? It's an emergency."

Annette comes to the phone sounding like she's out of breath. I explain the basics of my problem and she offers to go along with the plan provided I promise to treat her to an encore of this evening – and if I will play guitar on this song she says she just wrote.

I ask her what the song is and how much I'll get paid.

"It's called *If I Had A Dick*. Your pay is getting your girlfriend un-grounded before she's a seventy year old hag with no teeth."

I'd do anything for Nina Pennington. So I agree to my lawyer's terms.

The clock radio goes off at seven-thirty and I'm still tired. I hit the snooze button and go back to sleep for another ten minutes. The radio goes off again – but before I can smack the snooze button a second time I am assaulted by the voice of Chief Howard D. Watt. He's holding a press conference – so our guardians of liberty must have returned from their one day walkout.

"Speaking on behalf of the entire Clayton police department I must vehemently protest my removal from office this morning and the subsequent takeover of local policing duties by the Missouri State Attorney General's office. Throughout the years the Clayton police force has enjoyed unparalleled success in crime fighting and prevention. Had it not been for you effete crybaby snobs in the media my department would still be providing the same quality law enforcement service which our citizenry has come to rely upon."

A voice which I'm pretty sure belongs to Mary Ecclestone shouts a question, "How can you blame us? Your son, Patrolman Ronald Watt is the one who killed Brian Savage..."

FEED THE DOG

"Stop right there. My son did not kill Brian Savage. I have here the official coroner's report on the reporter's death. It says, and I quote, 'Brian Savage's accidental death was due to his coming in contact with a live electrical wire.' Nowhere does it mention my son, or anyone else connected with the Clayton police department being culpable in this tragedy.

As for the first part of your question let me answer it this way. You, the media, staged a riot at the Thibault crime family's house – and then, after getting your hands caught in the proverbial cookie jar and being put in jail where you belong, you cried to the Attorney General that we're unfair. You demanded special treatment. I'm sorry, but under my administration the Clayton Police department treated everyone equally – be they common citizen, criminal, or member of the press. When you broke the law in Clayton you went to jail. It was that easy. I ran a good operation here. That is why our town was one of the safest and most desirable communities in the United States to reside in."

"Chief Watt, if you administer justice so equally how do you explain your son not being charged with indecent exposure last night after being found naked from the waist down in the middle of Clayton Road?" a different reporter asks.

"My son was executing his official duties as a Clayton police officer."

"Was it official policy for him to execute his duties naked?" the reporter presses.

"He was undercover," Chief Watt says choosing his words poorly. Ronnie Watt was definitely not undercover. "My son is a good cop," the recently deposed Chief continues, "just yesterday he brought one of the biggest child pornographers in the country to justice. I don't hear any questions concerning the first class detective work that went into the apprehension of principal Basil O'Reilly."

Kristen yells I should come downstairs and watch the press conference on television, "they might show Basil O'Reilly in handcuffs."

Not wanting to miss the possibility of viewing a manacled Basil O'Reilly I join my sister in front of the TV. What I have heard about television adding ten pounds to everyone is wrong. In Chief Watt's case it makes him look at least another hundred pounds fatter.

Terry Madigan is asking Watt whether he plans on fighting his removal.

"Most definitely. You haven't seen the last of Chief Howard D. Watt. I will appeal to the Superior Court. If that doesn't work I will appeal to Federal Court. In fact you can say I will appeal ad nauseam, uuh, uuh, ugh..."

"Is something wrong with the TV?" Kristen asks, "Chief Watt's face is awfully red all of a sudden."

I look at the television screen, the rest of the colors seem okay. I think it's working fine, unlike Chief Watt who has just collapsed face first into a bank of microphones. I see Seymour Stankiewicz rushing to his fallen leader. He rips open Watt's shirt and appears to be administering CPR.

"He's had a heart attack! Move back and give him some air," someone screams at the horde of reporters and cameramen who are now crowding the dais to give us extreme close-ups of the slumped over Chief.

"Fuck off, we're exercising our First Amendment rights and giving the people the news," Mary Ecclestone states, forgetting that her microphone is on while she pushes her way closer to Watt, "this is good stuff. I bet we get picked up by Cronkite with this. I'll get the lead story!"

"I think he's dead," someone is saying.

It's no surprise to me, Chief Watt of all people should have known better than to say something in Latin.

While Channel 7 goes into stop action slow motion replays of Chief Watt's heart attack I let Duke out. He comes back a few minutes later with the *Globe Republican*. Judging from the out of breath man chasing my dog up the street – I deduce the paper must have formerly belonged to Mr. Harlow.

"I've finally caught the culprit who has been stealing my newspapers! Your dog is in big trouble Thibault. I'm calling the cops," he says grabbing the paper from Duke's mouth.

I close the door wondering whether Duke's rights will be properly protected by the judicial system. Will the cops read him his Miranda rights before busting him? Will he be entitled to a trial by his peers? Will he have to share a cell with that pervert, Basil O'Reilly? Since he can't afford a lawyer will he get a court appointed attorney? And, if he does get a freebie mouthpiece will it be Annette Stratton-Osborne? I hope not because I know he's a lot cuter than I am and I don't want him alienating her affection in case Nina is grounded for the next century and is therefore unable to elope with me. Before I can think of all the ramifications of my dog's imminent arrest there's a knock at the door.

I open it to see a pale Mr. Harlow standing on the porch with the paper. "Please forgive my anger and accept this newspaper as a token of my apology. I don't know what got into me. I'm so sorry. Would it be okay if I gave you a gift subscription for your own copy of the newspaper? It's the least I can do."

I thank him for his generosity while trying to figure out what could have possibly changed his mind so fast. Opening the front page I immediately understand. In big block letters the lead headline is:

MAFIA BOSS TO TESTIFY IN GRAND JURY PROBE
GANGSTER THIBAULT DENIES HE WILL TAKE 5TH

I look at the accompanying unflattering mug shot of my father before perusing the article. I'll have to remember to tell Johann not to stare wide eyed into the camera. It makes him look like a psychopathic ax murderer. I read the article.

> *Security around the Clayton Courthouse is expected to be extremely tight today when alleged Mafia Boss Johann Thibault testifies in a closed Grand Jury session. Sources in the District Attorney's office are hinting that the alleged Mafia Boss might break the Mob's sacred code of omerta.* *(Continued page 3)*

Before I can turn the page my eye is caught by another front page story. Under Neil Posavad's byline is a follow-up article on Archbishop Frontere:

> *According to documents filed in Probate Court yesterday the Archbishop of St. Louis, His Excellency Giuseppe Guglielmo Frontere, has been named executor of the estate of the late Vespucci family enforcer Salvatore Veneruzzo. Veneruzzo's company, Ace Industries, is purportedly the largest distributor of pornography in the midwest.*

> *This comes on the heels of allegations that the Archbishop intervened Monday with Clayton police authorities to gain the release of one of Ace Industries' leading pornographic models on assault charges.*

> *Raising the eyebrows of investigators, the Archbishop has recently been seen in public with both the porn starlet and rock star Ric Thibault, the teenage son of Johann Thibault, Veneruzzo's reputed successor* *(Continued page 3)*

I'm a certified rock star! *The Globe Republican* wouldn't print something if it wasn't true – I'm an overnight sensation! I quickly turn to page three;

> *in the Vespucci hierarchy. In a Court document filed yesterday the younger Thibault was bequeathed a late model Corvette from Veneruzzo's estate.*

> *Ironically, it was in a car owned by Johann Thibault's wife Lucretia that the bullet riddled bodies of Veneruzzo and Louis Palazarri were discovered last week.*

> *Attempts by this paper to reach the Archbishop for comment have been unsuccessful.*

Having finished the article on Archbishop Frontere, I skim the conclusion of the story on my father:

> *Prosecutors want to ask the reputed crime boss what he knows about the gangland*

executions of mobsters Salvatore Veneruzzo and Louis Palazarri. Reportedly the Grand Jury is also seeking to probe into Thibault's involvement with Ace Industries and its pornography business.

Informed sources say Thibault will be questioned about his relationship with Clayton High School principal Basil I. O'Reilly, who was arrested yesterday on child pornography charges. Thibault has two children currently attending Clayton High School and O'Reilly was reportedly a guest at a wild party in the Thibault home on the night of the Veneruzzo murders.

O'Reilly was taken into custody after investigators traced a widely circulated poster of an unidentified naked Clayton High student back to the principal. At the time of his apprehension O'Reilly was found in possession of several hundred pictures of nude students taken by a hidden camera in the girls' locker room of Clayton High.

The phone rings and Kristen answers it. It's Billy Bender wanting to know if we saw Chief Watt croak. Kristen tells Billy we were watching and hands me the phone.

"Since we saw him kick the bucket don't we get today off from school?" Billy asks.

"I don't think so. At most Watt is only worth a black arm band under Basil O'Reilly's latest guidelines. I don't think he even rates flags at half-mast," I reply.

"Yeah, but now that Basil's in jail don't they throw all his rules out the window?" queries Billy raising an interesting point.

"It probably depends on who they get to replace him," I answer, "but maybe we could call up everybody and get them to claim they are too traumatized to go to school. First our beloved principal, in whom we are supposed to place unquestioning trust, has been exposed as a child pornographer and now we have witnessed the tragic death of Chief Watt. It's too much for sensitive students like ourselves to handle. Did you see the newspaper this morning?"

"Yeah. Your dad's up shit creek."

"I know, but did you see they called me a rock star?"

"Yeah, that was cool. Dominique's gonna rip your pants off when she sees you. Hey man, I have to get going if I'm going to get hold of everybody before they go to school. I'll call everybody whose last names begin from A to K."

I agree to call L-Z. The first person I call is Justin Lafayette. He agrees with Billy and me that we should get the day off and volunteers to call everyone whose last names begin in the letter L to

FEED THE DOG

R. The lucky bastard gets to call Nina Pennington, but it's probably for the best since I'm not sure her father would let her talk to me.

I call Kevin Micheletti next. "I'm glad you called, I was just going to phone you," Kevin says. "I saw the story on your dad in the paper. Does he have one of those cool Godfather rings that everyone has to kiss?"

"I've never seen anyone kiss my dad's ring, in fact, I don't think I've ever seen anyone kiss my dad. Did you see the bit about me being a rock star?"

"Yeah, that was far out man."

I tell Kevin about our plan and he says he's all for it. He promises to call everyone from S through Z.

Having finished my calls I decide to go back to bed. But before I can get up the stairs the phone rings. I pick it up. It's Derek Irons, and he sounds hungover and angry.

"Did you see the paper this morning?" he asks.

"Yeah, it was great. They called me a rock star."

"Yes, but they didn't say what band you're in. We had you join Suckerpunch for your publicity value. For the money we're paying you the least you can do is make sure they include your band's name in any story about your family. Your name is no longer 'Ric Thibault', it's 'Ric Thibault of Suckerpunch'. I want to see Suckerpunch in big beautiful letters whenever I read your name in any paper."

"I didn't write the story. How can I control what they say?"

"I don't know, but you're a smart lad and I'm sure you'll figure it out. I'll see you tonight at rehearsal. Good-bye." Derek hangs up leaving me pissed.

I go upstairs to bed thinking how irrational Derek is. The guy drinks too much and has no concept of reality whatsoever. I guess that's why he's a manager.

I wake up at ten-fifteen to the sound of the doorbell ringing. I hope it's not the truant officer coming to bust my ass. I hear Kristen answering it, so I know she hasn't gone to school either and I'm safe.

"You can see the car for two dollars, or ride around the block in it for ten bucks," my sister is saying.

"Is it ten dollars per person or ten dollars per ride?" the stranger asks.

"It's ten dollars for the first person and seven dollars for each additional passenger," Kristen states.

She better not be messing with my Corvette, I think, throwing on some clothes and racing downstairs.

"My wife and I would like to buy two ride tickets."

"What the hell are you doing?" I ask my sister.

"That'll be seventeen dollars then. If you'll excuse me for just a second," Kristen says to the stranger, grabbing me by the arm and leading me out of earshot into the kitchen. "Ssh! I'm selling rides in the Deathmobile."

"The Deathmobile?"

"Yeah, we've got mom's car back from the cops and all these suckers have been calling wanting to see it. They're willing to pay for the privilege."

"Who gets the money?"

"Whoever sells the tickets."

"It won't work. We'll end up getting in fights over who can answer the door."

Kristen thinks about it for a second and sees my point, "What do you propose?" she asks.

"That we split the money evenly."

"How many ways?"

"Three ways," answers my greedy brother from behind me, "I heard you guys talking. I'm in on this."

"Okay," Kristen concedes.

"All right," I reluctantly agree, although I don't relish the prospect of being business partners with a sleaze bag like Stephan.

While Stephan goes and takes the customers out for a spin I share a marketing idea with Kristen. "We should capitalize on more than the Pontiac being the Deathmobile."

"What do you mean?"

"Well, why don't we take advantage of you being a centerfold and offer topless rides with a *Penthouse* pet? We could get a whole lot more than ten bucks per ride."

"How much more?"

"We'll offer topless rides around the block for fifty bucks per person, and for an additional twenty-five smackers the passenger will be allowed to sit in the front seat with Bambi Bosoms."

Kristen mulls it over for a second, "It's a good idea, but we need to advertise to get anyone willing to pay that much money – and I don't know if the newspapers will carry advertisements for topless car rides."

"Why worry about paying for advertising when we can get all the publicity we need for free? I'll call Mary Ecclestone and give her an exclusive on what we're doing. She'll cover it as a news story. I'll also tell Jimmy Leach and I'm sure he'll put it on his show."

"No one listens to Jimmy Leach except perverts," my sister reminds me.

"What's wrong with that? Perverts are our core market group," I reply while dialing Mary Ecclestone. She's not in. Her assistant says she will be busy providing live updates for the next few hours from Chief Watt's press conference.

"He's already dead. How much more can you update that?" I ask.

"You obviously don't understand the news business," sneers the assistant, "so do you want to leave a message?"

"Yes. Will you tell her Ric Thibault called and I'm willing to give her the exclusive interview she wanted?"

Suddenly she is a lot friendlier, "Johann Thibault's son, the rock star? I'll have Miss Ecclestone call as soon as I can get hold of her."

I hang up and call Jimmy. He says he'll plug the Deathmobile every five minutes if he can get five free topless rides. It's a small price to pay and I agree to it.

Stephan returns a few minutes later saying our customers were disappointed Lucretia's car has been fixed, "There aren't any bullet holes left in the car. They want to see blood and destruction."

The customer is always right. So I call Billy and ask him if we can borrow one of his father's guns.

"Why?"

"I need to shoot Lucretia's Pontiac."

"Won't she get mad?" Billy asks.

"No. We'll have made so much money by the time she gets out of the hospital that we'll be able to buy her a new car."

"Okay, I'll lend you a .45 magnum under one condition. You have to let me fire a few rounds into it," Billy offers.

"Only if you promise not to hit the gas tank."

"I'll be right over," Billy says.

"What are we going to do for blood?" Stephan inquires.

"Well, Kristen and I each donated a pint of blood a couple of days ago at school so we don't have any to spare. You're going to have to cut yourself and bleed all over the seats."

Stephan is scared, "I can't cut myself."

"I'll get a knife and do it for you," I volunteer, trying unsuccessfully not to sound too eager.

Kristen fetches a knife and we go out to the garage. I resist temptation and only give Stephan a small cut. As he bleeds all over the back seat Stephan states that this is a perfect example of free market economics at work.

I don't want to hear about any free markets. As far as I'm concerned Karl Marx can eat his heart out. We're captains of industry. We're going to be rich!

It's my turn to answer the phone, "Hello, Deathmobile Industries, may I help you?"

"I'd like to book a front seat ride."

"For a front seat ride I can fit you in next Tuesday at five-thirty. Would that be good for you?"

"Don't you have anything sooner?"

"I do have one opening for a back seat ride tomorrow night at nine-twenty-five, however the earliest front seat ride is Tuesday."

"Do you take credit cards?"

"No, I'm sorry we only take cash."

Jimmy Leach's ratings must have gone up, because it's one o'clock and the phone has been ringing off the hook for the last hour with people booking topless rides in the Deathmobile.

Kristen is out driving, and Stephan and I are alternating between running the photo concession (Ten bucks gets you a Polaroid of Bambi Bosoms and yourself leaning on the Deathmobile; for twenty dollars you get the same photo except Bambi is topless) and booking reservations.

Once Mary Ecclestone gets here and does her story business is going to be really booming. I call the phone company and order two additional lines. We'll probably have to add a few employees – maybe we can hire Kristen's stripper friends, Cherie and Tawny.

The phone rings again.

"Hello, Deathmobile Industries, may I help you?"

"What the hell is going on there? Why are you answering the phone like that – and what are you doing home from school?" It's Johann.

"Hi dad. School was canceled on account of everyone being traumatized by Chief Watt's dying on TV," I answer the easiest question. "Aren't you supposed to be testifying before the Grand Jury?"

"I've already finished."

"Did you break omerta? Are they putting you in the federal witness protection program and giving you a new identity while moving you to someplace so awful, like Arizona, that hitmen don't like going there to work?"

"I'm not in the goddamn Mafia and you know it."

"That's not what the newspapers say."

"Cut the crap you little schweinhund. I discovered some pretty interesting stuff from the Grand Jury today – and I think I know where all these Mafia rumors started. You and I need to have a nice long chat."

Feeling I might not want to have this discussion, I contemplate faking telephone problems again and hanging up on Johann. But since I don't have the luxury of the Atlantic Ocean separating us anymore and he can probably drive over here in five minutes, the odds are it would not work twice.

I try a different tactic. "I can probably fit you in when I get back from tour."

"Tour? What the hell are you talking about?"

"Did I forget to tell you? Don't you even read the papers? I'm a rock star now and I'm going out on tour opening for David Bowie."

"David who?"

For someone who can speak twelve languages my dad certainly isn't too smart. I can't believe he doesn't know who David Bowie is. "David Bowie is the biggest rock star in the world and I'm going to be on tour with him."

"You aren't going anywhere you little shit until we straighten a few things out and that's an order," my father says in a tone which seemingly contradicts his earlier denials of being in the Mob. "I'll be over in five minutes and you better be home when I get there."

I hang up in terror. Armageddon is five minutes away. The Bible was only slightly off – rather than riding in with the four horsemen of the apocalypse the end is riding in on the four Goodyear steel-belted radials of an air conditioned late model Ford Mustang. The sky is falling and existentialism is a fraud. I've got no control of my very purposeful universe. I am an idiot for not fucking Nina Pennington last night.

The doorbell rings its lugubrious melody. Mumbling the Lord's prayer, "our Father who art in heaven our kingdom come..." I trudge over and open the door.

Blessed are those who believe! Either God loves me or existentialism really works – which explains why Jean-Paul Sartre is still alive and fucking voluptuous Sorbonne girls in Paris – because standing in the doorway is Mary Ecclestone and her camera crew. She has come to do her story on the burgeoning jewel of Clayton's economy, Deathmobile Industries – and I know my father, be he in the Mafia or not, won't kill me in front of the Eyewitness News team.

Much to the chagrin of the twenty people queued up waiting for their rides I let the camera crew cut the line and give them a complimentary trip with Bambi Bosoms. "I bought a fifty dollar front seat ride and have been standing here waiting for over half an hour. How can you let those hooligans who started the Press riot jump in front of us? It's unfair," complains a fat balding fortyish guy in a raincoat.

"I'm sorry sir. Do you want a refund?" I reluctantly offer.

"No. All I want is my ride in the Deathmobile with Bambi Bosoms."

"Fuck the press – we want our rides," chants the crowd.

"Gentlemen, on behalf of Deathmobile Industries please allow me to apologize for any inconvenience. As a way of saying we're sorry Deathmobile Industries will throw in at no extra charge an autographed picture of Bambi Bosoms topless in the Deathmobile," I volunteer, sacrificing a goldmine in merchandising fees.

Our clientele seem satisfied with my offer and calm down. While Stephan goes and gets more Polaroid film I explain the concept behind Deathmobile Industries to Mary Ecclestone, "We're three students struggling to raise money for our college educations."

"What a crock of shit," she interrupts me, "you're trying to use me to get your pornographic scheme free publicity."

"Yeah, but don't your ratings go up when you have stories featuring scantily clad women?" I ask while out of the corner of my eye seeing Johann walking up the driveway followed by the camera crew who have just finished their ride, "and in exchange for the publicity I'll get you an exclusive interview with my father."

"Really?" she asks excitedly, wiping a bit of drool from her mouth. "When?"

"Now," I say, opening the door for Johann. "Hi dad, may I introduce you to Mary Ecclestone of

FEED THE DOG

Channel 7?"

Johann shakes her hand, but from the "what's-this-bimbo-doing-here?" look he shoots at me, he doesn't appear to be pleased to make her acquaintance.

"Is this guy trying to cut the line too?" yells the guy in the raincoat.

"Line? What line? What the fuck is going on here?" Johann demands.

"Did you guys get that? Are we rolling?" Mary Ecclestone asks the camera crew.

"Rolling," confirms the guy holding the camera.

"Mr. Thibault – traditionally Mafia leaders have been adverse to involving their children in pornography. Yet you are an exception. Does this have anything to do with your being apprehended wearing women's clothing in a Parisian brothel and does this signal a new direction in the Mafia's morality?"

Johann mumbles something about having no comment other than he's not in the Mafia as he turns around and runs out the door.

"He's trying to jump the line!" objects the guy in the raincoat, running after my father toward the Deathmobile. He grabs Johann and punches him in the stomach dropping my dad to his knees. My father's assailant reached into his pocket for a second and then shakes his head and runs off.

"Make sure you get this," shouts Mary Ecclestone to the cameraman, "This is Pulitzer Prize stuff – we've got exclusive footage of an attempted Mafia rubout."

It's three o'clock and the board of directors of Deathmobile Industries are reviewing the results of their first audit. Today we've sold seventeen front seat rides for $1,275, thirty-four back seat rides for $1,700, twenty-four viewings of the car for $217.50 and sixteen autographed pictures for $160. Less the $36.98 in film costs and nine dollars in gas, give us pretax revenues of $3,306.52. In a unanimous decision the board of directors declare a $1,102.17 special dividend to the three stock holders of record as of eleven o'clock this morning.

Stephan wants to know what we're going to do with the extra one cent left in the corporate treasury. To placate our rapacious brother we award it to him.

I provide my fellow capitalists with a summary of our projections. We have bookings clear into next month bringing in an estimated forty-six thousand dollars in revenue.

Stephan suggests Kristen should drop out of school thereby enabling us to add another eight hours daily to our operating schedule.

Kristen declines saying she doesn't want to do anything which might jeopardize her going to Stanford.

"Hey, stop talking so much and give us our rides," shouts an impatient customer.

"We'll be with you in a minute sir. I need to discuss one thing further with my partners," Kristen responds.

"I've been waiting twenty minutes and want my fucking ride now," the man protests.

"Me and some of my father's associates will take you for a nice long ride if you don't shut up," I threaten successfully. "Now, what did you want to discuss?"

"We have one potential obstacle looming in the future of Deathmobile Industries," my sister states.

"You mean Lucretia?" I question.

"Yes. Mom gets out of the hospital in two days and I think she's going to want her car back," Kristen says.

"Everyone knows she is crazy. Is there any chance we could get them to keep her longer?" Stephan inquires.

"Everyone knows you're crazy. Is there any chance we could get them to take you?" I ask my heartless brother.

"We could cut mom in," Kristen proposes.

"Or maybe we could buy her out," Stephan suggests as we get back to work.

"Where's Bambi Bosoms and the Deathmobile?" complains Kevin Futterman, "I've been waiting in line for over half an hour."

"She must have had to stop for gas," I reply looking at my watch, "she'll be back in a minute."

The phone rings again.

"Hello, Deathmobile Industries, may I help you?"

"Yes, this is Acting Detective Ganchar of the Clayton Police Department, may I speak with Ric Thibault?"

"This is he."

"Can you hold for a moment for Kristen Thibault?"

"Hi Ric, it's me. I've got a little problem..."

Deathmobile Industries has been dealt a severe setback. One of our principal corporate assets, Bambi Bosoms, has been busted!

According to Kristen, Officer Seymour Stankiewicz, the lone survivor of the Attorney General's purge of the Clayton police department, has just arrested her for indecent exposure and failure to have a chauffeur's license.

"They're arraigning me in an hour, can you get me a lawyer and also some clothes?" my sister asks, clearly on the verge of tears.

"Don't worry, it will all work out fine. I'll call Annette Stratton-Osborne."

I dial Annette and explain the problem.

"You know with all your family's problems you should put me on permanent retainer. It would be much cheaper," Annette proposes.

"Will you take the case?"

"Sure, I'll meet you down at the courthouse in an hour."

I hang up and begin the painful task of making $1,450 worth of refunds to the twenty-four people awaiting rides. This leaves the corporate treasury with only $625.

Stephan wants his share of the remaining money now. "We have to use it for Kristen's bail and lawyer," I explain.

"That's her responsibility. It isn't a corporate expense," Stephan solidifies his position as Chief Executive Asshole in our family.

"We'll vote on it at our next stockholders meeting," I grab the money and go into Kristen's room.

"I'll sue you for misuse of corporate funds," Stephan blusters from the doorway.

I'm not too bothered by Stephan's threats. I'd love to see my brother back in Court with Judge Heinz. I'll glue some tacks to Stephan's seat and when he sits down he'll scream so loud that the Judge will throw him back in jail for contempt of Court. I'm sure the sentences are longer for repeat offenders.

I go through Kristen's drawers and pick out a halter top and a pair of hot pants. From her closet I select her highest pair of stiletto heels. From all the movies I've seen this is the official uniform of women in prison.

I walk out the door and run into Nina walking up the front steps. She looks even more beautiful than I remember. Maybe her tits grew overnight – they look a little bigger.

"What are you doing carrying a pair of high heels?" she asks.

"I'm taking them down to the courthouse for Kristen."

"What's she doing there?"

"She got arrested for indecent exposure."

"Have you noticed that everyone in your family winds up in jail?"

I go through the list. Johann, Stephan, and Kristen have all been in jail this week. Lucretia broke the law with her suicide attempt and is in a mental hospital in lieu of jail. Even Nina was briefly incarcerated. Is there some hidden meaning here? Is she referring to herself as a member of my family? Am I on the verge of getting into her pants? "I guess I'm the black sheep in the family, I haven't even been arrested."

Nina asks if I want any company.

"I always feel better when you're with me," I respond, opening the car door for her like Amy Vanderbilt says a gentleman is supposed to.

On the way downtown Nina tells me her father believed the alibi and doesn't suspect a thing. "It was really sweet of Annette Stratton-Osborne to help me. I don't know how to thank her."

"I've already thanked her for you. Don't worry about it," I assure Nina.

Due to all the news vans surrounding the Courthouse there are no parking spots anywhere. We drive around until we find a space in front of Parizeau's Shoes. In Parizeau's window there is a sign announcing a special 1/2 price Charles Jourdan sale. Even though I didn't sell my story to the *National Enquirer*, having settled for Jasper Gilbertson and the *Midnight Sun* instead, I decide to buy Nina a pair of shoes.

"Hold my hand and close your eyes and you'll get a surprise," I instruct Nina.

"Why?"

"Trust me."

"Okay," she says, taking my hand.

I lead her into the store. A snotty man with a bad lisp, crew cut and a funny walk asks if he can help us.

"I'd like to buy my girlfriend a pair of Charles Jourdan black patent leather high heels."

Nina opens her eyes, squeals and gives me an extremely wet kiss.

"You want Fuck-Me pumps?" the salesman hisses.

"Exactly," I reply.

♪

"Taking into consideration the severity of the defendant's offenses and her links to the Thibault Crime Syndicate, the People feel Kristen Thibault, alias Bambi Bosoms, is a flight risk and request bail be set at ten thousand dollars," District Attorney Irwin Roberts pleads.

Ten thousand dollars? I do some quick arithmetic in my head; that's one hundred thirty-three front seat rides in the Deathmobile, or if we run full loads of three in the back and one up front, it's forty-four trips. If we are able to do twelve trips per hour we can have Kristen sprung in under four hours. Of course I don't think there is much of a market for front seat rides if Bambi Bosoms is in jail. On the positive side Kristen might get cast in one of those prison movies. She looks pretty sexy sitting at the defense table in her women in prison uniform. Of course she doesn't look as good as Nina, or Annette Stratton-Osborne either for that matter, but her high heels aren't Charles Jourdans and they probably didn't cost one hundred twenty-five dollars.

I look behind me. Sitting next to Mary Ecclestone is a sketch artist who is drawing the arraignment scene for tonight's newscast. His picture is pretty good except for his portrayal of Annette as having larger breasts than Kristen. I whisper my observation to Mary Ecclestone – but she is not interested in journalistic accuracy. I guess I shouldn't be surprised.

"Miss Stratton-Osborne, do you have anything to say on behalf of your client?" asks Judge Heinz.

"Yes, your Honor. The defense objects to the District Attorney's scurrilous remarks concerning my client's family. Her relatives are not at issue here. Yesterday you freed Officer Watt, a man accused of the same charges, on his own recognizance. My client is a straight A student, and an enterprising young businesswoman with strong ties to the community. She has no prior police record. Precedent has clearly been set, and we wish to be afforded the same treatment any other member of the public would receive."

Judge Heinz asks for the attorneys to approach the bench. He confers with the two lawyers while I hold Nina's hand and study her new Jourdans for a reflection. I think I must have bought a defective pair because there isn't one. But Nina doesn't notice any problems with the shoes, "I'm going to wear them to the Bowie gigs. I bet Dominique doesn't have a pair as cool as these."

"You're going to come on the road with me?" I ask torn between the desire to share a hotel room alone with Nina and the fear of her discovering I don't really know Bowie yet. But, maybe Bowie knows me. Now that I'm in Suckerpunch Dominique might have seen me in some special magazine catering to groupies. It's probably called *The Official Observers Guide to Rock Stars* and can be bought only in trendy clubs in New York, London and Los Angeles as well as backstage at any big concert. "What excuse are you going to use on your parents? If I recall correctly, I'm not number one on your dad's hit parade."

"My dad still hates your guts, but I really want to go on tour with you. It sounds so exciting. You're good at making up excuses. Can't you figure some way of getting my parents out of the way?" Nina asks with an 'accomplish-this-and-you-might-get-laid' look.

"Too bad Salvatore Veneruzzo is dead, because I'm sure he had friends who could kidnap your parents for a week or two," I say, only half-way facetiously.

"You can't go around kidnapping my parents. That wouldn't be nice," Nina says as the lawyers return to their tables.

"I was just kidding," I whisper, squeezing her hand. "Don't worry. I'll think of something."

"I'd like a brief recess while both lawyers and the defendant meet me in chambers," Judge Heinz announces.

Nina wants to go down to the newsstand to buy some gum. We take the stairs which is hard for Nina because she isn't good at walking in five inch heels. She has to go down sideways using me for support, which is cool because it gives me an excuse to wrap my arms around her chest thereby copping a few feels.

Coming back we run into Terry Madigan and he asks if he can speak with me. "How come you gave Mary Ecclestone an exclusive interview? Channel 12 would have outbid the competition for your story." He looks at Nina who is chewing gum and trying to adjust her shoe straps. "I'll give you two girls, one of whom made a porno movie and a beer commercial. Believe me that's a lot better than Ecclestone's bimbo who does topless posters."

"That's my fiancee you're talking about you bastard," I say, shoving Madigan against the wall, causing his toupee to slide forward over his face.

I see a bunch of flashes and spin around. Several photographers are busy clicking away while a bunch of reporters gather around. "The Mafia rock star kid nailed Terry Madigan with a Suckerpunch!" one of them says making up for his inaccurate description of my actions by getting my band's name right. At least Derek Irons will be happy.

Someone pulls me off Madigan. It's Kevin Bender. "Calm down Ric. You can't go around slugging reporters in public hallways – wait until you get them in a dark alley with no witnesses. It

FEED THE DOG

works much better."

"Hey! Isn't that Brother Theodore coming out of the Grand Jury?" hollers a reporter from down the hall. Except for Terry Madigan, all of the media herd run off to find out what the evangelist was doing with the Grand Jury.

Madigan is too busy adjusting his hairpiece to either join his comrades or see Nina tottering up to him in her high heels. She gives him a hard knee to the balls sending him sprawling to the floor.

"Good technique Nina," says Billy's dad admiringly.

"What are you doing here, Mr. Bender?" I ask.

"I have to testify in front of the Grand Jury. The District Attorney thinks I sold the bullets which killed those stupid Mafia guys," he says, kicking Terry Madigan in the balls. "I'm sorry Mr. Madigan. It was an accident. I didn't see you lying there," he apologizes, helping the moaning reporter to his feet.

Nina and I say good-bye to Kevin Bender and walk past Brother Theodore's impromptu press conference. I'm not sure what question was asked of Brother Theodore, but I hear him respond, "The Good Book says 'judge not lest ye be judged'."

We hurry upstairs to the courtroom. A few minutes later Judge Heinz, Kristen, and the two lawyers emerge from chambers. The Judge bangs his gavel and announces the case has been settled out of court. "Miss Bosoms, I mean Thibault, has signed a consent decree. She will no longer offer topless rides in her mother's automobile. Consequently the District Attorney will drop all charges against the defendant. Case dismissed."

I'm happy for Kristen but also depressed. The goose that laid the golden egg is lying dead in the middle of the courtroom. Deathmobile Industries is out of business.

I hope the $625 left in the corporate treasury is enough to fix the bullet holes in Lucretia's car because I'm sure Stephan will refuse to pay his share of the cost.

Jimmy Leach is furious. "You and I made a deal. I lived up to my end by mentioning at least twenty times you were offering topless rides with Bambi Bosoms in the Deathmobile. In exchange you promised me five topless rides with your sister. Now you're reneging by saying you have some court order prohibiting you from paying up. That's a crock of shit," he yells.

"I swear I'm telling the truth. Turn on the TV if you don't believe me. The news starts in two minutes. Mary Ecclestone will be doing a piece on us."

"I'd like to be doing Mary Ecclestone's piece," Jimmy says, switching on the television.

"Hello, this is Ted Hollinger and this is the Channel 7 news at six. Here are the headlines: Clayton police Chief Harold D. Watt dies during a morning press conference shortly after the Missouri Attorney General suspends him from office, a peace treaty with Vietnam has been signed in Paris, Spiro Agnew may be indicted on kickback charges, while Special Prosecutor Archibald Cox moves towards recommending the impeachment of President Nixon, a coup d'état in Chile, and 132 die in a plane crash in Dallas. But first here's our top story. Our Eyewitness News team has exclusive footage of an attempted Mafia assassination this afternoon at the Mob's topless taxi service headquarters. Here is Chief Investigative Reporter Mary Ecclestone with the latest details on the Thibault crime family. We warn our viewers some of the footage you are about to see is quite graphic and parental discretion should be used in allowing children to watch."

"An attempted underworld hit on alleged crime boss Johann Thibault failed when the hitman apparently forgot his gun," states Mary Ecclestone, offering her unique perspective on today's events. "Our Channel 7 cameras were on the scene when an unidentified man in a raincoat approached the reputed Mob chieftain. In slow motion you see here the hitman attacking Thibault with his fists and then reaching into his pocket for a gun. The assailant can't find his weapon, shakes his head and escapes.

According to our Channel 7 Mafia expert, Joey Angotti, today's attempted hit on the fast rising star of organized crime may be the work of disgruntled former associates of the late Salvatore Veneruzzo. They are said to be upset at the Thibault family's commercial exploitation of the car in which Veneruzzo and Louis Pellegrino were found shot to death.

In a Channel 7 exclusive, we were able to film the children of Johann Thibault giving X-rated rides in the bullet ridden car they have dubbed the 'Deathmobile'. For prices ranging up to seventy-five dollars members of the public were able to ride in the bloody automobile with Thibault's topless daughter.

Later in the day this operation was closed when the newly revamped Clayton police force arrested Kristen Thibault on charges of indecent exposure and failure to possess a chauffeur's license."

"Okay you weren't lying," says Jimmy. "I'll tell you what, for five Quaaludes I'll let you out of the deal."

"Ssh! I want to hear if Mary Ecclestone says anything about me."

"Do we have a deal?" Jimmy asks hopefully.

"Yeah," I respond, picking up the ringing phone.

It's Lucretia. I don't even have time to say hello before she is ranting.

"What the hell is going on? How could that motherfucker forget his gun? What's wrong with the Mafia? With so many people out of work and looking for jobs you would think they would be able to find a competent hitman who wouldn't forget his gun...and what happened to my car? You told me it was all fixed and now I see it on TV full of bullet holes...and tell your sister she's grounded for the rest of her life for going around topless on television and to put her shirt back on...Are you listening to me?"

"Yes ma'am, and how are you doing?"

Lucretia ignores me, resuming her harangue at an even more frantic pace, "What happened to the plastic Jesus that was on the dashboard and was blessed personally by Brother Theodore? I didn't see it on the news...and how much money did you get for those topless rides, and how much of it is my share...I get out of here in two days and there's going to be hell to pay...hey! I don't need one of those needles, I'm fine, it's everyone else who needs a shot – not me...I'm saner than anyone...give it to my asshole husband, the Mafia boss and my good-for-nothing kids...give me back the phone...Ouch!"

"I'm sorry," says a soothing female voice, "your mother is under a lot of strain and we've had to give her a shot to calm her down."

"Thank you very much. Was it a big shot?" I ask optimistically.

"It was her normal dosage, she'll be out for a few hours; until at least midnight."

"You mean past visiting time?"

"Yes. I'm afraid you won't be able to see your mother today."

"I'm so disappointed, but I'm sure you're taking excellent care of her. Good-bye." I hang up wondering if Dr. Tudor prescribes Thorazine in addition to Quaaludes.

The news is now covering Chief Watt's demise. Clayton's coroner, Dr. Hamilton is saying something about the cause of death being a heart attack. I don't know where Dr. Hamilton went to medical school – clearly he isn't very smart. Everyone knows the Chief died because he was speaking Latin.

"Just tell me where you keep the 'ludes and you can keep on watching TV," Jimmy offers, presuming me to be as stupid as Dr. Hamilton. There is no way I am going to let Jimmy help himself to my stash.

"I don't want to see the slow motion video tape of the Chief dying again so I'll get them." I run upstairs and count out the pills. I have thirty-one left.

I go downstairs and hand Jimmy the pills.

"Clayton's Court House was also the scene of another event today," Mary Ecclestone is saying. "Clayton businessman Zachary Pennington and televangelist Brother Theodore held a joint news conference on the Courthouse steps to announce he is forming a citizen's action committee to stamp out pornography."

They cut away to a clip of Nina's father speaking. "The citizens of Clayton can no longer stand idly by while our community is overrun by the scourge of pornography. It is a well known fact that pornography is a communist plot. It leads to hard rock music, drug use, and promiscuity thereby undermining the moral fabric which holds our free society together."

I'm all for hard rock music, drug use, and promiscuity, however I hate communists. I've seen tons of documentaries on communism and I've yet to see a commie girl wearing Charles Jourdan high heels and a tight sweater. Instead they are all fat and ugly with babushkas, loose drab clothing and names like 'Olga' and 'Svetlina'.

Zachary Pennington is an asshole. I hope he says something in Latin.

Nina's father continues, "which is why Brother Theodore and I have founded the Citizens Against Pornography, or C.A.P. I take great pride in serving as co-chairman with the most spiritual man I have ever met, Brother Theodore."

Channel 7 shows an excerpt from Brother Theodore's speech. "Jesus did not die for us to have filth in our schools. We must stop this disease which has already manifested itself once in Basil O'Reilly and is threatening to fester throughout society. Therefore I'm asking each and everyone of you to send C.A.P. a donation of fifty dollars to fight the proliferation of pornography. In return I'll send you a C.A.P. bumper sticker, a C.A.P. membership card, and at no extra charge a genuine plastic Jesus dashboard ornament which I personally have blessed."

"Brother Theodore refused to answer questions from the press concerning his testimony this afternoon before the Johann Thibault Grand Jury," Ted Hollinger reports.

Johann chases whores and isn't particularly religious so I wonder what connection there could possibly be between Brother Theodore and my father. They don't seem like the type of people who would hang out together.

FEED THE DOG

My thoughts are interrupted by the phone ringing. Again it's an irate person on the other end. This time it's Derek Irons.

"What's this shit about you not liking Suckerpunch?"

"What are you talking about?" I ask.

"I'm watching you slug out Terry Madigan on Channel 12 and they said you're through with Suckerpunch. We've got a contract. You can't leave us like this..."

"Hold on Derek. I think you misunderstood them. I'm sure they said I threw a sucker punch, which I didn't do. I'm not quitting the band."

Derek sighs in relief and moves to the next subject, "Claude Forey, the president of our record company, is coming to rehearsal tonight. Do you have any tight black leather trousers?"

"No, why?"

"You can't be in a rock and roll band if you're not wearing black leather. I want you to go down to Scarlet Leather on Euclid Avenue and get the tightest pair they have. They're open until nine and you can charge it to me."

"Okay."

"One more thing, I want you to wear the trousers to rehearsal."

"Why?"

"Claude Forey decides how much tour support bands get by how tight their trousers are."

"You're kidding."

"No I'm not," he says, hanging up.

I don't know anything about leather pants so I call Nina to see if she wants to help me.

"Hello?" Zachary Pennington answers.

"Hello. May I please speak with Nina?"

"Is this Ric Thibault?" he demands.

This seems like an occasion where the official Church sanctioned white lie is appropriate. I am protecting the vulnerable (me) in the hope of promoting the greater good – the goal of me getting into his daughter's pants. I know Archbishop Frontere would agree with me. "Ric who? This is Tim MacNeil the therapist at Clayton High School," I lie.

"Therapist? I never knew Clayton High had a therapist."

"Yes sir. I was originally hired to help students cope with the trauma caused by Mr. Apgar's and Sister Margaret's untimely deaths. Now with Principal O'Reilly being arrested on obscenity charges the School Board has hired me to provide counseling for the victims," I bullshit.

"I'm happy to see the School Board finally living up to its responsibility. That's one of the goals of my new committee, Citizens Against Pornography."

"I just saw it on the news sir, and it's a laudable project," I lie.

"Bless you. We have a long hard road ahead of us in the fight against pornography in the schools. We have to purge the libraries of indecent material..."

"Like *Lolita*?" I ask.

"That's a perfect example of the child pornography we need to get rid of."

"What about Hemingway?" I ask, remembering I haven't started *A Farewell To Arms*.

"It's been a long time since I read Hemingway and I don't remember anything obscene. Is there something wrong with it?"

"Take my word. Hemingway should be banned."

"Thank you so much for letting me know. I'll mention it to Brother Theodore at our meeting tonight. While I have you on the phone maybe you can tell me if the School Board is doing anything about removing undesirables such as known Mafia boss' children from the student body?"

"I wish we were able to. I'd like to see the Thibault children removed from school," I say truthfully since I need to skip classes so I can go out on tour with Suckerpunch. "But I have to talk to your daughter, is she available?"

"Yes. Let me get her. It was a pleasure talking with you. I'm glad to know there are still people who believe in decency working for the Clayton Board of Education."

I hear him yelling for Nina to pick up the phone. "It's Mr. MacNeil, the therapist from school."

Nina picks up the phone sounding depressed, "Hello?"

"Miss Pennington this is Tim MacNeil..." *click* I hear her father hang up. "Hi, it's me. Sorry for the bullshit, I had to make up a cock and bull story to get past your dad."

"Did you see him on TV?"

"Yeah, he was pretty scary."

"You should have to live with him. I was embarrassed enough by the poster but now he's gone totally off the deep end. If he ever gets near Basil O'Reilly, our ex-principal is going to be visiting Sal Veneruzzo."

"I guess it serves Basil right for taking the photos," I agree. "but, changing the subject, the reason I called is Derek Irons wants me to buy a pair of leather pants and I was wondering if you'd like to come shopping with me?"

Nina perks up, "Did you say shopping? When? Where?"

"In a few minutes."

"After today I love shopping with you. I'll be right over."

I put the phone down only to have it ring again.

"May I speak to someone from the Thibault family please," says a guy with a heavy Brooklyn accent.

"This is Ric Thibault, may I help you?"

"Yeah, this is Frankie Staniowski of Tequila Ike's Casino in Nevada. We collect famous cars for display in our lobby and we want to buy the Deathmobile."

"My mother is very attached to the car. I don't know if we want to part with it."

"I'm going to make an offer you can't refuse," he states firmly.

Alarm bells are tolling in my head. This guy works for a casino in Nevada. Everyone knows casinos are owned by the Mafia. Mafia guys all belong to the same fraternity and know each other; so Staniowski knows our family is not in the Mafia and isn't intimidated by the Thibault family. He's probably seen the *Godfather* at least five times and chose carefully the words he used when he said, "I'm going to make you an offer you can't refuse." He might even own that cigarette machine Billy and I knocked over in Pekin.

"Wha, a wha, what's your offer?" I stutter.

"Twenty-five thousand dollars."

The Mafia are not the type of people you want to rip off so I feel it incumbent to explain the car is not in perfect condition. "Um, Mr. Staniowski..."

"Call me Frankie."

"Okay, Frankie, but I have to tell you there are some bullet holes in the Deathmobile's body..."

"Cool! Thirty G's."

"One of the windows is blown out."

"Really? Great! Thirty-five thousand bucks."

"And the seats have bloodstains."

"All right, forty thousand smackers. Oh, could I put you on hold for a second? One of my associates needs to ask me a question."

"I can't believe it. I thought the Mafia was smarter. Every time I tell him something is wrong with the car he increases his offer by five thousand bucks," I tell Jimmy.

"Tell him it needs new tires and is missing its hubcaps," Jimmy advises.

"I'm back, now where were we?" Frankie Staniowski asks.

"I was telling you what was wrong with the car. The tires are bald and it's missing its hubcaps," for some reason I take Jimmy's advice.

"I'm sorry. Forty thousand dollars is my final offer. Do we have a deal?"

"Sold."

The impending arrival of Claude Forey is making Derek Irons nervous. "Okay guys, the equipment truck has to leave tomorrow for Detroit, so this is the last rehearsal before the Bowie dates. But more importantly we're having a little problem. I think it's only a technicality – but, as I was telling your new attorney, Miss Stratton-Osborne, I still haven't received the tour support check from Slipped Disk. Forey told me he has it with him and is going to give it to us after seeing you run through rehearsal. So please don't fuck anything up."

"Dr. Caley says I shouldn't be wearing these leather pants," Simon Q. Picasso complains while scratching his crotch. "Its animal powers have an atavistic effect on my psyche causing my superego to relinquish its hegemony over my id. Consequently I cannot be responsible for my actions."

"Herbie, do you see my fist?" questions Bernie Hrechkosy, holding up his hand.

"Don't call me Herbie, my name is Simon Q. Picasso."

Bernie punches Simon in the nose. "Now do you see my fist Mr. Simon Q. Picasso?" the guitarist asks.

"What did you do that for?" cries Simon.

"To prove that your shrink is a charlatan. You didn't punch me back which would have been the proper primitive response. Therefore there was no atavistic effect and your fragile superego is intact. Hence all you are suffering from is a case of rectal cranial inversion."

"Maybe it takes a while for the animal spirit to seep from the leather into my bloodstream and then into my brain," Simon snivels.

"Maybe it takes a while for reality to seep into your brain," Mick Masters corrects Simon.

"Would punching Herbie again help?" offers Rico.

"Stop it you guys," Derek orders, "Forey will be here any minute. Just in case any of you've

FEED THE DOG

forgotten I want to remind you how important your record deal is. Without it you'll be living in a trailer park and have your conversational skills limited to asking whether your customer prefers regular or premium petrol. Do I make myself perfectly clear? With this in mind I want you to be on your best behavior. This means no one (Rico are you paying attention to this?), no matter how true it is, should call Forey a queer. None of you should call him a faggot. Fairy, homo, pansy, fruit, poofter, and Nancy boy are all right out too."

"How about cocksucker?" Mick inquires.

"No. Try to remember the old expression 'you don't bite the hand that feeds you'."

"Can I take my leather pants off?" whines Simon.

"Only when Forey's around to enjoy it – although from what I hear there's not much to enjoy," snickers Mick.

"I'm taking Dr. Caley's advice and asserting myself," Simon shouts, swinging his bass at Mick's head. Mick manages to get his arms up enough to ward off the blow. Before it can escalate further Billy Jo Brackenbury leaps in and pulls Simon away.

"Hello Claude," I turn and see Derek greeting the small pudgy record company president who is wearing a silver lamé Liza Minnelli tour jacket. He is accompanied by a tall thin man dressed from head to toe in leather.

"This is Dickie Lafrenierre, my new head of Artist Relations," Claude Forey introduces his companion to Irons, "so where is the Mafia scion?"

Derek leads the two men over to where I'm standing with Nina and Bernie.

"Nice ass isn't it?" Forey asks Lafrenierre.

"Stupendous," replies the head of Artist Relations.

"Thanks," says Nina, blushing.

"Not yours sweetie, I was talking about the new boy's," sneers Forey.

"Allow me to present Ric Thibault, this is Claude Forey," Derek performs the introductions.

We shake hands. I wonder if Forey is feeling well because his hand is really limp and clammy. Remembering my Amy Vanderbilt manners I introduce Nina to the record company executives as my girlfriend.

"Those are beautiful Jourdans," Dickie Lafrenierre correctly identifies Nina's footwear, "they make your legs look fabulous. They're absolutely precious with your little feet. What are you, a size six?"

Nina nods.

"I wanted to buy Claude a pair just like yours but they don't make them in his size, so we had to settle for a pair of strapless Maude Frizons. They're cute – but there is nothing like a pair of Charles Jourdans to make a girl feel spectacularly sexy."

"But, Mr. Forey's not a girl," Nina points out.

"Not yet, but we're going to Switzerland next month and rectifying that," Lafrenierre smiles.

"You mean he's going to have his dick cut off?" asks Bernie.

"Among other things," replies Lafrenierre.

"Do you think he knows Miss Stumpf?" I whisper to Nina.

"What do they do with your dick after they cut it off?" questions Rico.

"Enough," interrupts Derek, "Claude didn't come here to talk about his personal life. Are you guys ready to play some music?"

"Oh, I am so looking forward to this," says Forey, sitting down on the couch with Derek and Lafrenierre. "They all look simply divine, don't they Dickie?"

"Absolutely marvelous," agrees Lafrenierre.

We launch into *I'm Stupid And So Are You* followed by a furious paced *Can't Keep Us Down*. Not wanting to live in a trailer park we demonstrate we're really cool rock and rollers by jumping around and making all the proper faces with our tongues hanging out during guitar solos.

Judging from Nina's reaction I think we're doing pretty well. She is dancing up a storm with her hair flying back and forth while her tits do likewise. I glance over at Forey. He's staring at my crotch and has a small wad of spittle leaking out the corner of his mouth running down his chin. His gaze makes me so nervous that I break a guitar string during *Swallow*. We finish the song and I hand Billy Jo my guitar so he can restring it.

While we wait for the roadie to return Annette walks in. She's wearing a mini-skirt and the same stiletto heeled patent leather knee length boots she wore last night but she must not have had a mirror when she got dressed, because she has a loose fitting ruffled blouse on which doesn't show how big her breasts are.

Derek manages to pry Forey's attention away from my crotch to introduce our lawyer. They exchange greetings and discuss the difficulties of procuring patent leather boots in large sizes.

Billy Jo Brackenbury returns my guitar and Derek asks us to play our new song, "Ric wrote this one," Irons explains to Forey, "It's called *Talkin' Nina Pennington Blues* and I think it'll make a great

FEED THE DOG

single."

"He can write too? How precious," replies Claude Forey again focusing his eyes on my crotch.

I never told Nina about my ode to her and her face lights up when she discovers she is being immortalized in song by Suckerpunch. While I'm checking my guitar's tuning Mick walks over and tells me he has changed a few lyrics to better fit his vocal style and also has added a new background vocal part for me to sing during the chorus. I'm supposed to join Simon and Bernie in singing 'blow me' at the end of each line.

> *Got a girlfriend who can't resist what I got*
> *Nina be her name*
> *She can't desist – she don't never stop*
> *Nina scream my name*
> *Nina, I wanna be on the tip of your tongue*
> *Blow me!*
> *Nina I'm gonna be a hard act to follow– Blow me!*

The new lyrics aren't bad. Forey and Lafrenierre are bopping to the music, holding hands, and tapping their feet. Forey gives the thumbs up sign to Derek, and mouths "This is a fucking hit."

Nina doesn't share their enthusiasm. She stops dancing and takes her shoes off and the next thing I know my face is absorbing the full impact of one hundred twenty-five dollars worth of Charles Jourdans, causing me to trip over my guitar chord and stagger into Simon Q. Picasso. Simon loses his balance and tumbles backwards into the drum kit which in turn sends the snare drum, tom toms and cymbals crashing back into Rico.

Finding no drum to assault with his drumsticks 'Bam Bam' elects to pummel Simon instead. However, Simon's bloodstream must have absorbed the full animal spirit from his leather pants because he retaliates by using his bass as a hockey stick and takes a slapshot at Rico's head. Luckily Simon's aim isn't very good and he misses his target. Unfortunately he connects instead with Bernie's Marshall amplifier propelling it to the floor where it explodes leaving Mick singing acappello:

> *Got a girlfriend who gets down on her knees and begs*
> *Nina be her name*
> *Got a girlfriend who wants what's between my legs*
> *Nina be her...*

Mick finally notices the music has stopped and turns around to see the escalating struggle between Simon and Rico. Deciding to join in the melee Mick takes the microphone stand and smashes it, with an ear shattering thud thanks to our monitors, squarely on top of Simon's head knocking him out cold.

"Thanks. Way to go man," congratulates Rico prematurely, failing to see Mick swinging the stand once more. With an equally loud thump it lands on top of the drummer's head.

However, Rico's head is much harder than Simon's and he is still ambulatory as he proves by grabbing Mick by the throat and attempting to throttle the singer.

Once again Billy Joe Brackenbury plays peacemaker, grabbing hold of Rico, enabling Mick to deliver a couple of kicks to Rico's balls before Derek enters the fray and wrestles Masters to the floor.

"I thought you loved me!" screams a crying Nina as I disentangle myself from my guitar chord, "How dare you write a dirty song about me?"

I don't have time to phone the Archbishop and get his opinion but this seems like another occasion to use an official Church sanctioned white lie, "Those weren't my lyrics. I didn't know Mick changed the words."

"You're lying. I heard you singing 'blow me', in the chorus," Nina bawls, slapping my face.

"Stop hitting me. I wasn't singing 'blow me', uh, I sang 'hold me'."

"Ric's telling the truth. I was singing 'hold me' too," says Bernie Hrechkosy coming to my rescue.

"'Blow me' is a much better lyric, don't you think Claude?" questions Dickie Lafrenierre.

Forey nods his head in agreement, "I must have heard a thousand songs with 'hold me' – it's such a cliché. 'Blow me' on the other hand would be original. It's so uplifting!"

"It's inspirational!" Dickie Lafrenierre adds enthusiastically.

"I was singing 'blow me'," shouts Mick, breaking free from the headlock Billy Joe had him in.

"Yes, I'm quite sure I heard him sing 'blow me'," states Derek, following Mick over to where Forey and Lafrenierre are sitting.

"These darlings do have a certain je ne sais quoi, I'm sure Suckerpunch are going to be the biggest band Slipped Disk has ever had!" exclaims Forey reaching for Mick's ass.

"Get your filthy hands off me you cocksucking faggot," says Mick, slapping the hand that feeds him, "Suckerpunch aren't going to be big because I'm not playing with these assholes any more. I'm going solo. I quit."

"I asked you not to call him a cocksucker or a faggot," complains Irons.

"I'm sorry for doubting you and breaking up your band," sobs Nina, hugging me. "How can I ever make it up to you?"

Time freezes and the universe goes into a state of suspended animation while I contemplate ways in which my girlfriend might atone for her sins. As Pope of the newly formed Church of the Amazingly Big Breasted Former Virgins I believe actions speak louder than words. I won't waste time doling out Hail Marys and Our Fathers as penance to sinners. Instead I want more meaningful and heartfelt acts of contrition such as blowjobs. However, although great leaders usually lead by example, I'm not sure if it's proper to hand out penance to a goddess. I may be opening a can of worms. There are some potentially serious union jurisdictional disputes here. It's a tough call. I'll have to ask a fellow theologian, like Archbishop Frontere, what he would do in this situation.

I look at Nina and time resumes. Her mascara is running down her cheeks in a trail of tears. I give her a hug and feel her boobs pressed up against my chest. "Don't worry. Everything will work out okay. It's not the end of the world."

"How could I have done this to you. What could I have been thinking?" Nina laments.

She's vulnerable. Take advantage of it stupid! "I think I might know," I bullshit, "it's kind of like a Freudian slip. In your subconscious mind you want to have sex with me, which caused your mind to transpose the phrase 'hold me' into 'blow me'. It's totally understandable and normal."

"Maybe. I never thought of it that way. Do you really think so?" Nina mumbles into my shoulder.

"You owe me big time," Bernie Hrechkosy whispers in my ear.

"I know," I reply to both Nina and Bernie.

"I'm not reconsidering. This time it's final – Suckerpunch do not exist," states Mick stomping out the door.

"I told you these leather pants would produce nothing but problems," the newly revived Simon Q. Picasso whimpers from the floor.

"I've got to hand it to Mick Masters he certainly has a lot of spunk," says Dickie Lafrenierre, getting up from the couch.

"How do you know he has a lot of spunk? You – you butch bastard," sputters a red faced Claude Forey, "You've been taking your job as head of artist relations too literally...two timing me with Mick Masters...I ought to claw your eyes out."

"No I haven't, what ever has gotten into you?" questions Lafrenierre.

"Then how did he know I was a cocksucker? Answer me that Mr. Ex-Vice President of Artist Relations," Forey demands.

"I hate to interrupt you Claude, but did you remember the tour support check?" inquires Derek.

Driving my Corvette to Shinske's Pizza Parlor I have mixed emotions. On the one hand I'm depressed. I've only been a rock star for three days and I'm already a has-been. I'm sixteen and already washed up. What am I going to tell all my friends? What is Dominique going to tell Bowie? In the "every cloud has its silver lining" department Nina feels so guilty for causing Suckerpunch's breakup that with a little luck, and maybe a Quaalude, I might finally get in her pants.

"You know I really liked the music to *Talkin' Nina Pennington Blues*," she says between sobs. "I wish I hadn't freaked out like that. I promise I'll make it up to you if it's the last thing I ever do."

The last thing she ever does? Why procrastinate? How do I tactfully and more importantly, successfully suggest she assuage her guilt immediately? "I remember a piece of advice Father O'Brien gave me once. He said it's bad for both your physical and spiritual health to carry guilt around with you. Physically you get ulcers, and spiritually God gets pissed off if you don't try to atone for your sins fast. That's why they're talking about putting in drive through confessionals."

"What do you think I should do?" Nina asks, turning on the radio. Jimmy Leach is actually playing a good song! Johnny Asthma & The Thalidomide Kids' *White Heat* is blaring:

> *I thought it must be a dream*
> *When I saw you standing there*
> *Nothing from the giant silver screen*
> *Could ever compare to your smiling face*
> *To your long long legs*
> *A five alarm blaze starts consuming me*
> *I can't take the heat*

Only divine intervention could force Jimmy to play something good, and probably even then it would have to be at gunpoint. It must be a sign from God.

"I think you should listen to your heart which is your subconscious voice. It will never steer you wrong."

"Maybe you're right," Nina says, snuggling up against me.

I make a right turn onto Big Bend Road and check the rear view mirror to make sure Annette and Bernie are still following us. They are right on my tail so I gun the motor.

The Johnny Asthma song ends and Jimmy introduces the next record, "Continuing our All Sincere marathon here's some friends of mine, Suckerpunch, with *I'm Stupid And So Are You*." Clearly Jimmy hasn't found out yet that we have broken up and no one is going to pay him to play the record anymore.

Nina turns down the radio. "What were the original lyrics you wrote to *Talkin' Nina Pennington Blues*?"

"I'm not sure I remember all of them, but it went something like this,

> *I'm in love with my beautiful girlfriend*
> *Nina Pennington be her name*
> *With her there's nothing that can contend*
> *Nina Pennington she's quite a dame*
> *Nina's the queen of my dreams*
> *Nina's more than she seems*
> *Nina's the queen of my dreams*

Mick really changed the lyrics a lot."

"I don't deserve you after what I did," Nina resumes her sobbing. "That's the sweetest thing anyone has ever said or written about me."

At the corner of Manchester we pull up to a red light and I give Nina a reassuring hug. She gives me a kiss on the cheek. I don't even have time to brush against the sacred twin mounds of Pennington before the light changes and I have to shift the car into gear and drive.

Two blocks down we come to another red light. Nina and I embrace. I stick my tongue as far down her throat as I can, coupling the maneuver with a brief massage of her boobs through the twin obstacles of her sweater and bra. Nina breaks the kiss to tell me she loves me. She then reinserts her tongue in my mouth. Annette honks her horn. The light has changed. Reluctantly, I disentangle myself from Nina and drive.

"Do you love me?" Nina questions in a husky voice.

"Yes."

"How much?"

"A lot."

"I love you too," she states, placing her hand in my lap.

"Really?" I ask, wondering whether Marge Bender's, Emily Wheldon's and Annette's theory about Corvettes making girls horny is true for all women – or if it's like one of those 'three out of four doctors recommend Bayer aspirin' things – with Nina being the dissenter.

"Really," Nina declares, running her hand across my leather pants.

"How much?"

"This much," she says reaching for my zipper. She unbuckles my belt. "I've never done this before."

The theory holds true! I must remember to buy a Mass Card in Sal Veneruzzo's memory next time I go to church and get Father O'Brien to include him in his novenas too. Maybe I should also have him throw in a few good words for General Motors and all the guys who work on the Corvette assembly line.

Nina pulls down my underpants and starts to give me a blowjob! After a moment I realize I might have built up my expectations for this moment too much. Nina is nowhere near as good as any of her predecessors – in fact she's not very good at it at all.

"It feels great, but try not to use your teeth so much," I guide her.

"I'm sorry. Is this any better?" Nina changes her technique for the better.

"Yes," I groan, trying to keep my eyes on the road, "but maybe try and move your head a little...you know...up and down."

"Like this?" Nina follows my directions but violates Amy Vanderbilt's admonition to never talk with one's mouth full.

I swerve to avoid a parked car. "That's perfect."

"I'm going to try something. Tell me if this feels better." Nina increases her up and down motion.

"It's amazing...I'm going to come!"

Nina accelerates her rhythm and smacks her head on the steering wheel.

Boom!

According to the copy of *The Diary of A Stud, How to Satisfy a Woman Every Time* I found tucked under Stephan's mattress you're supposed to hear rockets and explosions and feel the earth move when you're having a perfect orgasm. I feel the earth move, but although I've never been close enough to a rocket to hear it, the noise I experience is more like the dull thud of metal and fiberglass being smashed together.

I've just smashed into a silver Rolls Royce.

Nina's hysterical. "Oh my God...Are you okay...I'm sorry...I didn't mean to hit the steering wheel...I'm no good at blowjobs..."

I'm slightly dazed but I think it's more from the sex than the collision. "I'm okay," I interrupt her rambling, while zipping up my pants. "Let me look at you," she seems none the worse for wear, "and you were just getting good at giving blowjobs; all you need is more practice."

A concerned Annette runs over with Bernie and opens the door. Seeing we're all right she gives me some legal advice, "As your lawyer I advise you to shut-up and let me do all the talking."

The driver of the Rolls is attempting to restart his engine, so he's probably not hurt.

I get out and take a look. My sex life as I know it is probably over. The Corvette is smashed up big time and is impaled on the Rolls Royce's front bumper.

Meanwhile Annette is trying to talk to the other driver, but he won't open his window. He gets his motor going and puts the car into reverse, but can't disentangle his car from mine. Finally he shuts off the ignition and staggers out of the car. He looks familiar.

It's Brother Theodore!

"You little fucker, why didn't you watch where you're going?" he screams.

"I saw the accident, and it was your fault," Annette tells the evangelist, "you came barreling out of that parking lot and cut off the Corvette."

"You're a harlot, sent by the devil to bear false witness against me," slurs the still staggering televangelist.

"I'm a lawyer..."

"Same thing," Brother Theodore replies.

"It is not," Nina comes to Annette's defense.

Brother Theodore squints and focuses his bloodshot eyes on my girlfriend, "You're that heathen slut from the poster. Lord what have I done to be thrust into this modern day Sodom and Gomorrah? Is this a test of Thy willing servant? Do you want me to strike this Jezebel down?" Brother Theodore raises his hand as if to hit Nina.

"Leave my girlfriend alone," I yell. My seizing his arm puts us face to face and I am forced to inhale his fetid breath. He reeks of alcohol. No wonder he's so crazy – he's shitfaced drunk.

Brother Theodore finally calms down and I release him. Meanwhile an overly made-up woman wearing a mini-skirt, torn fishnet stockings and cheap non-reflecting high heels approaches the drunken evangelist. "I sure am sorry Mr. Smith, that's terrible what happened to your Rolls Royce. It's the most comfortable car I've ever worked in."

I get the feeling Brother Theodore Smith may be a long lost relative of Johann Thibault Smith formerly of the Pekin Days Inn.

The woman's insinuation enrages the evangelist, and he runs back to his Rolls. Reaching into the glove compartment he pulls out a gun.

"Just give me thy command Lord and I'll remove these infidels from Thy Kingdom," he bellows over the sound of an approaching police siren.

"Duck," I shout a warning to my friends and the streetwalker, "and don't say anything in Latin."

Brother Theodore fires a shot at me, but fortunately his impaired condition makes his marksmanship less than perfect as he blows out the Corvette's windshield. I dive behind my damaged car where Annette and Nina have already taken refuge.

A police car pulls up. Seymour Stankiewicz jumps out of his vehicle and orders Brother Theodore to freeze. However in his excitement at apprehending the gunman, Seymour Stankiewicz forgets to take his squad car out of gear and apply the parking brake. The car lurches forward and strikes Brother Theodore, knocking him to the pavement and causing his pistol to discharge. The bullet strikes the prostitute in the shoulder.

"After all the times I've had to get dressed up in a girl's school uniform so he can get his rocks off – the motherfucker goes out and shoots me," cries the hooker.

"Just keep quiet. It's not serious, you'll be fine," Annette comforts the woman. "I'm a lawyer and if you let me represent you, by the time we get through with Brother Theodore you're going to be a very rich woman."

I walk over to where Brother Theodore's leg is pinned underneath the police car. He is delirious, ranting about how he has to get out of here fast or the world will end, but he's not going anywhere until the paramedics and a tow truck get here to lift the police car off his leg.

Seymour Stankiewicz tells Brother Theodore to, "shut the fuck up. You're under arrest. You have the right to remain silent. Stop your moaning, it doesn't say anything here on my Miranda card about your having the right to be noisy..."

"Don't worry about his rights, ask him if he has any car insurance. My Corvette is fucked," I tell the policeman, but he ignores me and continues alternating reading Brother Theodore his rights and yelling at him to shut-up.

FEED THE DOG

"You must be traumatized," Nina says giving me a hug. "You're so brave sticking up for my honor and wrestling that crazy bastard. I really love you – and," she sticks her tongue in my ear and whispers, "I've got my own special home remedy for trauma."

I'm no longer interested in Brother Theodore's insurance status.

We walk back over toward where Bernie is standing as a silver limousine pulls up alongside us. The back window rolls down and a voice calls my name. It's former state trooper Kelly O'Shea.

"Could you come over here for a second please?" the Archbishop's head of security asks.

I walk to the limo and see Archbishop Frontere and Sister Marie are in the car as well.

"You won't believe what just happened..." I try to explain.

"We saw the whole sordid affair unfold." Archbishop Frontere interrupts. "It's a shame when a man of the cloth like Brother Theodore suffers a nervous breakdown like that...a wretched horrible shame. Ric, I was wondering if you would do us a favor. I think there might be a canvas bag which belongs to me in the back seat of Brother Theodore's Rolls. Would you go check, and if it's there, bring it here to me. I would consider it a personal favor."

"Sure," I say, although I'm wondering why the Archbishop can't get the bag himself. After all I've just been shot at and am traumatized and in dire need of Nina's special therapeutic home remedy.

I walk over to the Rolls and find the canvas bag lying upside down on the floor. I pick it up but its contents have spilled out. Lying on the floor are at least twenty, one inch thick packages of hundred dollar bills.

"Get away from my car. Leave my fucking money alone," yells Brother Theodore.

Seymour Stankiewicz looks up at the mention of money and walks over to the Rolls.

"Shit, get this goddamn car in gear and let's get the fuck out of here," I hear the Archbishop shout. I guess this must be his day off and he gets to swear like everyone else. Otherwise he's in big trouble with his boss.

"Holy fucking shit," Seymour Stankiewicz echoes the Archbishop's sentiments upon seeing the money. However, I don't think this is Seymour's day off and I'm pretty sure he's in even bigger trouble with God – especially since he's trying to slip a packet of money into his pocket.

"Hey lawyer lady," Brother Theodore shouts at Annette, "I want to hire you to protect my property."

"I'm afraid I'm already working for this poor woman you shot. It would be a conflict of interest," replies Annette.

"I've got a lot more money than she does."

"How much?" asks a suddenly interested Annette.

"Millions," Brother Theodore grimaces.

"Actually ma'am, I think you only have a minor flesh wound and need a Band-Aid rather than a lawyer," Annette tells the prostitute. Turning to Seymour Stankiewicz she says, "You have neither probable cause nor a warrant to search my client's automobile so take the money out of your pocket and give it to me."

The policeman reluctantly hands it to her. "Thanks," Annette says, stashing the money in her purse. "This should be sufficient for an initial retainer. Is that okay with you Brother Theodore?"

He winces and nods his agreement.

"You poor man, I can't believe you have been so mistreated. First that asshole kid in the Corvette broadsides you and then this crook of a cop runs you down in his patrol car. You've got quite a lawsuit here. We're talking millions."

"Hey, you're supposed to be my lawyer and I'm not an asshole," I protest.

Annette walks over to me and pleads, "Come on Ric, I'll make it worth your while if you let me out of representing you."

"How? By suing me? What happened to legal ethics?"

"Ethics? Be serious. Who believes in ethics any more?" Annette asks, watching the paramedics free her prospective client from underneath Seymour's squad car.

"I do," I reply.

"Me too," Nina concurs.

"I don't," states Bernie Hrechkosy.

"How about a compromise?" Annette proposes while gathering the rest of the money from the Rolls. "Brother Theodore will agree not to sue you if you let me be his lawyer."

"What about my lower back pain?" asks Bernie.

"You weren't even involved in the accident," Annette points out.

"I meant Ric's lower back pain," Bernie corrects himself.

"I don't have any back pain," I state.

"Sure you do, and so does Nina, you just don't know it yet," Bernie says, "you're both in shock."

Annette goes and talks to her new client for a moment while they lift the Rolls off of him. She returns with a new deal. "Brother Theodore has agreed not to sue you and will admit his responsibility for the accident. His insurance company will make a settlement with you for any possible complications stemming from the crash if you let me be his lawyer."

I agree to her terms. So does Brother Theodore as they load him into the ambulance. He's got no choice – Annette is holding all the cash.

"Now you really owe me big time," Bernie says.

"Yeah, I know. How can I repay you?"

"Do you have any of Dr. Tudor's 'special entertainment tablets'?"

"A few."

"How many?"

"Around twenty-five," I answer, knowing I have thirty-one.

"That ought to be just about right for saving your ass with Nina and getting Annette to back off with Brother Theodore."

A tow truck driver pulls up and asks me where I want the Corvette taken. "Ace Auto Body," I respond quickly. After all – the work they did on the Deathmobile was pretty good.

Annette accompanies her new client to the hospital leaving Bernie, Nina and me stranded. Bernie wants to drop by my house and pick up his payment so we call a taxi.

A few minutes later a gum chewing cab driver who looks like he hasn't slept in the last two decades picks us up. "WheretoMac?" he asks quickly, making me wonder if he worked for the sisters of Carmelite for a few years.

I answer him, "We'll be making two stops driver, the first is..."

"No. We'll be making only one stop," Nina corrects me, "7220 South Meramec please. I don't want to go home. I want to spend the night with you – if that's okay?"

It takes me roughly a billionth of a second to mull over and accept Nina's proposition. I give her a full-on roto-rooter kiss while a thought gnaws at my mind. We break off the kiss and I come up for air. There is no way to avoid it. I have to ask her, "What are you going to tell your parents?"

"I'll think about it tomorrow," says Scarlett O'Hara Pennington.

Arriving at my house Bernie asks the cab driver to wait for him while he runs in and picks something up. I open the door and while Nina goes to the bathroom I run upstairs and take six Quaaludes out of my bottle, leaving them on my dresser and go back downstairs. I hand the remaining twenty-five to Bernie and wish him good luck.

"With these babies," Bernie leaves, fondling the bottle of pills, "luck has nothing to do with it.

I'll call you tomorrow."

Nina returns and I escort her to my bedroom for our first night together. I turn on the radio for some mood music but KDNA is playing an introspective depressing wimpy Jackson Browne song which is tailored more for slashing one's wrists than getting laid. Leave it to Clyde Zanussi to program a radio station catering to people contemplating suicide at one A.M. Even Clyde should know that the population segment planning to off themselves is a far less loyal audience than those who are trying to get laid. They certainly aren't going to be around to buy the advertisers' products.

I switch stations to KSHE and they're playing Janis Joplin's *Move Over*:

> *...you know that I need a man*
> *you know that I need a man...*

KSHE understands its audience. Joplin serves as the proper inspiration for Nina who responds by removing her clothes in a slow striptease. She isn't a very good stripper because she folds each item of clothing neatly after taking it off – which diminishes the sexiness of her routine. Nina should enroll in a class for strippers – I'm sure they teach it at a junior college – or better yet maybe I could get Kristen to call Tawny and Cherie to come over and provide some private tutoring.

She finally completes her folding chores and places her clothes on top of my bookcase. "I'm nervous," she blushes, crawling into bed.

"So am I," I admit, kissing Nina on the neck and debating whether watching her fold her clothes constitutes foreplay, and if so, whether it is sufficient to satisfy the foreplay requirement I read about in *Diary of A Stud; How To Satisfy A Woman Every Time*.

The little voice in my head tells me I should go that extra mile to make this a pleasurable experience for Nina. This way she'll likely be hooked on sex with me. But don't go too far, the voice says, because she might become a nymphomaniac like Marge Bender and want to fuck everything that doesn't have to squat to piss.

So I romantically lick and fondle her breasts for a couple of minutes. Nina moans passionately. She's ready.

I'm more than ready.

The moment I have practiced for and dreamed about is here! I crawl on top of my love of life and stick my tongue down her gullet. Nina grabs my dick and guides me toward its sacred target.

I thrust forward and Nina sighs, "Oh Ric, that feels so good."

"It does?"

"Yes," she grunts, "fuck me."

"I thought virgins were supposed to be in pain the first time."

"I was, now come on and fuck me."

"The pain sure doesn't last long."

"It hurt like hell," she groans in pleasure.

"You sure don't act like it."

"This isn't my first time."

"What?" I'm flabbergasted. "I thought you said in the car it was your first time."

"Yes, it was the first time I blew anybody in a car."

"You mean you're not a virgin?"

"Of course not silly. I'm sixteen. Nobody's a virgin when they're sixteen unless they're a geek. Now are we going to fuck or talk?"

I decide to fuck. I hope she doesn't find out I was a geek until a few weeks ago.

"Wake up you little schweinhund."

I open my eyes to my father's warm morning greeting from outside my bedroom door. I check my alarm clock. It's seven thirty. How did he get here? What is he going to do when he finds Nina in bed with me? I'm in shock and, contrary to Bernie's theory, my back hurts. Was it from the accident or fucking Nina, and, more importantly, can I make any money out of it?

"What are you doing here? Are you moving back in?" I ask in a groggy tone while motioning for Nina to hide in my closet.

"Have you seen this morning's newspaper?" Johann demands. I assume someone has been messing with Clayton's water supply because it's a stupid question to ask a person who, until now, has been sound asleep.

"No. Why?" I open the door.

Johann answers my first question by throwing Friday morning's *Globe Republican* in my face. The headline reads:

CASINO BUYS VENERUZZO DEATH CAR FOR $50,000 FROM THIBAULT CRIME FAMILY

Can't the press get anything right? I read on:

> *The son of reputed Mafia boss Johann Thibault, ex-rock star Ric Thibault has sold the car dubbed the 'Deathmobile' in which mobsters Salvatore Veneruzzo and Louis Palazarri were murdered to Tequila Ike's Casino. (See related story on Deathmobile, page 2)*

That sucks. Word has already gotten out that I'm a washed up ex-rock star. What am I going to tell all my friends? Is there anyway I can get a day or two off from school to cope with the trauma?

"What the fuck have you been up to? What do you know about this?" Johann demands.

"My bass player and drummer had a fight and the band broke up. We're not doing the Bowie tour," I lament.

"I don't care about your goddamn band. What's this about selling the Pontiac for fifty grand?"

"They're lying, the deal was only for forty thousand."

"You sold my car for forty thousand dollars?" Johann asks.

"No, I sold Mom's car for forty thousand dollars," I correct him.

"So what happened to the other ten grand?" my father persists.

"I know it's hard to believe, but the press has made a mistake. Tequila Ike's would only agree to pay me forty thousand."

"Pay you? It's in joint names and you don't have the pink slip," my father taunts me.

Pink slip? I can't believe he's so open about being a transvestite. No wonder everyone is saying all this stuff about Johann being unsavory. I hope Nina doesn't hear him bragging about being a pervert. It's embarrassing. "Of course I don't have a pink slip, I don't have any women's underwear."

"The pink slip is a document which you need to produce to legally transfer title to a car you idiot – and as for your not having women's undergarments how do you explain this?" he asks, picking up Nina's bra from the top of the bookcase.

I know what a heart attack must feel like. I'm fucked. How am I going to explain this one? I panic. I can't tell him Nina is hiding in the closet. He'll kill me or maybe do something even worse, like grounding me until I start collecting Social Security and then stealing my checks. Think man think. "Uuh..."

"Not you too!" Johann groans, collapsing onto the bed. Burying his head in his hands he mumbles, "The Bible is right – the sins of the father are visited upon the son...I never knew my sickness was hereditary. I've hit rock bottom. I know I've set a bad example for you Ric, but I want to be a good father." He sits up and takes my hand, "Believe me, I know what you're going through. It's lonely when you're different like us and have no one to talk to. We both need help and we'll get it together. Don't worry I'll be with you all the way. We'll lick this problem together."

"Get away from me you queer," I break free of his grasp, "I don't want to lick anything with you. You really do need professional help."

"You're just as sick as I am buddy boy."

"No I'm not," I open the closet, revealing a naked Nina, "the bra belongs to my girlfriend."

"Oh my God! I mean thank you Lord. I mean you're fucking grounded. How could you – with the daughter of the son-of-a-bitch who is trying to throw you out of your home?" Johann spots the pile of Quaaludes on the dresser and plops two of them in his mouth, "I've got a splitting headache."

And I only have four Quaaludes left.

"Give me back my clothes," Nina shrieks, shutting herself back in the closet.

I walk over to retrieve Nina's remaining clothes but my father beats me to it and snatches them from the bookcase. In the process her panties slide off and fall behind the bookcase. Johann reaches behind it and pulls out both the panties and Nina's poster.

The phone rings while my father stares aghast at Basil O'Reilly's photograph of my girlfriend. "What's this?" he demands, "is Zachary Pennington's bank handing out promotional dirty pictures of his daughter instead of those stupid calendars this year? Talk about the pot calling the kettle black; he has some fucking nerve to accuse me of being from a side of the community he refuses to do business with. At least none of my children is involved in pornography!" he says. Clearly he hasn't either gotten to page two of the newspaper or watched television last night and is the only person in Clayton still unaware of the existence of Bambi Bosoms – although now is probably not the best time to break the news to him. Enraged, Johann throws the poster and Nina's clothes at me and storms out of the room.

Nina emerges from the closet clad in my Blues hockey jersey. "How could you have that dirty poster?" she cries.

"I stole it from Ronnie Watt when he arrested you," I lie, "I didn't want the police giving it out to the press; so I brought it home. I was going to rip it up, but I've heard ripping up someone's image brings a curse upon them and I didn't want that happening to the woman I love."

"I'm sorry. I should have trusted you," Nina says, taking off the jersey and embracing me while rubbing her naked boobs against my chest. I have a hard on, and my back doesn't hurt so much any more.

Kristen spoils my dick's enthusiasm by shouting, "Mom's on the phone and she wants to yell at you."

Nina collects her clothes and I go to speak with Lucretia – but Johann has already grabbed the phone and is engaged in a conversation with his future former wife.

"Your kid claims it was only for forty thousand...I don't believe him either...It's weird how something like this can make us talk civilly to each other...How are you?...No I'm not being nice to you because I want something from you – how can you possibly say that?...I care about you – in fact I even miss you...wait a goddamn second; according to the pink slip it's my car too and I'm not signing my half over unless we split the profits fifty-fifty...Okay, a brand new fully loaded Pontiac costs seven grand tops; how about we buy a new one for you and split the remaining money?...I'll come visit you...bring a bottle of Smirnoff? No problem."

My own parents are uniting in a conspiracy against me! The assholes are trying to screw me out of my deal with Frankie Staniowski. I better call Annette and find out what my legal rights are in this matter. I don't think it will conflict with her Brother Theodore case.

"Your mother wants to talk to you," Johann hands me the phone.

"Are you trying to pocket the extra ten thousand bucks for yourself, or are you being a good kid and hiding it from your father for me?"

"There is no ten thousand extra."

"Too bad. When do I get my money? Will they pay cash? I don't want to pay taxes on it."

"What's my share?" I ask ignoring her questions.

"Your share?"

"Yes, if I hadn't been rammed by the car full of nuns the Deathmobile would never have been at Ace Auto Body and Salvatore Veneruzzo wouldn't have been rubbed out in it. Furthermore if Billy and I hadn't shot out the windows and the doors you'd only be getting twenty-five thousand, I would never have been able to talk Staniowski up from the twenty-five thousand they originally offered."

"You shot out my car's windows?"

"Uh-huh."

FEED THE DOG

"Your father is right, you are a little bastard. You're grounded."

"Okay, but I'm going to have to tell Frankie Staniowski that there is no deal and then you aren't going to get a red cent for your Pontiac." I threaten.

"You wouldn't dare."

"You want to bet five dollars?"

"You would do that to your bedridden mother in the hospital?" she asks meekly before summoning her strength, "you should have left me to die in peace so I wouldn't have to experience this callous disrespect you're showing me..."

I hold the phone away and let her rant away for a minute before interrupting her, "Do you want to make a deal?"

"What sort of deal?"

"Cut me in on the forty thousand."

"What do you propose?"

"My manager takes fifteen percent as his rate for making deals, so I should get the same which comes to six thousand bucks."

"That's highway robbery," she screams, "No fucking way – that's my goddamn money...Get away from me with that needle...I'm not ranting or crazy I'm just negotiating with my no good son...Please no...I promise to be calm...I'm not paranoid... it's just the bastard is trying to rip me off...Argh!"

"Hello, this is Nurse Ouimet, and I'm afraid Mrs. Thibault needs to relax and is going to be unavailable for the next several hours. Could you please call back later?"

Hanging up I hear Kristen imploring my father for her share of the Deathmobile monies, "I had as much to do with the Deathmobile as Ric. I want my share of the profits too!"

The phone rings before I can hear Johann's response. I pick it up. It's Derek Irons. I wonder if he read about my Deathmobile deal and is trying to exact his management percentage. "Hi Derek."

"Ric I'm coming over to your house with Claude Forey and I want you to have your leather pants on when I get there."

"Why?"

"We'll explain it to you when we get there. Look good and I'll see you in ten minutes." *Click.*

I go into my room and tell Nina that Derek and Claude are on their way over to see me.

"After last night I promise to keep my mouth shut – no matter what," she says.

"I'd rather you didn't," I propose, kissing her on the lips despite the fact her breath stinks.

"Is it all right if I take a quick shower before they get here?" she asks, "I don't want Forey and Derek to think I'm an unkempt slut."

I appreciate Nina not wanting to be known as unkempt – she should start by doing something about her breath – but I don't think anything is wrong with being a slut. It certainly makes those on the receiving end happy.

The doorbell rings. I hope is isn't Derek and Forey. Irons promised me he wouldn't be here for ten minutes and I'm not even dressed yet. I throw on my pants, go into the hall and peek downstairs.

Kristen gets the door. It's Billy.

Even though someone beat me to her virginity, I'm still proud of my conquest of the High Priestess of the Church of the Amazingly Big Breasted (confirmed) Former Virgins. I want the whole world to know – it will make up for my loss of rock star status. So I invite Billy Bender, The Biggest Mouth In Clayton, to my room so he can see the ravished Nina and start spreading the news. He works far faster and cheaper than Jimmy Leach, which is of no small importance since I'm down to my last four Quaaludes.

I open my bedroom door as Nina is getting ready to shower. She squeals a protest and slams the bathroom door shut while I apologize claiming I forgot she was naked.

Billy is suitably impressed, "Wow, I was coming over to console you about being a former rock star, and you've got Nina Pennington naked in your bedroom. Did you guys do it?"

"Do what?" I ask, knowing damn well what he means.

"You know," he whispers, "go all the way."

"It's not for me to say," I act suave and sophisticated like Sean Connery in one of those James Bond movies, "but you're welcome to smell my pillow for her perfume."

Billy inspects the sheets and finds a wet spot. "Far out man – you actually fucked Nina Pennington!"

"One doesn't fuck Nina Pennington," I correct Billy, "you make love to her. There's a difference."

"Jesus," Billy says, still engrossed in his examination of the bed linens, "Kevin Futterman wasn't lying. Nina wasn't a virgin."

My James Bond nonchalance goes right out the window, "How do you know? How does Kevin know? What are you talking about?" I demand, not sure if I want to hear Billy's answer since the last time I saw Kevin he was complaining about not being able to take a ride with Bambi Bosoms in the Deathmobile and admiringly extolling the virtues of my steel toed cowboy boots which are, according to the school bully, "perfect for kicking the shit out of anyone who looks at your girlfriend."

"Kevin told me he fucked Nina in the bathroom at the Tropicana bowling alley after the Stanley Komadoski Memorial Ball. I can't wait to tell Justin Lafayette. I'm sure I can get good odds betting on whether Kevin beats you up."

"Which side are you betting on?"

"I'm going to bet he beats the crap out of you. That way if he doesn't I'll be happy for you – and if he does I'll take consolation in my winnings."

Our conversation is disrupted by Johann barging in. The Quaaludes must not have kicked in yet because he doesn't seem horny and is still agitated. "There is absolutely no way either your mother or I am sharing the Deathmobile money with anybody. Is that fucking clear?" He turns around and leaves, slamming the door behind him.

I now know where Stephan inherited his greed from.

My father stomps down the stairs and asks Kristen to open her bedroom door because he wants to feed her the same bullshit he just gave me. Kristen tells him she's getting dressed and to wait a second.

A few seconds later I hear Johann pounding on Kristen's door and shouting, "What's going on in there? Who's in there with you?"

He opens the door and Kristen pleads, "Hold on a second Dad, I can explain."

"You better start explaining. Start with who the hell this is. What is going on in this house? Since I moved out it's become some sort of bordello!" screams Johann. From what I've heard about bordellos you have a lot of naked women hanging around the place. Maybe Cherie and Tawny spent the night; so, curious to find what is fueling my father's accusations, Billy and I tiptoe downstairs to investigate.

"Hello Mr. Thibault, I'm a friend of Ric's and your daughter's," says a familiar voice, "my name is Bernie Hrechkosy."

My opinion of my father's intelligence skids to an all time low. I can't believe how dumb he is. After all, according to the newspapers, Johann has had recent experience in bordellos and should be able to recognize the difference between a brothel and my sister hanging out with Bernie and his twenty-five Quaaludes.

While Johann is ordering Bernie to get the hell out of here I hear Duke barking. I look out the window to see Claude Forey and Derek Irons coming up the front steps.

I open the door and walk out onto the porch. "Hi, Derek. Hello Mr. Forey."

"Hi Ric," says Forey, "aren't you going to invite us in?"

"Now might not be the best time. My dad is a little upset," I explain.

"Don't worry. Claude has a business proposition which will cheer him up," says Derek.

Bernie comes running out the door followed by Johann.

"Oh good, Bernie's here. It saves us the trouble of trying to track him down," remarks Derek.

"Yes, and he's wearing those magnificent black leather trousers. So you must be Ric's father, Mr. Thibault, or is it 'Don' Thibault?" exclaims Forey, extending his hand to Johann.

"Who the hell are you?" grumbles my father.

"Dad this is Claude Forey, the president of Slipped Disk Records – you two should talk – you have a lot in common, and this is Derek Irons, my manager."

"You have a manager?"

"All rock stars have managers," Billy correctly interjects.

"Yeah, but according to the paper you're an ex-rock star – and according to me you're a grounded ex-rock star – and grounded ex-rock stars don't need managers," my father yawns. Maybe he's finally beginning to feel the effect of the Quaaludes.

"You should hear me out before you do anything so rash," says Forey. "I think your son is an extremely talented songwriter and performer. His song *Talkin' Nina Pennington Blues* is the best song I've heard in years. I want to sign him to a recording contract. I'm going to make your son rich and famous!"

"Rich?" Johann asks.

"Famous?" I ask.

"Yes. I want you to replace Mick Masters and record *Talkin' Nina Pennington Blues* with Suckerpunch immediately in my studio in Los Angeles. But I want you to sing 'blow me' not that trite 'hold me' garbage. I'm prepared to turn on the star making machinery for you right now."

"Didn't you say something about rich?" Johann asks.

"Oh yes, I'll give your son fifty thousand dollars if he'll sign now."

"I was just joking about Ric being grounded, do you have a pen for him to sign with?" my father yawns again.

"What's in it for me?" Bernie inquires.

"I won't kill you for a start," mumbles Johann wearily.

"The band gets seven hundred fifty bucks a week salary plus per diems," Derek promises.

"But Nina will kill me if I sing 'blow me'," I interrupt, while watching a police car pulling up along with Mary Ecclestone's news van.

"Fuck Nina Pennington," reply Bernie, Claude, Derek and my father loudly in unison.

"Ric already did – and I'm betting Kevin Futterman is going to beat the crap out of him for doing it," Billy says, while I watch Seymour Stankiewicz and another policeman who I don't know get out of the car with an extremely irate looking Zachary Pennington.

"Did you hear that? I was right. Those criminals have my daughter and now they're chanting for one of those mobsters to molest her. Shoot them – or better yet give me your gun," screams Nina's father, reaching for Seymour's weapon.

"Duck," I yell for the second time in less than twelve hours. I dive along with everyone else behind the porch railing, as Zachary Pennington fires a round in our direction.

Again we are lucky. No one said anything in Latin and the bullet harmlessly strikes the front door. The other cop quickly disarms Zachary Pennington and tells us it's safe to get up after Seymour Stankiewicz finishes handcuffing Nina's father.

"Is that savage from a rival Mafia gang?" asks Claude Forey, clutching a motionless Johann on the floor. "Oh my God, I think Don Thibault has been hit!"

I run over and check out my father. There's no blood anywhere, and he's breathing normally. He's passed out from the Quaaludes. I tell Forey my dad is fine explaining, "he's still suffering from jet lag and is a little rundown."

"Your father is one cool cucumber. No matter how rundown I was I couldn't fall asleep when someone is shooting at me. I guess he must be so used to Mob rubouts that they've become routine to him. He must lead an exciting life."

I'm able to wake my father up and sit him down on the front porch.

"What did you mean when you said we have something in common?" asks Claude Forey admiringly.

"Um...you both like to travel and experience different cultures. My father just got back from Europe and you're about to go," I respond, thinking now is not the best time to discuss current trends in transvestism.

I go out to the street and watch the cops shove Zachary Pennington into the back seat of the police car.

"You should be arresting criminals like those kidnapping child molesters, not honest citizens like me," he protests.

Neither policeman has their Miranda card handy and Seymour Stankiewicz apologizes to Nina's father for being unable to read him his rights.

"I know them," I volunteer while out of the corner of my eye spotting Mary Ecclestone pulling up in the Channel 7 news van. "You have the right to remain silent, you have the right to an attorney, and if you have to spend all your money on your daughter's wedding and consequently can't afford one, an attorney will be appointed for you. Do you understand your rights?"

Nina has finished her shower and comes outside to see what is going on. "What's my father doing handcuffed in the back of a police car?"

"He went berserk and tried to kill me," I explain.

"I'm standing in front of the Clayton home of alleged Mafia boss, Johann Thibault, where another attempted gangland hit has taken place. According to eyewitnesses to the incident this time the assailant remembered his gun. I have with me one witness, rock star Bernie Hrechkosy..." Mary Ecclestone is saying.

"Now I get it. This is another of your famous publicity gimmicks. Irons you're brilliant!" Forey exclaims.

"I saw the whole thing. It was a setup – the pigs were in on it from the start," Bernie tells Mary Ecclestone, "they brought the hitman with them and I bet they're going to let him escape as soon as they get out of sight. Someone should arrest the cops as accessories."

"I can't believe my own father would try and kill my boyfriend," Nina begins to cry again, "I'm so sorry."

Derek taps me on the shoulder and whispers into my ear, "I don't want you to think I'm callous and uncaring, but now is the perfect time to ask Nina whether she'll let you sing 'blow me'."

I escort Nina back upstairs to my room and try to calm her down. "What's going to happen to my dad? He could go to jail," she sobs, while pacing back and forth.

"Don't worry. From what I've seen of both the District Attorney and the police I'm sure he'll get off," I console her, hoping that I'm wrong.

"This is giving me a fierce headache," Nina says leaning on the dresser.

Shit! In all the excitement I still haven't put the remaining Quaaludes away and Nina is reaching for them.

"Wait a second!"

"Why?"

"Um, oh yeah, those aspirin are too old – they're past their expiration date."

"I don't care," she says, taking two and plopping them into her mouth.

I'm down to two Quaaludes, which I throw in my pocket.

"I almost forgot to ask you, what do Forey and Derek want?"

"They want me to record your song for Slipped Disk. Forey says *Talkin' Nina Pennington Blues* is a huge hit and he's going to make me a star. He's going to give me fifty thousand dollars!"

"That's great," Nina says, giving me a hug. Too bad the Quaaludes haven't kicked in yet – because I wouldn't be adverse to celebrating with more than a hug.

"Can you imagine everybody in the world will know your name? *Tiger Beat* will want to do a story on the woman who inspired rock star Ric Thibault's hit. I bet you *Cosmopolitan* will want to do a feature on you too. So will *Playboy* and *Penthouse*..."

"I'm not taking my clothes off for any magazine," Nina states unequivocally.

"You're so beautiful you won't have to take your clothes all the way off. They'd kill just to have pictures of you in a bikini."

"If that's all they want it's okay. You told Forey you're going to do it, didn't you?"

"Well there is one small hitch."

"What's that?"

"Forey liked the song better the way your subconscious wrote the lyrics. He wants me to sing 'blow me' rather than 'hold me'."

"You can't," Nina bursts into tears again.

"Since it was your idea, you would be listed as co-writer."

"What difference does that make? I don't want to go through life being known as the 'blow me' girl," Nina sobs harder, causing her mascara to run down her face.

"You'd get a lot of money."

"Is money all you can think about?"

"No. I care about you most of all. That's why I haven't said yes."

Nina's sobbing slows and she reaches for a Kleenex and blows her nose. "How much money do you get for co-writing a song?" she whimpers.

"You get money every time they play it on the radio in addition to the royalties you get for each record sold."

"Jimmy Leach would play it wouldn't he?"

"You can count on at least ten or twenty pairs of Charles Jourdans worth of airplay from Jimmy alone."

"Really?"

"Uh huh."

"Eventually I am going to get married – and when I do my last name won't be Pennington any more," the future Nina P. Thibault cracks a smile. "You're going to be bigger than Bowie. Let's go talk to Forey – but first let's call Jimmy Leach and make sure he's going to play the record."

Mrs. Babin is unsympathetic, "I'm sorry Mr. Thibault, Miss Pennington and Mr. Bender, without a signed note from each of your parents explaining your tardiness you will have to see Mr. Campbell, the acting principal. Please take a seat outside the principal's office."

"I'm scared. I've never been sent to the principal's office before. Do you know anything about this Campbell guy?" Nina asks as we trudge down the hall.

"Yeah, Justin Lafayette told me he's an ex-Marine. He's supposed to be a real hard ass who loves to hand out detentions and kick people out of school. Too bad Basil O'Reilly isn't principal any more," Billy says, "we wouldn't have anything to worry about."

"What do you mean?" questions Nina, slumping down on the bench outside of the office.

"Last time when we got sent to Basil's office Ric found..."

"Out the Bloodmobile was going to be here," I cut Billy off while giving him a 'You're about to join Salvatore Veneruzzo and Louis Palazarri in the back of the Deathmobile if you don't shut-up' look.

"I don't get it. What did the Bloodmobile coming have to do with not having anything to worry about?" Nina inquires.

"Um, Basil used to let you out of detention for donating blood," I lie, "one pint would wipe out all your demerits."

Nina takes my hand and gives it a squeeze. I look at her and she smiles back at me. "Kiss me,"

FEED THE DOG

she whispers.

I comply with her request, giving her a tongueless kiss on the cheek.

"You can kiss better than that," she moans, pulling me closer to her and inserting her tongue into my mouth.

I tentatively return the kiss while glancing at the clock outside the principal's office. It's nine-fourteen. Nina took the Quaaludes twenty-five minutes ago and I think they're beginning to work, because she moves my hand to her tits.

"You better quit it. Campbell is going to freak if he catches you making out," Billy points out.

I agree with him reluctantly and break off our kiss. Nina, however doesn't share Billy's point of view. "Don't be a wimp. You're a rock star, you don't need Clayton High. Fuck Clayton High. Fuck Campbell, and most of all fuck me," she purrs, sticking her tongue back down my throat.

Nina's dexterity with her tongue quickly converts me to her thinking. Rock stars don't worry about getting kicked out of school. They view their expulsions as merit badges. Some day I'll be at that special country club in England which all rock stars belong to. David Bowie, Keith Richards, and I will be drinking brandy and discussing how we got expelled from school. "I got thrown out for getting a blowjob from Dominique in second period Biology during my senior year," David will be saying. "I got tossed for getting a blow job from Dominique in first period English during my freshman year," Keith relates, "how about you mate?" "I got Nina Pennington to swallow two Quaaludes and made out with her outside the principal's office," I say proudly. "I'm jealous," says Bowie. "Me too," pipes in Keith, "do you still have any of those Quaaludes?"

I tell Billy to mind his own business and resume our makeout session, worming my hand down Nina's sweater and under her bra. This is the way sex education should be taught in school. Hands on experience is much better than listening to Coach McCrimmon's boring lectures about the twin evils of sexually transmitted diseases and teenage pregnancy.

"Hi, Kevin. What are you here for?" I hear Billy saying. Good try Billy. You think you're going to make me take my hands off Nina's breasts for the old 'look behind you' trick. I wasn't born yesterday. I watch television. That trick never works. I should know, having tried it unsuccessfully on your mother.

"That Hucul bastard kicked me out of Biology for beating up Mark Noris. Hey, what the fuck is he doing with Nina Pennington?" grunts a pissed off sounding Kevin Futterman.

I hastily remove my hands from Nina's tits, and dispatch an emergency silent prayer to God,

"Since You are the one who had one of your Saints utter 'blessed are those who believe', please make Kevin still believe I'm a Mafia Boss's kid. And Lord could you give Futterman an I.Q. booster shot and make him bright enough to understand the inadvisability of messing with Mafioso's offspring. Amen."

Gambling on the effectiveness of prayer, I turn around and face the school bully. "I was kissing Nina and feeling her breasts. Got any problem with it?"

The impact of Kevin's punches is accompanied by several major theological revelations:

1. The Church of the Amazingly Big Breasted Former Virgins needs to fill up some collection plates and raise some cash so we can grease some palms and be competitive with those other big money religions in our lobbying efforts with the big guy upstairs. Otherwise I will have to listen to the patron saint of bureaucrats (Whoever the low level flunky who got the cushy patronage job is) saying, "I'm sorry, but Mr. God has an extremely busy schedule today and isn't listening to any new prayers and to be frank with you He has a huge backlog of them – He's still dealing with requests from the sixteenth century – and isn't going to be able to get around to yours until, let me check my schedule, sometime late in the next millennium. So, you'll have to complete this L246-6969b triplicate prayer request form in Latin and make sure you use a number two lead pencil. Then throw the first two copies away, and take the remaining form to our prayer fulfillment center two doors down. There you should take a number and stand in line like every other infidel." Priority service from God and His minions is essential during moments like this.

2. Existentialism is bullshit. Man does not control his own destiny, because there is no way in hell I would willingly allow anyone to clobber me as hard as Kevin just did.

3. Jesus is not the one to consult concerning certain earthly matters such as brawling. His 'turn the other cheek' admonition is particularly suspect because with Kevin's second blow both sides of my face are hurting instead of only one.

4. If you are stupid enough to get in a fist fight with the Lord, and if the Bible is correct and man is created in God's own image, then you should make sure you're wearing cowboy boots with pointed steel reinforced toes because if you kick God in the balls real hard you can win a fight even when you're overmatched, as I discover with a well placed boot to Kevin's crotch.

Kevin writhes on the floor in pain, "You don't fight fair, you cheater," he moans.

Billy is pleased, "I'm glad you decided to get in a fight before I had a chance to place any bets with Justin. You saved me some serious dough."

I assure Nina I'm okay while she examines my face for any bleeding. "You've got a swollen lip which looks like it must hurt," she giggles and whispers, "Maybe I should kiss it and make it feel better just like my mother used to do when I was a kid."

If I were the American Medical Association I would have my researchers study the healing power generated by Pennington kisses, because after a few smooches the pain is gone and the only swelling I'm feeling is in my pants. Nina offers to kiss that swelling too. The Quaaludes must be in full gear. She drops to her knees and unzips my pants.

I've often heard Father O'Brien say, "You can't keep a good man down." Apparently you can't keep assholes down either, because Kevin Futterman is back on his feet and charging me like one of those wounded rhinos on *Mutual of Omaha's Wild Kingdom*, but unlike Marlon Perkins I don't have a tranquilizer gun.

"You motherfucker," Futterman shouts.

How does he know? Deciding it's imperative to shut him up before he blabs about Marge Bender to Nina and Billy I lash out with my best Bruce Lee imitation sidewinder karate kick just as the principal's door opens, and deliver another effective steel tipped cowboy boot to the balls. Unfortunately the balls do not belong to Kevin Futterman. Instead I have dropped a fortyish looking guy whose khakis have a rapidly growing wet spot in the crotch area. I notice this while I am falling from the force of the Neanderthal left fist of Kevin Futterman.

"Look at it this way; if they expel you you won't have to finish that stupid book by Hemingway – and besides, you won't have to skip school to tour with Suckerpunch," Billy attempts to console me while we wait outside the faculty disciplinary committee's meeting room.

I see the merit in Billy's reasoning, but I'm still not ready to choose him as my advocate before the disciplinary committee. With his astute guidance I'm sure I could be the first Clayton High student to receive the death penalty.

Nina is still under the influence of the Quaaludes and is feeling no pain – leaving that particular domain exclusively to me. My jaw hurts, my left eye is half closed, my lower lip feels like a basketball and I can taste blood oozing from somewhere in my hopefully still-toothed mouth. When she isn't giggling and playing with her hair Nina is hugging me and saying how brave I was to stand up to Futterman. I decide against disillusioning her by pointing out that being knocked flat on the floor does not exactly constitute standing up to anyone.

The door opens and Kevin Futterman is escorted out the door by a limping Mr. Campbell and one of the new Clayton police officers sent by the Attorney General. "Now that I've been kicked out of school we'll have plenty of time to visit each other," Futterman sneers.

"The only way you're going to see Ric after they kick him out of school is if you buy a ticket and get lucky enough to score a backstage pass to one of his band's gigs. He's going to be a mega rock star!" Billy Bender, the eternal optimist, taunts the poster boy for Future Thugs of America.

"Fuck you," Futterman tells Billy, thereby using up all the remaining words in his vocabulary.

Campbell tells Kevin to shut-up and collect his personal belongings (which probably consist of several pairs of brass knuckles, a lead pipe, a switchblade and a semi-automatic sawed-off shotgun) from his locker.

"I'm looking for Ric Thibault." I hear Bernie Hrechkosy's voice coming from Mrs. Babin's office down the hall.

"Mr. Thibault is going before the disciplinary committee and is unavailable," Campbell shouts down the hall.

"He's my lawyer," I say, "Aren't I entitled to an advocate?"

"Kevin Futterman didn't have an advocate," the acting principal replies.

"That's because everyone wants him out of here. No one wants to help a guy who is just going to beat you up if he stays in school." says Billy.

"I know my rights. The student constitution stipulates that I'm allowed to have an advocate before the disciplinary committee," I insist.

"Okay. Since we all know what the outcome of your case is already I'll allow you to have your precious advocate. You can have five minutes to confer with counsel before we expel you," Campbell graciously allows Bernie to talk to me.

"Jesus. What happened to your face?" Before I can answer, Bernie is relating exciting news, "You're not going to believe it! Derek booked us on the *Midnight Special* which tapes tomorrow afternoon in Los Angeles. He wants us to play *Talkin' Nina Pennington Blues* – and guess who the guest host is? David fucking Bowie! We've got to rehearse this afternoon and then catch a four o'clock plane. So we've got to blow this joint."

FEED THE DOG

"Oh my God! David Bowie? Los Angeles? What should I wear? Do you think David will like my Charles Jourdans? What else should I wear? Let's hurry and get kicked out of school. I need to go shopping." Nina emerges from her stupor.

"You're not going anywhere," Campbell states.

"I thought you said you were going to expel me?"

"That's what you want me to do, so I've changed my mind. You're staying right here – in school where you belong."

"Fuck you," I attempt to provoke Campbell.

"Nice try, but it won't work. I'm withdrawing the charges. Go back to class all of you."

"I'm skipping school."

"You will do no such thing. You will stay here until four o'clock when school is over. Officer Hughes here will escort you to each of your classes and stand guard outside of the door for the remainder of the day. You better cancel your reservations, because you will be here until four o'clock when school is over."

"Why don't you kick Campbell in the balls again and see if he changes his mind," Billy suggests.

"Don't worry," Bernie shouts as we're marched off to first period English class at gunpoint, "I've got an idea. I'll pick you up at four."

I hope his plan is a good one. It's all I can think of during English, especially during the surprise test our substitute English teacher, Mrs. Ruff, springs on us. It's on *A Farewell To Arms*, and I still haven't read it – so I copy from Nina's paper. I never knew Hemingway wrote a book set in Los Angeles whose hero is named "David Bowie".

"Will Ric Thibault please report to Acting Principal Campbell's office," the school public address system blares during third period French class.

"I gotta go," I get up and excuse myself.

"Ric Thibault asseyez-vous! Ici nous parlons francais seulement!" Madame Bourbonais orders.

"But.."

"Non, en francais! Mais..." she cuts me off.

"D'accord. Mais le principal Campbell veut moi, donc je sors."

"Non, il faut utiliser l'imperatif de 'sortir'," she corrects me.

"Shit." I try to remember the imperative of sortir.

"Que'est-ce c'est 'shit'? En francais s'il vous plaît," Bourbonais angrily slams her book on the desk.

"Pardon, merde, je sortis," I remember the imperative and head for the door.

"Merde? Ne dit pas de grands mots! Je vais parler avec Monsieur Campbell..." Bourbonais screams after me as I escape into the hall. I hope Campbell speaks French and she does talk to him. Maybe she'll be more successful than I was at getting me kicked out of school.

While I'm escorted to the acting principal's office by my personal cop, Officer Hughes, I try to figure out what Campbell wants. Maybe Bernie has effected his plan and it's on to Los Angeles, the setting of Hemingway's much neglected classic, *A Farewell To Arms*!

My optimism evaporates when I open the door. Assholes don't smile unless there is bad news, and Campbell is beaming, flashing more teeth than a Rose Bowl Queen on lithium. He is not alone in the office. District Attorney Irwin Roberts is sitting on the couch with Seymour Stankiewicz and a fidgety looking guy wearing a baseball cap and a blue windbreaker with FBI stenciled on it in big yellow letters.

The FBI guy introduces himself as Special Agent Frank Quinn. As soon as the G-man opens his mouth I understand how the FBI got their own TV show and why they are regarded as the elite amongst police forces. While Seymour Stankiewicz looks on with envy, Quinn recites the Miranda warnings by heart, "You have the right to remain silent..."

"I'm sorry, Miss Stratton-Osborne is out of the country on holiday and hasn't left a phone number. May I take a message?"

"Is she going to call in?" I ask.

"I'm not sure," says the voice on the phone.

"Yes, could you tell Miss Stratton-Osborne her client Ric Thibault is calling from the Clayton jail. I need her help. It's important."

"You're not in the jail's hospital ward are you?" the voice asks.

"No," I answer, watching the FBI guy fondling Seymour Stankiewicz's nightstick, "not yet, why?"

"Oh Miss Stratton-Osborne has another client in the Clayton prison ward who keeps calling every five minutes looking for her," says the voice.

"Who's that?"

"Some demented guy who calls himself 'Brother Theodore'. He claims she ran off with a million dollars of his. Can you imagine that?"

I can.

I hang up the phone and tell Special Agent Quinn, "My lawyer isn't available, I need to get a new one."

"Regulations allow you only one phone call, so you're shit out of luck," he replies, "Besides only guilty people need lawyers. Are you feeling guilty about something? Is that why you want a mouthpiece?"

Guilt? Me? I'm a rock star. Rock stars don't feel guilt. I know; I read it in an interview with Keith Richards. But before I can issue a denial there is a huge, yet strangely peaceful, jolt causing the walls to fly open revealing a genuine (even more genuine than Brother Theodore's green glow in the dark plastic Jesuses) Holy vision, in the form of a tall blond angel with great legs, leather pants, Charles Jourdan boots and humongous tits barely hidden behind a black lace corset. She's carrying a small yellow and black booklet. I catch sight of the title – *Cliff's Notes Version of the Newer Than New Improved Testament*. My Holy vision speaks in a husky voice which apparently only I can hear, "My name is Saint Lolita. I'm the patron saint of rock stars and teenagers. Don't try looking me up in the *Book of Saints* because I'm not in it – I'm an unlisted saint. Anyway, I've been sent by thy Maker with a few new Commandments concerning the operation of the Church of the Amazingly Big Breasted Former Virgins. Thou shalt be the first Pope. Thou shalt institute a quick guilt absolution program. Thou shalt not have Hail Marys. Thou shalt not have Our Fathers. Instead thou shalt say unto thyself, I'm sorry and promise to try and not to do it again. Thou shalt not need priests hearing confessions thereby saving countless dollars in overhead. Thou shalt thereby eliminate the middle man freeing countless dollars in priest salaries which can be put to much better use. Therefore thou shalt be able to attract and afford better looking recruits as nuns. Thou shalt dress thy nuns better. Halter tops, fishnet stockings, mini skirts and stiletto heeled fully reflecting patent leather boots from St. Charles of Jourdan shall be the uniform. And thou shalt retire nuns as soon as they hit thirty-five or their tits sag, whichever comes first. And finally, thou shalt keep the wine but get rid of those awful tasting wafers. Thou shalt not fuck this up." Saint Lolita looks at her watch, "Oh shit, I've got to split; I've got to catch a plane 'cause I have backstage passes to Bowie at the *Midnight Special* tomorrow in L.A.... ciao!" She takes a step backwards and disappears in a cloud of smoke. I ponder the meaning of her words and the fact that pilgrims laden with prayers and tourist dollars will be coming here to the Clayton police department, the scene of my religious revelation, for years to come. Someone is going to make a fortune off the merchandising...

"Wake up Thibault," Quinn is shaking me, "did you fall asleep trying to wrestle with your conscience or was it just too taxing for your criminal brain to come up with some bullshit fabrication? What is it you're feeling so guilty about that you need a shyster?"

"I'm not a criminal and I'm not feeling guilty of anything. The only reason I want a lawyer is because you arrested me," I say while looking around the room for any signs of my Holy vision. Sadly I see only Seymour Stankiewicz, Irwin Roberts, a fat stenographer with crooked teeth and too much make up whose name is Helga Snepsts and Quinn. None of them are the sort you want to go around spreading the gospel of the miracle at the Clayton police department. Matthew, Luke, John, and Mark they're not – they are not good disciple material. No one is going to convert to the Church of the Amazingly Big Breasted Former Virgins due to the eyewitness accounts of apostles named Seymour, Irwin, Frank and Helga.

"We haven't arrested you," Roberts returns me to the secular world.

"Then why did you read me my rights if you weren't arresting me?"

"Because according to our files you're one of those liberal do-gooder ACLU types who make our lives crazy if we don't do everything proper and in accordance with the latest Supreme Court decision. Quite frankly we've got better things to do than spend the rest of our lives sweating in a room full of mealy-mouthed lawyers while giving depositions on whether you were properly treated. Now are you going to cooperate or are we going to throw you in the slammer for obstructing justice?"

Although being an ex-con probably looks good on a rock star's resumé I prioritize. If all I have to do is answer a few questions to get out of here, thereby allowing me to catch a plane to Los Angeles for the *Midnight Special*, "I'll cooperate."

"Good, let's start with the Corvette. Tell us about your car."

"The whole front end is fucked, the windshield was shot out by that creep Brother Theodore and..."

"I don't care about any of that. I want to know how you got the car," Quinn cuts me off.

"Salvatore Veneruzzo gave it to me," I reply honestly.

"I know that. Why did he give it to you?"

"He gave it to me as a loaner when my mother's car was being fixed."

"If it was a loaner, how do you explain the title being transferred into your name?

"He left it to me in his will."

"How long did you know Salvatore Veneruzzo?" Irwin Roberts takes over the questioning.

"I met him last Wednesday, after a car full of nuns hit my mother's car."

"And considering he has been dead for one week, you only knew him for two days?"

"Yes."

"What in the world could have happened over the space of two days which would so endear you to the enforcer of the Vespucci crime family that he would bequeath you a brand new 1973 Corvette?"

Out of nowhere Saint Lolita reappears. She's holding a plane ticket and the new issue of *Circus* featuring David Bowie on the cover. "I almost forgot one more commandment sweetie," she says while searching for something in her purse, "thou shalt not protect Archbishop Frontere. Your Corvette is totaled and he isn't giving you another one, so let him look after his own ass. Whew! What a relief! I remembered to bring my knee pads – they make it so much more comfortable to pay for my backstage pass, as well as insuring I don't rip my stockings, they're Dior. Remember, thou shalt tell the truth and fry the pervert. Got to run – Ta-ta darling!" She vanishes, leaving me on my own to face my inquisitors.

Who am I to disobey the specific instructions of a messenger of God? That would be taking existentialism too far. One doesn't try to control one's own destiny when God is ordering you to do a simple thing like telling the truth.

I take Saint Lolita's advice. "He did it as a favor to Archbishop Frontere."

"You're saying Salvatore Veneruzzo, a Mafia enforcer, and Archbishop Frontere were friends?" Roberts asks.

"Don't you read the newspapers?" I ask, astonished.

"I read the funny pages every day. That Little Orphan Annie gets herself into so many messes," Seymour Stankiewicz interjects.

"No, I'm talking about yesterday's newspaper's front page. They had it in the article which called me a rock star."

Irwin Roberts ignores me, "Little Orphan Annie is okay, but for my money Nancy is the funniest comic strip ever, although Blondie and Family Circus give her a good run for the money..."

"I don't read the comics," Quinn interrupts. He leans forward shoving his face two inches from mine. He should pick his nose – he's got a huge booger dangling from his left nostril, "and I don't have time for any liberal communist slanted crap masquerading as news either. Just tell us whether Archbishop Frontere and Salvatore Veneruzzo knew each other and were friends."

"Yes, they were."

"How do you know?" Quinn persists.

"The Archbishop told me."

"Have you ever met the Archbishop, face to face?" District Attorney Roberts finishes his discussion with Seymour Stankiewicz on the humor inherent in Beetle Bailey and turns his attention back to me.

"Sure."

"And you're saying he is the executor of Salvatore Veneruzzo's estate?" Quinn asks.

"That's what he told me, and also what both the *Globe Republican* and the *Evening Tribune* say," I answer.

Quinn and Irwin Roberts leave the room to talk leaving me with Helga and Seymour. Helga uses the break to trowel another layer of make-up onto her face while Seymour occupies himself by playing with his nightstick. A few minutes later they return.

"Would you be able to pick Archbishop Frontere out of a line up?" the FBI agent queries.

"Uh huh."

"Okay, go pick Archbishop Frontere up and bring him in for a line up," the District Attorney instructs Seymour Stankiewicz, "but watch out, he knows Latin."

"You're looking through a two way mirror. The people in the next room can not see you, but you can see them. There are six people in the line up each of whom is standing under a number. All I want you to do is identify the man you know as Archbishop Frontere by his number," Irwin Roberts directs me. "If you need any of the men to speak just tell me what you want them to say and I'll get them to repeat it.

All right?"

As I look through the mirror I feel like I'm on some perverse form of the *Dating Game*. It would get really good ratings with questions like "Suspect Number Two, can you tell me whether it is okay

FEED THE DOG

for nuns to kiss on the first date?" or, "Suspect Number Three, what would you do on a date with Saint Lolita?" or, "Suspect Number Five, do nuns have hair?"

"Do you see the Archbishop?" Quinn returns me to reality.

I survey the line up. It isn't difficult to pick the Archbishop out. Number One is a short Hassidic Jewish looking guy replete with hat, a long coat and beard. Number Two is a tall black man with an afro and bell bottom pants. Number Three looks like the Pakistani pharmacist who filled Dr. Tudor's prescription for the Quaaludes. Number Four is Jimmy Leach and Number Five looks like a depressed Hare Krishna who must have been rousted from the airport and had his books confiscated. I look at Number Six. Standing underneath the official Vatican issue silly hat and wearing his regulation Archbishop uniform is Archbishop Frontere. Seymour Stankiewicz and two other cops have guns pointed at the handcuffed cleric's head.

"Don't let Special Agent Quinn hurry you. We have plenty of time. We want a positive identification," Roberts says. "Do you want to hear any of them say anything?"

"Yes. Can you have Number Four say, 'I am a sleazy no talent Quaalude addicted asshole who no one in their right mind would listen to'?"

Roberts presses an intercom switch, "Number Four say, 'I am a sleazy no talent Quaalude addicted asshole who no one in their right mind would listen to' please."

"I'm not going to say that. This is bullshit. You said all I had to do was stand here and say nothing and then you would fix my parking ticket..."

"Would one of you officers please point your gun at Number Four and tell him to shut-up," Quinn orders.

"But I wanted him to say it," I complain.

"All right. Officer Stankiewicz point your gun at Number Four and tell him to say 'I am a sleazy no talent Quaalude addicted asshole'."

"Don't forget the 'who no one in their right mind would listen to'," I remind Quinn.

Jimmy grudgingly complies with my request.

"That's obviously not the Archbishop," Roberts says, "so let's get on with it. Do any of those men look like Archbishop Frontere? Number six perhaps?"

I still want to have fun with Jimmy Leach. "You want me to make an absolutely positive identification so don't rush me. I'm still not sure Number Four isn't the Archbishop. Let me hear him say one more thing, 'I swear to God I will not try to get into Bambi Bosoms' pants'."

Roberts sighs while passing on my instructions to Number Four.

"What is this, some kind of a joke?" Jimmy protests before Seymour points his gun back at the deejay. "Okay, you've made your point already. I swear to God I will not try to get into Bambi Bosoms' pants. Are you satisfied?"

I am. If Kristen were here she would probably be satisfied too.

"I'm ready to tell you which one of them is the Archbishop," I tell Roberts. If this was in a Hollywood police station I'd get a musical crescendo, or at the very least a drum roll, while making such a momentous identification, but since this is boring Clayton all I can hear is the humming of the fluorescent lights overhead. "Archbishop Frontere is Number Six."

"We've cracked the case and got our man! That was textbook police work...real crackerjack stuff," Irwin Roberts congratulates Quinn. Pushing the intercom button the District Attorney tells Seymour, "take the Archbishop to the back room and see if you can get a confession out of him."

"The Archbishop doesn't do confessions," Seymour replies, "He's an executive. You've got to go to Father O'Brien for confessions."

"Stankiewicz is right," Quinn agrees.

"Okay. Pick up Father O'Brien and see if he'll confess," Irwin Roberts orders, "and then get Officer Hughes to drive Thibault back to school."

"That's okay, I'll walk."

"No, the least we can do is drive you back to school," Roberts insists.

"When Chief Watt brought me here for questioning he didn't give me a ride back. A precedent has been clearly established," I protest.

"We do things differently now."

I change tactics, "Don't you think Clayton's tax paying citizens would prefer Officer Hughes being deployed on the front line combating the recent local crime wave rather than wasting his valuable police training by escorting me to school?"

"Now that we've got Brother Theodore, Archbishop Frontere, Basil O'Reilly and Zachary Pennington put away the only crime investigation around here is going to be conducted by the Officer Involved Shooting Board. They'll be investigating whether it was a justified shooting when Officer Hughes fired at you when you refused to go back to school. And, I can assure you, they will rule in favor of Officer Hughes," Roberts threatens.

I'm marched into the patrol car and driven back in time to be deposited into Mrs. Ogilve's sixth period Social Studies class. She's talking about Thomas Jefferson's epitaph, 'Rebellion to tyrants is obedience to God'. The Church of the Amazingly Big Breasted Former Virgins agrees wholeheartedly with Jefferson's beliefs.

♪

Won't somebody kick the clock and get it moving again? It says it's 3:55 but I'm sure it hasn't budged in at least five minutes. Seconds are taking lifetimes to click off, and I'd be willing to swear someone is playing a dirty trick and holding the minute hand from its progress thereby enabling Mr. Dennis to drone on overtime about hypotenuses of right angled triangles. I know he gets paid to teach geometry but does Dennis really think anyone is interested? Does he go to nightclubs at night and try to pick up girls with come-on lines like, "Hey good looking, I bet I can tell you what the area of that triangular pendant hanging between your tits is." I doubt he has ever been laid – he's far too dull for anyone to voluntarily spend time with. Instead he probably goes home every night and jerks off to posters of isosceles triangles.

I glance at Nina. I'm not sure if it's due to Mr. Dennis being so boring or if it's on account of the Quaaludes she swallowed this morning, but she's passed out face down in her books. I take a look around the room. Even my chaperone, Officer Hughes, has dozed off, Billy Bender is staring out the window, Roger Lefley is looking at the well-worn copy of *Playboy* he has hidden inside his geometry book, Justin Lafayette is whispering something to Kevin Micheletti – they're probably making a bet on how many people will be bored to death before the end of class.

My eyes return to the clock. Whoever has been messing with the clock has decided to parole off another minute. It's 3:56, but I'm sure the clock is still not working properly. What sort of bastard would want to slow down the clock? It couldn't be a student – they all want to get out of here as soon as possible. I doubt whether it could be the custodian, Willie Kannigieser. He just wants to collect his paycheck and get the hell out of here so he can make post time at Cahokia Downs racetrack. A few weeks ago Kannigieser told me he's going to hit the super trifecta and use the money to open a mercenary commando training school in Paraguay. He promises to bring his students north for their final examination, which will consist of blowing Clayton High School up. Who is the culprit who is screwing with the clock? Someone should hire Barnaby Jones to find the sadist. It's probably Mr. Dennis. Holding us captive in his class is the only way he can get anyone to pay the slightest bit of attention to him.

The asshole who has been messing with the clock decided to release another minute. It's 3:57. I bet David Bowie never was forced to take geometry. He probably had a roadie attend class for him while he was getting a blowjob in the special groupie girl's bathroom they had at his school. I'm sure Keith Richards just outright skipped geometry. "Excuse me, but you must have mistaken me for someone who could give a flying fuck. Now get out of my way before I have my security person, Kevin 'Bonecrusher' Futterman, beat the shit out of you; I've got to catch a plane to Los Angeles and be on the *Midnight Special* with David Bowie," Keith would say. I bet they take your special rock star identification card away for enjoying geometry, "I'm sorry Mr. Donovan, but you're no longer allowed to throw your television out the window and fuck *Vogue* models. You no longer get to ride in limos and instead have to take the bus. No one is buying your records any more. You should have thought of the consequences before you started enjoying geometry."

I look up and out of the corner of my eye I notice another small miracle has happened. It's 3:58. Come on clock, you can make it! There's only 120 more seconds to click off until freedom. One Mississippi, two, Mississippi... come on fortify yourself, eat some Wheaties or snort some of that white powder which Jimmy Leach and Clyde Zanussi claim gives them so much energy. You sure managed to move quickly enough when the Blues were on the power play against the Bruins in the Stanley Cup finals, so I know you can go faster than that. This isn't football, there's no two minute warning and stopping the clock so you can have a stupid commercial. I know it's been longer than a minute. It's been at least an hour – maybe even a whole day since you last decided to move...

"Mr. Thibault, I'm talking to you,"

"Huh? What?" Why is Dennis calling on me, and why hasn't the clock moved?

"I asked you what degree angle is necessary to complete a triangle whose isosceles sides have sixty-six degree angles?" Mr. Dennis is standing right in front of my desk.

"Um," the clock moved there is only one minute to emancipation, sixty ticks and we're out of here, fifty-nine...fifty-eight...fifty-seven...

"This is a simple question, haven't you been paying attention? This oral quiz will determine five percent of your grade, a grade which appears might not be to your liking..." Dennis rattles on. Fifty-one...fifty, "Well Thibault, the least you can do is hazard a guess with so much riding on the answer. You must have a number in your head." Forty nine...

"Forty-eight."

"Please accept my apology, you're right. How refreshing, you appear to have some aptitude in this class after all..."

Forty-three...forty-two...forty-one...Bernie better have a good plan. I better wake up Nina, we're going to have to tear out of here. I nudge her desk. She awakens with a yawn and I point to the clock. She nods and winks at me. My God she's beautiful. David Bowie you're going to take one look at Nina and be eating your heart out tomorrow. Come on clock! Move your stupid fucking hand, is that too much to ask? I know it's been at least a week since I started watching you...

"Your homework is to complete questions 1-20 on page 180 and..." ring! the bell goes off! Nina and I run out the room. "Mr. Thibault and Miss Pennington stop, I haven't finished handing out the homework yet," Dennis is yelling as we bolt out the door.

We run at full speed down to the parking lot and find Bernie and Derek Irons standing outside a stretch limousine. We jump in and we're off to the airport. David Bowie here we come!

"What's your plan?" I ask Bernie, after finally regaining my breath.

"We're booked on the last flight to L.A. which leaves at four-thirty. I didn't know Nina is coming with us."

"I'm a rock star and I'm not going anywhere without my girlfriend," I state, surveying the limo. Along with tacky red velvet seats, the car has a bar and a color television.

"But there is no money in the budget for Nina's ticket..." Derek causes Nina's eyes to well up with tears.

"I'll pay for it, don't worry," I say, clutching Nina's hand.

"But Ric, the flight is at four-thirty. There is barely enough time to get to the airport. There is no way we're going to have enough time to stand in line and buy Nina a ticket," Derek claims. He should use the same clocks Clayton High have. There is always plenty of time.

"I have an idea. Driver, pull over at the next phone booth," Bernie orders.

"What are you doing Bernie? We don't have time to pull over," Derek's voice belies concern as the limo pulls over at a gas station.

"I guarantee there will be no problem making the flight. Just give me two minutes. What flight are we taking and what's the telephone number of the airline?" my bandmate asks, picking up the phone.

"We're flying Eastern flight 69. Their number is 1-800-555-2000," Derek replies.

Bernie dials Eastern. "Hello, I want you to listen very carefully," Bernie puts on a strange ethnic accent which I can't place, "this is Commander Zero of the People's Revolutionary Committee Against American Cultural Imperialism in Albania. We have placed a bomb on board your flight 69 to Los Angeles which is scheduled to detonate at five o'clock this evening. If the plane takes off, the blood of its passengers will be on your hands. That is all," Commander Zero hangs up.

"Take it easy driving to the airport," Bernie instructs the chauffeur while turning on the television, "we have plenty of time."

Derek is congratulating Bernie for his ingenuity when I hear Mary Ecclestone's voice on the television, "...interrupt our regularly scheduled program to join a news conference here at Clayton city hall. District Attorney Irwin Roberts is taking the podium for an announcement presumably concerning the arrest of Archbishop Frontere. Here's Mr. Roberts."

"Ladies and gentlemen, I am pleased to announce both the smashing of a major organized crime operation and the apprehension and indictment of the men we believe to be the murderers of Salvatore Veneruzzo and Louis Palazarri. As the result of tremendous police work by federal and local law enforcement agencies working together, we have this afternoon filed multiple charges of conspiracy to commit murder, extortion, federal and state income tax evasion, and distribution of pornography against His Excellency Archbishop Giuseppe Guglielmo Frontere. We have further filed murder, attempted murder, income tax evasion, and mail fraud charges against Gustavio Favio Roberto, who is known to many of you by his alias 'Brother Theodore'. The case was cracked when we received the results of ballistic tests conducted on the gun seized from Brother Theodore during last night's attempted assassination of rock star Ric Thibault..."

"What happened to Ric Thibault of Suckerpunch?" Derek glares at me.

"I can't control what the District Attorney says. Maybe he'll get it right later on, let's listen," I say, hoping Derek will shut-up so I can hear the rest of the news conference.

"...bullets fired from Brother Theodore's pistol matched slugs taken from the bodies of Louis Palazarri and Salvatore Veneruzzo. Upon routine examination of Brother Theodore's fingerprints we discovered that Brother Theodore is actually Gustavio Favio Roberto. Roberto is a fugitive who faked his death five years ago in a plane crash over the Atlantic Ocean. He is wanted by Pennsylvania authorities for his role in the disappearance of ten million dollars from the International Brotherhood of Teamsters pension fund. Sister Marie Baptiste Roberto, Archbishop Frontere's mistress and the sister of Gustavio Roberto, has entered into a plea bargain. In exchange for her testimony concerning the criminal conduct of her brother and Archbishop Frontere she has agreed to plead guilty to misdemeanor drug possession charges stemming from her possession of two hundred tabs of LSD. Miss Roberto will testify that Archbishop Frontere and Brother Theodore were silent partners in Ace Industries. She will further testify that the deceased men, Salvatore Veneruzzo and Louis Palazarri were murdered by Gustavio Roberto on orders from Giuseppe Frontere. Now I am prepared to answer any questions from the press."

Ernie Skidmore, looking recovered from the pummeling he took a few days ago, has the first question, "Can you tell us what the Archbishop's and Brother Theodore's motives were?"

"According to our information Archbishop Frontere and Gustavio Roberto were incensed when they discovered Veneruzzo and Palazarri were skimming money from Ace Industries' lucrative plastic manufacturing operations," Roberts replies.

"What sort of plastics were Ace Industries manufacturing?" Neil Posavad queries.

"Religious icons, you know iridescent plastic Jesuses, commemorative plates of the Saints, religious candles Virgin Marys and so forth, as well as um, sexual aids," the District Attorney stammers.

"What do you mean by sexual aids?" Mary Ecclestone asks.

"We confiscated a large quantity of several different items from Ace Industries. They seem to be a leading manufacturer of penile substitutes," an uncomfortable looking Roberts tugs at his collar, "as well as merkins and inflatable dolls."

"Did you bring any of these items to the press conference for us to inspect?" Ecclestone follows her question up in a husky voice.

"We will put the items on display after the conference in my office."

"What is the involvement of your previous suspect, Johann Thibault, in all of this," a reporter from the *Globe Republican* asks.

"After a lengthy investigation we have found no evidence whatsoever linking Mr. Thibault to this or any other crime. Allegations that Mr. Thibault is now, or ever was, a member of organized crime are entirely unsubstantiated."

"What? You fucking lying piece of shit, conning your way into the band by telling me your father was a Mafia boss," Derek Irons screams at me.

"I never said my dad was a Mafioso, and I didn't con my way into the band either. If you remember you called me up and asked me to audition."

"Maybe I did call you," Derek concedes, "but you never said your father wasn't a Mob boss."

"It's not my fault you never asked me."

"And I suppose you're going to claim it wasn't your fault they didn't mention Suckerpunch either?" Derek shouts, as Channel 7 interrupts there coverage of Irwin Roberts' press conference.

"...we interrupt this interruption for a fast breaking story at the St. Louis Airport. We go now to our correspondent Terry Hollinger at Lambert Field."

"This is Terry Hollinger live at Lambert Field. Eastern Airlines has just announced it has received a bomb threat from a man identifying himself as Commander Zero of the People's Revolutionary Committee Against Culture in Alabama. According to Eastern spokeswoman Holly Buchanan, the airline's 4:30 flight to Los Angeles has been delayed so bomb squad personnel can search the aircraft. What? Oh. Whoops! I'm terribly sorry, Miss Buchanan has informed us that it was Commander Zero from the People's Revolutionary Committee Against American Cultural Imperialism in Albania who called in the bomb threat and not Commander Zero of the People's Revolutionary Committee Against Culture in Alabama. I apologize to Commander Zero of the People's Revolutionary Committee Against Culture in Alabama. That's all the information we have here; so let's return you to our previous interruption with Mary Ecclestone at Clayton city hall."

It's 5:15 and the bomb squad still hasn't finished checking flight 69 for Commander Zero's bomb. Derek has finally calmed down, probably due to the four shots of Jack Daniels he downed in quick succession at the bar.

Nina is on the phone informing her mother that she won't be home for dinner for a couple of days, and I've just realized I better figure out how I am going to avoid having Nina discover I haven't actually met David Bowie when we get to Los Angeles.

I consider several options:

1. Tell Nina that Bowie is jealous of my overnight success and is now snubbing me.
2. Convince Nina that it is improper rock and roll etiquette for the girlfriend of a rival band to hang out with the headliner.
3. Ply her with my two remaining Quaaludes, and hope she passes out during the taping of the *Midnight Special* thereby missing Bowie.

I'm leaning towards using Option One, while keeping Option Three in reserve in case the former doesn't work. Not sure I'm making the right decision I consider an alternative option which is so insidious it doesn't get a number. Option X is telling her the truth. I think about it briefly but can't see the upside in it.

Further deliberations are interrupted by the airport's public address system, "Eastern Airlines paging Los Angeles passenger Derek Irons. Derek Irons please pick up the red courtesy phone for a message."

Bernie and I preserve the airport's Jack Daniels supply by retrieving Derek from the bar and ushering him to the courtesy phone.

"This is Derek Irons...did he leave a number?...okay," Derek hangs up and tells us he has to call Sammy Grant, the producer of the *Midnight Special*.

We walk him over to the pay phones and he places a credit card call to Grant. "Hello this is Derek Irons calling for Sammy Grant...Hi Sammy, Derek Irons here...you what?...that's bullshit...we had an agreement...you're going to believe the Clayton police? You know they've been wrong before...I don't care if the Thibault kid's father is in the Mafia or not, Archbishop Frontere is the kid's godfather and he'll fix your fucking wagon...hello?...hello?...fucking wanker," Derek slams the phone down.

"What's the problem?" I ask.

"The fucking *Midnight Special* found out your father is not in the Mafia and they no longer want us to play. They've canceled our plane tickets. It's over."

I'm devastated. For the second time in twenty-four hours I'm an ex-rock and roll star. What was the geometry homework Dennis assigned? And now that the word is out on my dad not being in the Mob, is Mr. Hucul going to decide that his biology test wasn't culturally biased against gangsters' children and reinstate my failing grade? I feel myself inexorably being drawn to a career in petroleum distribution. Hello Century 21? Do you have any trailers for rent behind Moe's Fina all night gas station in West Bumfuck Missouri?

It's Saturday and I've got the blues so bad that I should lose my eyesight so I could call myself Blind Ric Thibault and get a recording deal with some exotic record label whose records are only bought by rich white people who are trying to show how liberal they are. Even though it's the weekend and we don't have school I can't think of one positive thing in my life. My band is toast, my Corvette is crashed, Stephan is still my brother, Lucretia is due to be released from the loony bin this morning, and I still live in Clayton Missouri. Meanwhile Nina claimed she was so depressed about not going to Los Angeles that she couldn't give me a blowjob much less fuck me last night. I put on my sunglasses and pick up my guitar and try to explore the depth of my blues. I come up with a riff to a new song *My Life Sucks - and My Girlfriend Doesn't*. It's pretty good but I realize I'll probably need a more commercial title if I want to get on the 'All Sincere' radio format, so I rename it *Free*.

I go downstairs and let Duke out. He takes a leak all over the Benders' rose bushes and brings in the newspaper. I open the front page and see the full color special pull out section dealing with the arrest of Archbishop Frontere and Brother Theodore. I skim the articles and don't find one mention of me. I guess I used up those fifteen minutes in the limelight Andy Warhol is always talking about. I'm only sixteen years old and it's all downhill from here.

Too depressed to read any more about the fall from grace of the local clergy I look for the sports pages to see how the Blues did last night. As I go through the paper searching for the sports section the editorial page's headline catches my eye:

AN OPEN APOLOGY TO JOHANN THIBAULT

With the same morbid curiosity exhibited by people who slow down and stare at traffic accidents I read the apology:

> *Sometimes even the news media goofs. We did, and now we feel compelled to offer our most humble apologies to Mr. Johann Thibault, who previously in this paper has been falsely alleged to be a member of organized crime...*

Before I can finish the apology the telephone rings. I pick it up. It's Johann.

He tells me he feels somewhat vindicated by the letter of apology, "but I'm going to have my lawyer file a one million dollar slander lawsuit in case we can scare up some cash from the bastards. Changing the subject – I called your bluff and spoke with Frankie Staniowski at Tequila Ike's. He's sending your mother and me the forty grand directly. You're not getting one red cent. Furthermore your mother and I have decided we really love each other and should get back together, so I need you and your brother to load up the U-Haul and bring all my stuff back, while I'm over at the lawyer's canceling the divorce and filing the lawsuit against the papers. Have a nice day." *Click*

Have a nice day? Give me an Uzi and a few clips of ammunition and I'll show you a nice fucking day, but until then I'm even more depressed than I was before. It's too bad I'm not in Los Angeles performing *Talkin' Nina Pennington Blues* on the *Midnight Special*. I know I could sing the 'blow me' choruses with incredible passion and conviction.

Duke starts barking and I notice a delivery man coming up our front walk. I open the door and sign for a gift wrapped package addressed to the Thibault family. I carry the parcel in and am about to open it when I notice it came from Zachary Pennington. "Don't panic," I tell myself. Calming down I think about it for a millisecond. What with the way everything is going I should panic – it's probably a small thermonuclear device. So I gingerly take the package outside and place it on the driveway. Leaning over I press my ear against it and listen for ticking.

"I was coming to find you. What are you doing lying on the driveway?" Marge Bender nearly causes me to have a heart attack.

"We got this package from Zachary Pennington," I explain.

"Oh, your little bimbo's father, the one who tried to kill everybody yesterday? My bail bondsman told me Pennington made his bail. Is it a bomb?"

"Be quiet and let me listen," I tell her, putting my ear back to Zachary Pennington's parcel. I don't hear anything. "No, I don't think so."

"Good," Marge says, "because I want the pleasure of killing you myself."

"What did I do?"

"Let's go somewhere more private."

"There's no one here but us," I respond not wanting to be behind closed doors and ending up being forced to have sex with her.

We glare at each other.

"Okay," she whispers, "I'm pregnant."

It was a bomb. And it just exploded.

"Are you sure?"

"Trust me the rabbit is dead."

"Are you sure it's mine?"

"Absolutely."

"Can't you have an abortion?"

"I'm Catholic, and so are you."

"No, I'm not. I've converted."

"To what?"

"To the Church of the Amazingly Big...um...you haven't heard of it; but we believe in abortions. In fact we even have a patron saint for abortions," I assure Marge. Sister Lolita can add those duties to her job description. Maybe she can get a raise from God.

"I can't have an abortion," Marge defiantly states.

I have an inspiration, "maybe we should go talk to Father O'Brien and see what he recommends."

"I'll call Planned Parenthood and schedule an appointment," Marge leaves, becoming the first convert to the Church of the Amazingly Big Breasted Virgins – the world's fastest growing new religion. Blessed are those who believe.

I hear the phone ring and race back into the house to answer it. It's Jasper Gilbertson. He claims I misled him about Johann being in the Mafia and wants his money back. I tell him to fuck off and hang up.

No sooner have I hung up than the phone rings again. It's some guy named Sam Peckinpah calling from Hollywood. He claims he's a movie director. He's been following our family on the news and wants to make a movie about us. "If I send you a plane ticket, would you come out here and talk to me?" he asks.

Hollywood? The movies? Movie stars are more famous than rock and rollers. Although they don't get to go on tour and smash hotel rooms they have casting couches and morally casual long legged starlets with bigger breasts than fashion models. Yes, Hollywood would be the perfect place for the Church of the Amazingly Big Breasted Former Virgins to hold nun auditions.

The doorbell rings again and I ask the guy to hold on while I get it. It's Nina, she's come to see if we got her dad's peace offering. I tell her it came but I haven't opened it yet, but I'm on the phone with some guy named Sam Peckinpah who wants to make a movie about me.

"Sam Peckinpah? The movie director who makes all those violent movies?"

"I don't know. Hold on and I'll ask him," I say picking the phone back up. "Sorry about that Mr. Peckinpah. I had to open the door for my girlfriend. She wants to know if you're the director who makes all those violent films."

"That's me," Peckinpah proudly admits, "but before I forget I wanted to ask you what the final body count around your house is."

"Body count?"

"Yeah, how many people died?"

"Give me a second. Let's see there was Salvatore Veneruzzo and Louis Palazarri, the midget reporter, Chief Watt and the three Latin teachers – bringing the total to seven. And Brother Theodore

FEED THE DOG

had his leg run over by a police car," I add, trying to inflate the figure slightly to impress Peckinpah.

"That's a good start. Was there lots of blood?"

"Yeah. You should see the Deathmobile. There's blood everywhere," I respond, "and if you need more I have this friend, Kevin Futterman..."

"No, I don't need more," Peckinpah laughs, "by the way is your girlfriend still the girl from the poster?"

"Yes. Why?"

"She's a very beautiful girl. Do you think she'd want to come with you to meet me?"

I ask Nina. She squeals and hugs me tightly. "I think she'll come," I tell Peckinpah while fending off Nina's enthusiastic kisses.

Peckinpah says he is going to have two first class plane tickets delivered to us by messenger, and hangs up.

"See," Nina says between full tongue kisses, "we don't need Suckerpunch to be famous. We're going to be movie stars. Let's celebrate by going shopping for cool clothes. I don't have anything to wear to Hollywood."

I tell Nina I like her better when she has nothing to wear, but she's not listening. She goes into Kristin's room to see if my sister has the new issue of *Cosmopolitan*. Its cover story is on what movie stars are wearing in Hollywood.

The phone rings. A man identifying himself as Jake Awrey from Jake's Bail Bonds and Bounty Hunters wants to speak to me about the possibility of steering potential clients to his firm. "You seem to know an awful lot of people who are frequently in need of my services and maybe we could make a deal and work together," he proposes. "I'll give you a ten percent referral fee for each criminal you send my way."

"What about innocent people who need bail money after being wrongly arrested?" I ask.

"I didn't think you were so naive kid. Trust me, everyone's a criminal. We're born that way. It's just whether the cops can collar you on a charge that sticks," the bail bondsman says, clearly endorsing the concept of Original Sin – a theory which the Church of the Amazingly Big Breasted Former Virgins is not prepared to take a stand on. Movie stars don't care about guilt any more than rock stars. They care about seeing their name in lights, getting laid, going to cool parties, making money, and trying not to throw up when they're being photographed while emerging from their limousines at the Academy Awards.

I need to think this one through better, so I tell Awrey that I'm intrigued by his proposition, but am in a hurry to catch a plane. I will have to talk with him after I return from Hollywood.

I hang up just in time for the phone to bother me again. It's Stephan. He wants to rub it in about me not being on the *Midnight Special*. Maybe Sam Peckinpah is into cinema verité and can cast my brother as Louis Pellegrino. I'd love to be the lucky bastard who gets to play Brother Theodore, but I probably would get sacked when it took me too many takes to properly shoot Stephan.

I tell Stephan the news about Johann. "Dad put his girlfriend on waivers and is moving back in. He says you're supposed to meet him in Creve Couer and load everything into a U-Haul."

"What about you? You have to help too."

"I can't. Nina and I have a plane to catch," I state, hanging up.

It's noon. The messenger just got here with the tickets to Los Angeles. We're to leave on the three o'clock flight. Hopefully Nina has finished her shopping and is on her way here with her suitcase. My bags are packed and by the front door.

The phone rings. It's Derek Irons. He's already heard I'm meeting with Peckinpah and wants to remind me that he is still my manager and gets fifteen percent of everything I make. "I always knew you had talent," he claims, "and I'll be with you every step of the way."

The front door opens as I hang up. It's Johann and Lucretia. She's waving a doctor's certificate proclaiming her sane. Probably somewhere in St. Louis right now there is a psychiatrist popping champagne corks and rejoicing at my mother's discharge. "All I had to do to get rid of the bitch was write some bullshit on a piece of paper and Lucretia Thibault's out of my fucking life. She's not my problem anymore!" he says, dancing a jig.

My parents are all gooey and acting like a pair of doves in heat. Frankie Staniowski wired the Deathmobile money into their bank account and they are going to celebrate by taking a vacation. They're catching the five o'clock American Airlines flight to Hawaii.

"Great!" I congratulate them, "And as long as you're going to the airport anyway can you drop Nina and me off at Eastern?"

"What do you mean 'drop you and Nina off at Eastern?'" my father demands, pouring a shot of vodka for Lucretia.

"We're on the three o'clock flight to Los Angeles."

"Our plane doesn't leave until five, so we're not leaving for the airport until 3:30," my mother says.

"That's no problem. Our plane will be running at least a couple of hours late," I state with certainty. I've got it all worked out. A friend of Commander Zero's will be calling Eastern any minute now. "Hello Eastern Airlines? Listen carefully. This is Commander One, Commander Zero's boss at the People's Revolutionary Committee Against American Imperialism in Albania. Commander Zero was fired for forgetting to put the bomb on yesterday's flight, but we managed to get the device on today's three o'clock flight to Los Angeles instead. So you know the routine – if the plane takes off the blood of its passengers will be on your hands. Have a nice day."

"I don't care when your plane leaves. You're not going anywhere. You're not a rock star any more. You're grounded," Johann says.

"I may not be a rock star any more, but now I'm something better. I'm going to be in the movies."

"Your father and I have had enough of your bullshit. You're grounded and that's final. You're staying here and doing your homework," Lucretia hiccups while downing her second shot of vodka and opening Zachary Pennington's box. "Oh look Johann honey, it's a bottle of Dom Perignon from Zachary Pennington with a note of apology. Let's drink it."

"Go to your room and do your goddamn homework," Johann orders.

I'm pissed. I'm going to Hollywood with Nina and my two remaining Quaaludes if it's the last thing I do. It's times like this when people turn to God for divine intervention. The Church of the Amazingly Big Breasted Former Virgins has incorporated a few old Catholic traditions into its liturgy. White lies for one. They are not a sin. The Church condones this sort of fib to protect the vulnerable in the hope of promoting the greater good, and this definitely qualifies as greater good. "The only homework I have is in Latin, and I need a little help with it."

"Both your father and I know Latin. What help do you need?" Lucretia asks, popping the champagne's cork.

"Do you know the Latin word for 'the end'?"

Epilogue

It's three weeks later but I only just now got a return phone call from Annette Stratton-Osborne in Costa Rica, except her name isn't Stratton-Osborne anymore – it's the Contessa something or other. Annette claims she's been trying to call me every day but either the phones are messed up in Costa Rica or our phone has been busy and she hasn't been able to get through.

Somehow Annette has heard that Sam Peckinpah is interested in my story and she wants to know if I'm going to be rich and famous, and if so, she maintains I am still going to need her as my lawyer since she is the only one who can give me the personal attention that I require.

"But what happened to the conflict of interest with your representing Brother Theodore?"

"Brother who?"

"Brother Theodore, the one who gave you that cash retainer on the night of the accident."

"What accident? I never saw you hit anyone in a Rolls Royce with your Corvette, and anyone who claims to the contrary is mistaken. Now tell me what's with you and the famous movie director, Sam Peckinpah? Has he done his casting yet? Do you know if he personally does the casting, or who does and what he likes in a woman?"

"I'm not sure about any of the casting stuff," I tell Annette, "but Sam told me to write everything down exactly like it happened, and he said he would take it from there...and I could swear that Nina and I saw you take the money from Brother Theodore..."

"Ric, I'm an officer of the Court and it would be a grievous violation of legal ethics to tell you a lie, so your faulty recollection of any dealings between Brother Theodore and myself must be due to the trauma you suffered in the accident. An accident, if I may point out, which would have been totally avoidable if you had not been getting a blowjob from your girlfriend right in the open where everyone could see while you were driving. But that's not important now. As your lawyer I have to warn you, you have to change everyone's name and attach some sort of disclaimer swearing that your story isn't true and any similarity between real people and events is purely coincidental, or someone's going to sue your ass for everything you have now or may ever possibly have in the future."

"You mean like on *Dragnet* where the names have been changed to protect the innocent even though everyone wants to know who the guilty assholes are?" I ask.

"Unless you want to lose everything including what's left of the Corvette, your guitar and however many of those Quaaludes you have left that Jimmy Leach told me you've been trying to disguise as aspirin."

"You mean I can't call Stephan 'Stephan' or even refer to that well known criminal Basil O'Reilly as 'Basil O'Reilly'?" I ask, making a mental note to shove the two surviving Quaaludes down Nina's gullet tonight, by force if necessary, lest one of Chief Watt's successors comes and tries to fuck with me.

"Trust me. You've got to change everyone's name, and I mean everyone's, especially, um, I mean including mine!"

18 May 1973

Sam Peckinpah
Hollywood, California 90028

Dear Mr. Peckinpah:

I'm sorry that I haven't sent you my account of what happened yet, but under the advice of my lawyer, known hereafter as the Contessa Bridget Vopat, I have to change the name of everyone in my story including my girlfriend (hereinafter known as Hillary Berenson).

I also have to change the location of Clayton to somewhere where everyone isn't always trying to make a fast buck by hauling you into court every second and suing me for everything I have – so how would you feel if the setting was someplace cooler like Malibu? I'm sure it would be easier for you to cast a movie where there are already movie stars...and you would be able to save a lot of money by not having to ship your couch out here to Clayton.

Oh yeah, one other thing, Annette, I mean the Contessa Vopat, told me is that I have to warn you that this book is a work of fiction. The names, characters, places, and incidents herein described are the products of my vivid imagination and any resemblance to actual persons, living or croaked, events, or locales in this story is entirely coincidental...Honestly.

Sincerely,

Ric Browde

Ric Browde – the writer formerly known as Ric Thibault

P.S. Please find enclosed a topless picture of my friend Bridget Vopat who I think would be perfect for the role of my lawyer in the movie. She says she doesn't mind if you have to put all sorts of fake blood all over her for her to get a part.

P.P.S. When do I get paid?

P.P.P.S. I've got this great new band Ric Thibault's Suckerpunch to do the soundtrack!

Liner Notes

¹*Talkin' Nina Pennington Blues* (single version) (Ross – Ross – Almeida – Browde) Slipped Disk made us hire some out of work asshole record producer who forced us to record this, the 'Blow Me' version, while wearing our leather pants. The sadistic bastard did not care that he permanently traumatized Simon Q. Picasso, he was unconcerned with any potential damage to my relationship with Nina, and worst of all the schweinhund buried my rhythm guitar in the mix.

²*I'm Stupid and So Are You** (Paruszkiewicz) Simon Q. Picasso, a/k/a Herbie Paruszkiewicz, wrote this song on the advice of his shrink, Dr. Caley. Caley claimed that it would have a cathartic calming effect on Simon to hear Mick Masters embarrass himself by announcing for all the world to hear that he is stupid. Dr. Caley was wrong...Mick took great delight in it.

¹*White Heat* (Browde – Engel – Voxx) It is with mixed emotions that I allowed Slipped Disk to put this song by Johnny Asthma & The Thalidomide Kids on the record. This is Nina's favorite song. She says it always makes her horny when she hears it. But what happens if I'm not there when she hears it? I might have to break her parent's stereo, the jukebox at Shinske's Pizza parlor, Kevin Futterman's eight track...

^{1,3}*If I Had A Dick* (Ross – Davalos) I pay my debt to Annette Stratton-Osborne (Or is it the Contessa Vopat?) and, with the rest of Suckerpunch, play on her demo. She says this is a protest against macho rock and rollers who brag about being able to go all night and then when the going gets tough wimp out after three or four times. In my opinion this weak song is just another case of everyone wanting to be a rock star, however my guitar does lift it from the mundane...

²*Still Monday** (Paruszkiewicz – Drossin) Recorded without leather pants, this ballad is Suckerpunch selling out by trying to get on the new 'All sincere – all the time' radio format. Clyde Zanussi alleges the song tested really well by making the sample group of Texan shitkicker's palms sweat and has ordered Jimmy Leach to put the song in heavy rotation.

[1,2]Can't Keep Us Down (Paruszkiewicz – Dietrich) We hereby serve notice, this is the theme song for the Church of the Amazingly Big Breasted Former Virgins' future recruiting efforts. I think I played a pretty cool solo on this one.

[1]Free# (East) Led Zeppelin didn't write *Stairway to Heaven* until they were well into their thirties. I wrote this and I'm only sixteen. I think that says a lot.

[1]Zero King# (East) Jimmy Leach asked us to write a song about him. We did.

[1]While I'm Dead...Feed The Dog Underture (Ross – Ross – Browde) You may have wondered what happened to those last two Quaaludes. The day after Mick Masters quit the band we were recording my new soon to be smash single. Well that scumbag has-been producer kept trying to tell me what to do, so I finally slipped my last two 'ludes into his Johnny Walker on the rocks, which he maintained was only iced tea. Kristen, who was at the studio necking with Bernie, saw me do this, and after the idiot passed out, she threatened to rat me out unless I let her sing too and make it a duet. I have to admit I nailed my vocals. As for Kristen I'll withhold comment, but if anyone wants to marry her and get her out of my life her address is, 7220 South Meramec, Clayton Missouri 63105. Her bedroom is the one on the ground floor and her window is usually open. So drop by...please.

[1]Looking Up At Her Thighs (All Fall Down) (Almeida – Roach – Ross) One of Rico 'Bam Bam' Ross's contributions to the band. According to Rico the song is about the confusion he experiences when he has sex...What's her name? Did I tell her I loved her? Am I going to need a doctor? Am I going to need a lawyer? Did I use up all my Quaaludes?

[2]Let Me In (Paruszkiewicz – Drossin) I often think Simon Q. Picasso is some sort of idiot savant. The guy is a total geek, but has the unique ability to put into words and music feelings that everyone experiences, such as my attempts to get into Nina's pants. One of my finest pieces of guitar playing.

[2]Take It Away (Paruszkiewicz – Drossin) This is Simon complaining about Derek Irons forcing us to wear our leather pants. Incidentally we were wearing them when we played the song – you can notice the aggression in Simon's bass playing.

Talkin' Nina Pennington Blues (Special collector's version) (Ross-Ross-Almeida-Browde) Usually record companies wait until you croak before digging this deep into the vaults and releasing original versions of songs recorded in a star's bedroom. Then after hiring some lame writer to scribble some bullshit liner notes proclaiming how this rare version shows the true genius of the artist, they slap a sticker on it saying "FREE BONUS contains unreleased rare track." But Slipped Disk didn't even wait for me to have some spectacular rock star drug overdose before financially sodomizing me and including this, the original version of my masterpiece. But even though it is a total rip off it does show how talented I am.

Please note: Claude Forey, the bastard who runs Slipped Disk, will not allow us to include Suckerpunch's single *Pulling A Train* on the album. He claims to be protecting America's youth by not releasing an obscene song, although I think it has more to do with the fact that he's covering his ass because he secretly harbors the desire to be the first transsexual elected as a Republican Congresswoman.

Produced by: Ric Browde

All songs ASCAP. [1]Capitalist Bloodsuckers of Doom. [2]Timbo Music. [3]Nickie's Juke Joint Music.
Except * Produced by Tim Paruszkiewicz
Produced by Bobby East

Executive Producer for Slipped Disk: Mark Fine
Engineered by Rod O'Brien, Greg D'Angelo, Ric Browde & Bobby East
Recorded at Jake's Place, Studio City (Home of many a casting couch) California
Mixed at Cherokee Studios, Hollywood (Home of even more and plusher casting couches) California
Mastered & Mistressed by: Patricia Sulliivan at A&M Recording Studios (Charlie Chaplin's old digs where the casting couch was invented) Hollywood, California

Photography: Bam Ross
Model: Jenteal

Quotations taken from:

Lolita by Vladamir Nabokov. Copyright 1955. Used by permission of Random House Books. All rights reserved.

L'Etranger by Albert Camus. Copyright 1942. Used by permission of Random House Books. All rights reserved.

Move Over by Janis Joplin. Copyright 1970 by Strong Arm Music. All rights reserved.

For information on how you can buy ACE INDUSTRIES best selling poster of Nina Pennington, as well as genuine *While I'm Dead...Feed The Dog* T-shirts, sweatshirts, baseball hats. and anything else they can make money off of, send an e-mail to: ap054@lafn.org

Special Thanks

Nina quite rightly points out that I will very likely win some sort of Academy Award just as soon as we get out to California and Mr. Peckinpah makes his movie about me. She says I should start practicing my acceptance speech now so I'll be prepared and won't end up like one of those liquored up blathering celebrities gushing on about how they want to thank all the little people who helped them get off the casting couch and into their huge Beverly Hills mansions. So here's what I've come up with:

I want to thank all the big people who helped get me off the casting couch and into my Beverly Hills mansion. Specifically I want to thank the greatest friends anyone could ever have – Bam & Share Ross, Jo 'I'm not Glam' Almeida, Rod & Sherri 'Talk Slowly I'm Canadian' O'Brien, Dr. Gail Charnley, Tim Paruszkiewicz, Jeffrey & Chris 'they play hockey on Monday nights too' Light and Stephanie Lund. Thanks for the music and the good times to Terry Messal, Richie D'Albis, and Howard Drossin formerly of Flies On Fire and now of Vitamade, Bobby East, Dave Roach, Ted Hutt, Greg D'Angelo, Susan Donaldson and Peter Schrock. Extreme thanks to Ted Green for a decade of advice and help. A tip of the hat to Cory I. (which stands for 'I haven't read it yet but here are your fifty copies') Weisman. A big merci beaucoup to the lawyers Drew You have the right to, and should, remain silent' Ryce, and Seth 'Small Print' Lichtenstein, Gracias to Mark & Cynthia Fine for providing me my very own casting couch, Susan Yannetti for her energy and being the coolest person I know, Vivid for putting the ass back into class, and to Jeff Sydney and Steve McKeever for making me believe this was worthwhile, and to Sean Perkin. Viellen danke to the members of my family, who always accepted me unconditionally – Opus Biallystock Browde, Basil O'Reilly Browde, and Duke Browde – my father, Anatole Browde, and mother, Francis Browde, for making me laugh, my grandparents whose spirit lives on, and above all to Holly T. Browde, who should see a shrink (Dr. Caley might be available) for voluntarily spending twenty years as best friend, companion and model for Nina Pennington...if she only would put on that blond wig, and these Charles Jourdan black patent leather pumps...

Let me say in closing that this is an honor I will remember for as long as I can...

ALSO AVAILABLE FROM COMENT PUBLISHING

A COMPREHENSIVE
GUIDE DEDICATED TO
EVERYTHING MUSIC